TypeScript Microservices

Build, deploy, and secure microservices using TypeScript combined with Node.js

Parth Ghiya

BIRMINGHAM - MUMBAI

TypeScript Microservices

Commissioning Editor: Merint Mathew
Acquisition Editor: Denim Pinto
Content Development Editor: Priyanka Sawant
Technical Editor: Ruvika Rao
Copy Editor: Safis Editing
Project Coordinator: Vaidehi Sawant
Proofreader: Safis Editing
Indexer: Aishwarya Gangawane
Graphics: Jason Monteiro
Production Coordinator: Arvindkumar Gupta

First published: May 2018

Production reference: 1290518

Published by Packt Publishing Ltd.
Livery Place
35 Livery Street
Birmingham
B3 2PB, UK.

ISBN 978-1-78883-075-1

www.packtpub.com

`mapt.io`

Mapt is an online digital library that gives you full access to over 5,000 books and videos, as well as industry leading tools to help you plan your personal development and advance your career. For more information, please visit our website.

Why subscribe?

- Spend less time learning and more time coding with practical eBooks and Videos from over 4,000 industry professionals

- Improve your learning with Skill Plans built especially for you

- Get a free eBook or video every month

- Mapt is fully searchable

- Copy and paste, print, and bookmark content

PacktPub.com

Did you know that Packt offers eBook versions of every book published, with PDF and ePub files available? You can upgrade to the eBook version at `www.PacktPub.com` and as a print book customer, you are entitled to a discount on the eBook copy. Get in touch with us at `service@packtpub.com` for more details.

At `www.PacktPub.com`, you can also read a collection of free technical articles, sign up for a range of free newsletters, and receive exclusive discounts and offers on Packt books and eBooks.

Contributors

About the author

Parth Ghiya loves technologies and enjoys learning new things and facing the unknown. He has shown his expertise in multiple technologies, including mobile, web, and enterprise. He has been leading projects in all domains with regard to security, high-availability, and CI/CD. He has provided real-time data analysis, time series, and forecasting solutions too.

In his leisure time, he is an avid traveler, reader, and an immense foodie. He believes in technological independence and is a mentor, trainer, and contributor.

Thank you is the best prayer that anyone can say, and I will say that a lot. I would like to thank God, my family, teachers, and all my extended family for their support of me and for making me a humble person and giving me their time. I would like to thank the entire Packt team (Nitin, Priyanka, Ruvika, and Tanvi especially) for their support and this opportunity. I would like to thank everyone who bore with me during the entire journey.

About the reviewer

Dhaval Marthak has a wealth of experience in AngularJS; Node.js, other frontend technologies such as React, server-side languages such as C#, and hybrid applications with Backbase. Currently, he is associated with an organization based in Ahmedabad as a senior frontend developer, where he takes care of projects with regard to requirement analysis, architecture design, high-availability, security design, deployment, and build processes to help customers.

Packt is searching for authors like you

If you're interested in becoming an author for Packt, please visit `authors.packtpub.com` and apply today. We have worked with thousands of developers and tech professionals, just like you, to help them share their insight with the global tech community. You can make a general application, apply for a specific hot topic that we are recruiting an author for, or submit your own idea.

Table of Contents

Preface

In the last few years or so, microservices have achieved the rockstar status and are right now one of the most tangible solutions in enterprises to make quick, effective, and scalable applications. Microservices entail an architectural style and pattern in which a huge system is distributed into smaller services that are self-sufficient, autonomous, self-contained, and individually deployable.

The apparent rise of TypeScript and the long evolution from ES5 to ES6 has seen lots of big companies move to ES6 stack. TypeScript, due to its huge advantages like class and module supports, static type checking, and syntax similarity to JavaScript, has become the de facto solution for many enterprises. Node.js, due to its asynchronous, non-blocking, lightweight nature, and for, has been widely appointed by many companies. Node.js written in TypeScript opens doors to various opportunities.

However, microservices have their own difficulties to be dealt with, such as monitoring, scaling, distributing, and service discovery. The major challenge is deploying at scale, as we don't want to end up with system failures. Adopting microservices without actually knowing or addressing these issues would lead to a big issue. The most important part of this book concerns the pragmatic technological independence approach for dealing with microservices so as to leverage the best of everything.

In three parts, this book explains how these services work and the process to build any application the microservices way. You will encounter a design-based approach to architecture and guidance for implementing various microservices elements. You will get a set of recipes and practices for meeting practical, organizational, and cultural challenges to adoption. The goal of this book is to acquaint users with a practical, step-by-step approach for making reactive microservices at scale. This book will take readers into a deep dive with Node.js, TypeScript, Docker, Netflix OSS, and more. Readers of this book will understand how Node.js and TypeScript can be to deploy services that can run independently. Users will understand the evolving trend of serverless computing and the different Node.js capabilities, realizing the use of Docker for containerization. The user will learn how to autoscale the system using Kubernetes and AWS.

I am sure readers will enjoy each and every section of the book. Also, I believe this book adds value for not just Node.js developers but also others who want to play around with microservices and successfully implementing them in their businesses. Throughout this book, I have taken a practical approach by providing a number of examples, including a case study from the e-commerce domain. By the end of the book, you will have learned how to implement microservice architectures using Node.js, the TypeScript framework, and other utilities. These are battle-tested, robust tools for developing any microservice and are written to the latest specifications of Node.js.

Who this book is for

This book is for JavaScript developers seeking to utilize their Node.js and TypeScript skills to build microservices and move away from the monolithic style of architecture. Prior knowledge of TypeScript and Node.js is assumed. This book will help answer some of the important questions concerning what problems a microservice solves and how an organization has to be structured to adopt microservices.

What this book covers

Chapter 1, *Debunking Microservices*, gives you an introduction to the world of microservices. It begins with the transition from monolithic to microservice architectures. This chapter gets you acquainted with the evolution of the microservices world; answers to frequently asked questions that come up about microservices, and familiarizes you with various microservice design aspects, twelve-factor applications for microservices; and various design patterns for microservice implementations along with their pros, cons, and when to and when not to use them.

Chapter 2, *Gearing up for the Journey*, introduces necessary concepts in Node.js and TypeScript. It begins with preparing our development environment. It then talks about basic TypeScript essentials such as types, tsconfig.json, writing your custom types for any node module, and the Definitely Typed repository. Then, we move to Node.js, where we write our application in TypeScript. We will learn about some essentials such as Node clusters, Event Loops, multithreading, and async/await. Then, we move to writing our first hello world TypeScript microservice.

Chapter 3, *Exploring Reactive Programming,* gets into the world of reactive programming. It explores the concepts of reactive programming along with its approaches and advantages. It explains how reactive programming is different from traditional approaches and then moves to practical examples with Highland.js, Bacon.js, and RxJS. It concludes by comparing all the three libraries along with their pros and cons.

Chapter 4, *Beginning Your Microservices Journey,* begins our microservices case study—the shopping cart microservices. It begins with the functional requirements of the system, followed by overall business capabilities. We start the chapter with architectural aspects, design aspects, and overall components in the ecosystem, before moving to the data layers of microservices, wherein we will have an in-depth discussion on the types of data and how the database layer should be. Then, we develop microservices with the approach of separation of concerns and learn about some microservices best practices.

Chapter 5, *Understanding API Gateway,* explores the designs involved in an API Gateway. It tells why an API Gateway is required and what its functions are. We will explore various API Gateway designs and the various options available in them. We will look at the circuit breaker and why it plays an important role as part of a client resiliency pattern.

Chapter 6, *Service Registry and Discovery,* talks about introducing a service registry in your microservices ecosystem. The number of services and/or location of services can remain in flux based on load and traffic. Having a static location disturbs the principles of microservices. This chapter deals with the solution and talks about service discovery and registry patterns in depth. The chapter further explains various options available and discusses Consul and Eureka in detail.

Chapter 7, *Service State and Interservice Communication,* focuses on interservice communication. Microservices need to collaborate with each other in order to achieve a business capability. The chapter explores various modes of communication. It then talks about next-gen communication styles including RPC and the HTTP 2.0 protocol. We learn about service state and at where the state can be persisted. We go through various kinds of database system along with their use cases. The chapter explores the world of caching, sharing code among dependencies, and versioning strategies, and details how to get client resiliency patterns to handle failures.

Chapter 8, *Testing, Debugging, and Documenting,* outlines life after development. We learn how to write test cases and plunge into the world of BDD and TDD through some famous toolsets. We see contract testing for microservices—a way to ensure that there are no groundbreaking changes. We then see debugging and how to profile our service and all the options available to us. We move on to documenting and understanding the needs of documentation and all the toolsets involved around Swagger, the tool that we will use.

Chapter 9, *Deployment, Logging, and Monitoring*, covers deployment and various options involved in it. We see a build pipeline, and we get acquainted with continuous integration and continuous delivery. We understand Docker in detail and dockerize our application by adding Nginx in front of our microservice. We move on to logging and understand the need for a customized, centralized logging solution. We finally move on to monitoring and understanding the various options available, such as keymetrics, Prometheus, and Grafana.

Chapter 10, *Hardening Your Application*, looks at hardening the application, addressing security and scalability. It talks about security best practices that should be in place to avoids any mishaps. It gives a detailed security checklist that can be used at the time of deployment. We will then learn about scalability with AWS and Kubernetes. We will see how to solve scaling problems with AWS by automatically adding or removing an EC2 instance. The chapter concludes with Kubernetes and its example.

Appendix, *What's New in Node.js 10.x and NPM 6.x?*, covers about the new update in Node.js v10.x and NPM v6.x. The Appendix is not present in the book, but it is available for the download int the following link: `https://www.packtpub.com/sites/default/files/downloads/Whats_New_in_Node.js_10.x_and_NPM_6.x.pdf`

My aim for the book was to have this book's topic be relevant, useful, and, most important of all, focused on practical examples useful to career and business-based use cases. I hope you enjoy reading the book as much as I loved writing the book, which surely means that you will have a blast!

To get the most out of this book

This book requires a Unix machine with prerequisites installed. A basic understanding of Node.js and TypeScript is very much needed before proceeding with the book. Most of the code will work in Windows too but with different ways to install it; hence, Linux (Oracle VM Box with Ubuntu is also a perfect fit) is recommended. To get the most out of this book, try to work out the examples and apply the concepts to examples of your own as soon as possible. Most of the programs or case studies in these programs utilize open source software that can be installed or set up with ease. However, a few instances do require setting up a few paid setups.

In Chapter 9, *Deployment, Logging, and Monitoring*, we need an account on logz.io so as to have a complete ELK setup ready rather than individually managing it. A trial version is available for 30 days, but you can extend some plans. An account for key metrics is needed to uncover its full potential.

In Chapter 10, *Hardening Your Application,* you need to procure an AWS account for scaling and deployment purposes. You also need to procure Google Cloud Platform for independently testing out Kubernetes rather than going through the manual setup process. The free tier is available for both accounts, but you need to sign up with a credit/debit card.

Download the example code files

You can download the example code files for this book from your account at www.packtpub.com. If you purchased this book elsewhere, you can visit www.packtpub.com/support and register to have the files emailed directly to you.

You can download the code files by following these steps:

1. Log in or register at www.packtpub.com.
2. Select the **SUPPORT** tab.
3. Click on **Code Downloads & Errata**.
4. Enter the name of the book in the **Search** box and follow the onscreen instructions.

Once the file is downloaded, please make sure that you unzip or extract the folder using the latest version of:

- WinRAR/7-Zip for Windows
- Zipeg/iZip/UnRarX for Mac
- 7-Zip/PeaZip for Linux

The code bundle for the book is also hosted on GitHub at https://github.com/ PacktPublishing/TypeScript-Microservices. In case there's an update to the code, it will be updated on the existing GitHub repository.

We also have other code bundles from our rich catalog of books and videos available at https://github.com/PacktPublishing/. Check them out!

Download the color images

We also provide a PDF file that has color images of the screenshots/diagrams used in this book. You can download it here: https://www.packtpub.com/sites/default/files/ downloads/TypeScriptMicroservices_ColorImages.pdf.

Conventions used

There are a number of text conventions used throughout this book.

`CodeInText`: Indicates code words in text, database table names, folder names, filenames, file extensions, pathnames, dummy URLs, user input, and Twitter handles. Here is an example: "An example of all the operators in the preceding table can be found at `rx_combinations.ts`, `rx_error_handing.ts`, and `rx_filtering.ts`."

A block of code is set as follows:

```
let asyncReq1=await
axios.get('https://jsonplaceholder.typicode.com/posts/1');
console.log(asyncReq1.data);
let asyncReq2=await
axios.get('https://jsonplaceholder.typicode.com/posts/1');
console.log(asyncReq2.data);
```

Any command-line input or output is written as follows:

```
sudo dpkg -i <file>.deb
sudo apt-get install -f # Install dependencies
```

Bold: Indicates a new term, an important word, or words that you see onscreen. For example, words in menus or dialog boxes appear in the text like this. Here is an example: "Open up your instance and then go to the **Load Balancing** | **Load balancers** tab."

 Warnings or important notes appear like this.

 Tips and tricks appear like this.

Get in touch

Feedback from our readers is always welcome.

General feedback: Email feedback@packtpub.com and mention the book title in the subject of your message. If you have questions about any aspect of this book, please email us at questions@packtpub.com.

Errata: Although we have taken every care to ensure the accuracy of our content, mistakes do happen. If you have found a mistake in this book, we would be grateful if you would report this to us. Please visit www.packtpub.com/submit-errata, selecting your book, clicking on the Errata Submission Form link, and entering the details.

Piracy: If you come across any illegal copies of our works in any form on the Internet, we would be grateful if you would provide us with the location address or website name. Please contact us at copyright@packtpub.com with a link to the material.

If you are interested in becoming an author: If there is a topic that you have expertise in and you are interested in either writing or contributing to a book, please visit authors.packtpub.com.

Reviews

Please leave a review. Once you have read and used this book, why not leave a review on the site that you purchased it from? Potential readers can then see and use your unbiased opinion to make purchase decisions, we at Packt can understand what you think about our products, and our authors can see your feedback on their book. Thank you!

For more information about Packt, please visit packtpub.com.

Debunking Microservices
1

"If I had asked people what they wanted, they would have said faster horses."

– Henry Ford

Whether you are a tech lead, developer, or a tech savant eager to adapt to new modern web standards, the preceding line represents your current life situation in a nutshell. Today's mantra for the successful business, fail quickly, fix and rise soon, quicker delivery, frequent changes, adaption to changing technologies, and fault-tolerant systems are some of the general daily requirements. For the very same reason, during recent times, the technology world has seen a quick change in architectural designs that have led industry leaders (such as Netflix, Twitter, Amazon, and so on) to move away from monolithic applications and adopt microservices. In this chapter, we will debunk microservices and study their anatomy, and learn their concepts, characteristics, and advantages. We will learn about microservice design aspects and see some microservice design patterns.

In this chapter, we will talk about the following topics:

- Debunking microservices
- Key considerations for microservices
- Microservice FAQs
- How microservices satisfy the twelve-factors of the application
- Microservices in the current world
- Microservice design aspects
- Microservice design patterns

Debunking microservices

The core idea behind microservice development is if the application is broken down into smaller independent units, with each group performing its functionality well, then it becomes straightforward to build and maintain an application. The overall application then just becomes the sum of individual units. Let's begin by debunking microservices.

Rise of microservices

Today's world is evolving exponentially, and it demands an architecture that can satisfy the following problems that made us rethink traditional architecture patterns and gave rise to microservices.

Wide selection of languages as per demand

There is a great need for technological independence. At any point in time, there is a shift in languages and adoption rates change accordingly. Companies such as Walmart have left the Java stack and moved towards the MEAN stack. Today's modern applications are not just limited to the web interface and extends its need for mobile and smartwatch application too. So, coding everything in one language is not at all a feasible option. We need an architecture or ecosystem where multiple languages can coexist and communicate with each other. For example, we may have REST APIs exposed in Go, Node.js, and Spring Boot—a gateway as the single point of contact for the frontend.

Easy handling of ownership

Today's applications not only include a single web interface, but go beyond into mobiles, smart watches, and **virtual reality** (**VR**). A separation of logic into individual modules helps to control everything as each team owns a single unit. Also, multiple things should be able to run in parallel, hence achieving faster delivery. Dependencies between teams should be reduced to zero. Hunting down the right person to get the issue fixed and get the system up and running demands a microservice architecture.

Frequent deployments

Applications need to constantly evolve to keep up with an evolving world. When Gmail started, it was just a simple mailing utility and now it has evolved into much more than that. These frequent changes demand frequent deployments in such a way that the end user doesn't even know that a new version is being released. By dividing into smaller units, a team can thus handle frequent deployments with testing and get the feature into customers hands quickly. There should be graceful degradation, that is, fail fast and get it over with.

Self-sustaining development units

A tight dependency between different modules soon cascades to the entire application and it goes down. This requires smaller independent units in such a way that if one unit is not operational, then the entire application is not affected by it.

Now let's understand in depth about microservices, their characteristics, their advantages, and all the challenges while implementing a microservice architecture.

What are microservices?

There is no universal definition of microservices. Simply stating—*a microservice can be any operational block or unit, which handles its single responsibility very efficiently.*

Microservices are modern styles to build autonomous, self-sustaining, loosely coupled business capabilities that sum up as an entire system. We will look into the principles and characteristics of microservices, the benefit that microservices provide, and the potential pitfalls to keep an eye out for.

Principles and characteristics

There are a few principles and characteristics that define microservices. Any microservice pattern would be distinguished and explained further by these points.

No monolithic modules

A microservice is just another new project satisfying a single operational
business requirement. A microservice is linked with business unit changes and thus it has
to be loosely coupled. It should be that a microservice can continuously serve the changing
business requirements irrespective of the other business units. For other services, it is just a
matter of consumption, the mode of consumption should not change. Implementations can
change in the background.

Dumb communication pipes

Microservices promote basic, time-tested, asynchronous communication mechanisms
among microservices. As per this principle, the business logic should stay inside the
endpoint and not be amalgamated with the communication channel. The communication
channel should be dumb and just communicate in the communication protocol decided.
HTTP is a favorable communication protocol, but a more reactive approach—queues is
prevalent these days. **Apache Kafka**, and **RabbitMQ** are some of the prevalent dumb
communication pipes providers.

Decentralization or self-governance

While working with microservices, there is often a change of failure. A contingency plan
that eventually stops the failure from propagating to the entire system. Furthermore, each
microservice may have its own data storage need. Decentralization manages just the need
for that. For example, in our shopping module we can store our customer and his
transactions-related information in SQL databases, but since the product data is highly
unstructured, we store it in NoSQL-related databases. Every service should be able to take a
decision on what to do in fail case scenarios.

Service contracts and statelessness

Microservices should be well defined through service contracts. A **service contract** basically
gives information about how to consume the service and what all the parameters are that
need to be passed to that service. **Swagger** and **AutoRest** are some of the widely adopted
frameworks for creating service contracts. Another salient characteristic is that nothing is
stored and no state is maintained by the microservice. If there is a need to persist
something, then it will be persisted in a cache database or some datastore.

Lightweight

Microservices, being lightweight, help to replicate a setup easily in any hosting environment. Containers are more preferred than hypervisors. Lightweight application containers help us to maintain a lower footprint, thus by binding a microservice to some context. Well-designed microservices should perform only one function and do that operation well enough. Containerized microservices are easily portable, thus enabling easy auto-scaling.

Polyglot

Everything is abstract and unknown behind the service API in microservice architecture. In the preceding example of shopping cart microservices, we can have our payment gateway entirely as a service deployed in the cloud (serverless architecture), while the rest of the services can be in Node.js. The internal implementations are completely hidden behind the microservices and the only concern to be taken care of is that the communication protocol should be the same throughout.

Now, let's see what advantages microservice architecture has to offer us.

Good parts of microservices

Adopting microservices has several advantages and benefits. We will look at the benefits and higher business values we get while using microservices.

Self-dependent teams

Microservices architecture enables us to scale any operation independently, have availability on demand, and introduce new services very quickly without zero to very few configurations. Technological dependence is also greatly reduced. For example, in our shopping microservice architecture, the inventory and shopping module can be independently deployed and worked upon. The inventory service will just assume that the product will exist and work accordingly. The inventory service can be coded in any language as long as the communication protocol between inventory and product service is met.

Graceful degradation of services

Failure in any system is natural, graceful degradation is a key advantage of microservices. Failures are not cascaded to the entire system. Microservices are designed in such a way that microservices adhere to agreed service level agreements; if the **service level agreements** (**SLAs**) are not met, then the service is dropped. For example, coming back to our shopping microservice example, if our payment gateway is down, then further requests to that service are stopped until the service is up and running.

Supports polyglot architecture and DevOps

Microservices make use of resources as per need or effectively create polyglot architecture. For example, in shopping microservices, you can store products and customer data in a relational database, but any audit or log-related data you can store in **Elasticsearch** or **MongoDB**. As each microservice operates in its bounded context, this can enable experimentation and innovation. The cost of change impact will be very less. Microservices enables **DevOps** to full level. Many DevOps tools and techniques are needed for a successful microservice architecture. Small microservices are easy to automate, easy to test, contaminate the failure if needed, and are easy to scale. **Docker** is one of the major tools for containerizing microservices.

Event-driven architecture

A well-architected microservice will support asynchronous event-driven architecture. Event-driven architecture helps as any event can be traced into—each action would be the outcome of any event, we can tap into any event to debug an issue. Microservices are designed with the publisher-subscriber pattern, meaning adding any other service that just subscribes to that event will be a mere task. For example, you are using a shopping site and there's a service for add to cart. Now, we want to add new functionality so that whenever a product is added to a cart, the inventory should be updated. Then, an inventory service can be prepared that just has to subscribe to the add to cart service.

Now, we will look into the complexities that microservice architecture introduces.

Bad and challenging parts of microservices

With great power comes greater challenges. Let's look at the challenging parts of designing microservices.

Organization and orchestration

It is one of the topmost challenges while adapting microservice architecture. This is more of a non-functional challenge wherein new organizational teams need to be formed and they need to be guided in adopting the microservice, agile, and scrum methodologies. They need to be simulated in such an environment that they can work independently. Their developed outcome should be integrated into the system in such a way that it is loosely coupled and is easily scaled.

Platform

Creating the perfect environment needs a proper team, and a scalable fail-safe infrastructure across all data centers. Going to the right cloud provider (**AWS** or **GCP** or **Azure**), adding automation, scalability, high availability, managing containers, and instances of microservices are some of the key considerations. Further microservices demand other component needs such as an enterprise service bus, document databases, cache databases, and so on. Maintaining these components becomes an added task while dealing with microservices.

Testing

Being completely independent testing out services with dependencies is extremely challenging. As a microservice gets introduced into the ecosystem, proper governance and testing are needed, otherwise it will be a single point of failure for the system. Several levels of testing are needed for any microservice. It should start from whether the service is able to access cross-cutting concerns (cache, security, database, logs) or not. The functionality of the service should be tested, followed by testing of the protocol through which it is going to communicate. Next is collaborative testing of the microservice with other services. After that is the scalability testing followed by fail-safe testing.

Service discovery

Locating services in a distributed environment can be a tedious task. Constant change and delivery is the dire requirement for today's constantly evolving world. In such situations, service discovery can be challenging as we want independent teams and minimal dependencies across teams. Service discovery should be such that a dynamic location can be provided for microservices. The location of a service may constantly change depending on deployments and auto-scaling or failures. Service discovery should also keep a lookout for services that are down or are performing poorly.

Microservice example

The following is a diagram of shopping microservices, which we are going to implement throughout this book. As we can see, each service is independently maintained and there are independent modules or smaller systems—**Billing Module**, **Customer Module**, **Product Module**, and **Vendor Module**. To coordinate with every module, we have **API Gateway** and **Service Registry**. Adding any additional service becomes very easy as the service registry will maintain all the dynamic entries and will be updated accordingly:

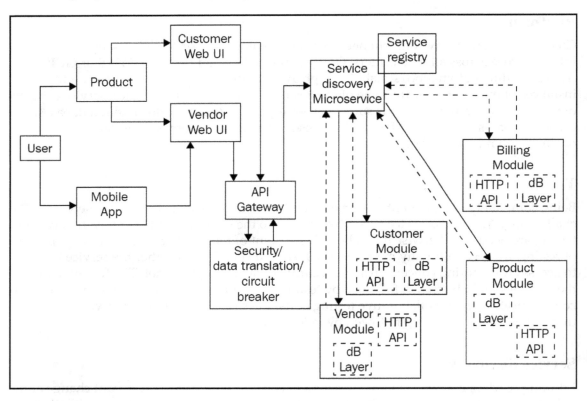

Key considerations while adopting microservices

A microservice architecture introduces well-defined boundaries, which makes it possible to isolate failures within the boundaries. But being like other distributed systems, there is likely a chance of failure at the application level. To minimize the impact, we need to design fault-tolerant microservices, which react in a predefined way to certain types of failure. While adapting to microservice architecture, we add one more network layer to communicate with rather than in-memory method calls, which introduces extra latency and one more layer to manage. Given next are a few considerations that if handled with care while designing microservices for failure, will benefit the system in the long run.

Service degradation

Microservices architecture allows you to isolate failures, thus enabling you to isolate the failures and get graceful degradation as failures are contained within the boundaries of the service and are not cascaded. For example, in social networking sites, the messaging service may go down, but that won't stop the end users from using social networks. They can still browse posts, share statuses, check-in locations, and so on. Services should be made such that they adhere to certain SLAs. If a microservice stops meeting its SLA, then that service should be restored to back up. **Netflix's Hystrix** is based on the same principle.

Proper change governance

Introducing change without any governance can be a huge problem. In a distributed system, services depend on each other. So when you introduce a new change, the utmost consideration should be given as if any side or unwanted effects are introduced, then its effect should be minimal. Various change management strategies and automatic rollout options should be available. Also, proper governance should be there in code management. Development should be done via TDD or BDD, and if the agreed percentage is met upon, only then should it be rolled out. Releases should be done gradually. One useful strategy is the *blue-green* or *red-black* deployment strategy, wherein you run two production environments. You rollout the change in only one environment and point out the load balancer to a newer version only after your change is verified. This is more likely when maintaining a staging environment.

Health checks, load balancing, and efficient gateway routing

Depending on business requirements, the microservice instance can start, restart, stop on some failure, run low on memory, and auto-scale, which may make it temporarily or permanently unavailable. Therefore, the architecture and framework should be designed accordingly. For example, a Node.js server, being single-threaded, stops immediately in the case of failure, but using graceful tools such as **PM2** forever keeps them running. A gateway should be introduced that will be the only point of contact for the microservice consumer. The gateway can be a load balancer that should skip unhealthy microservices instances. The load balancer should be able to collect health information metrics and route traffic accordingly, it should smartly analyze the traffic on any particular microservice, and it should trigger auto-scaling if needed.

Self-curing

Self-curing design can help the system to recover from disasters. Microservices implementation should be able to recover lost services and functionality automatically. Tools such as Docker restart services whenever they fail. Netflix provides wide tools as an orchestration layer to achieve self-healing. Eureka service registry and Hystrix circuit breaker are commonly used. Circuit breakers make your service calls more resilient. They track each microservice endpoint's status. Whenever timeout is encountered, Hystrix breaks the connection, triggers the need for curing that microservice, and reverts to some fail-safe strategy. **Kubernates** is another option. If a pod or any container inside the pod goes down, Kubernates brings up the system and maintains the replica set intact.

Cache for failover

Failover caching helps to provide necessary data whenever there are temporary failures or some glitches. The cache layer should be designed so that it can smartly decide how long the cache can be used in a normal situation or during failover situations. Setting cache standard response headers in HTTP can be used. The max-age header specifies the amount of time a resource will be considered fresh. The stale-if-error header determines how long the resource should be served from the cache. You can also use libraries such as **Memcache**, **Redis**, and so on.

Retry until

Due to its self-healing capabilities, a microservice usually gets up and running in no time. Microservice architecture should have *retry logic until condition* capabilities, as we can expect that the service will recover or the load balancer will redirect the service request to another healthy instance. Frequent retries can also have a huge impact on the system. A general idea is increasing the waiting time between retries after each failure. Microservices should be able to handle idempotency issues; let's say you are retrying to purchase an order, then there shouldn't be double purchases on the customer. Now, let's take time to revisit the microservice concept and understand the most common questions asked about microservice architecture.

Microservice FAQs

While understanding any new terms, we often come across several questions. The following are some of the most frequently asked questions that we come across while understanding microservices:

- **Aren't microservices just like service-oriented architecture (SOA)? Don't I already have them? When should I start?**

  If you have been in the software industry for a long time, then seeing microservices would probably get you remembering SOA. Microservices does take the concept of modularity and message-based communication from SOA, but there are many differences between them. While SOA focuses more on code reuse, microservices follow the *play in your own bundled context* rule. Microservices are more of a subset of SOA. Microservices can be scaled on demand. Not all microservice implementations are the same. Using Netflix's implementation in your medical domain is probably a bad idea as any mistake in the medical report will be worth a human life. The simple answer for a working microservice can be to have a clear goal of the operation that the service is meant to perform and if it doesn't perform then what it should do in failures. There have been various answers to when and how to begin with microservices. *Martin Fowler*, one of the pioneers in microservices, states to start with the monolith and then gradually move to microservices. But the question here is—*is there enough investment to go into the same phase again in this technological innovation era?* The short answer is going early in microservices has huge benefits as it will address all concerns from the very beginning.

- **How will we deal with all the parts? Who's in charge?**

Microservices introduce localization and self-rule. Localization means that the huge work that was done earlier will no longer be done by the central team. Embracing self-rule means trusting all teams to let them make their own decisions. This way, software changes or even migrations becomes very easy and fast to manage. Having said that, it doesn't mean that there's no central body at all. With more microservices, the architecture becomes more complex. The central team then should handle all centralized controls such as security, design patterns, frameworks, enterprise security bus, and so on. Certain self-governance processes should be introduced, such as SLAs. Each microservice should adhere to these SLAs and system design should be smart in such a way that if SLAs are not met, then the microservice should be dropped.

- **How do I introduce change or how do I begin with microservice development?**

Almost all successful microservice stories have begun with a monolith that got too big to be managed and was broken up. Changing some part of the architecture all of a sudden will have a huge impact, it should be introduced as gradually kind of *divide and rule*. Consider asking yourself the following questions for deciding which part to break in the monolith—*How is my application built and packaged? How is my application code written? Can I have different data sources and how will my application function when I introduce multiple data sources?*—Based on the answers of these parts, refactor that part and measure and observe the performance of that application. Make sure that the application stays in its bounded context. Another part that you can begin is the part whose performance is worst in the current monolithic. Finding these bottlenecks that hinder change would be good for organizations. Introducing centralized operations will eventually allow multiple things to be run in parallel and benefit the greater good of the company.

- **What kind of tools and technologies are required?**

While designing microservice architecture, proper thought should be given to the technology or framework selection for any particular stage. For example, an ideal environment for microservice features, cloud infrastructure, and containers. Containers give heterogeneous and easy to port or migrate systems. Using Docker brings resiliency and scalability on demand in microservices. Any part of microservices, such as the API Gateway or the service registry should be such that it should be API friendly, adaptable to dynamic changes, and not be a single point of failure. Containers require shifting on and off to a server, track all application upgrades for which proper framework either—**Swarm** or **Kubernates** for orchestrating framework deployments. Lastly, some monitoring tools to keep health checks on all microservices and take actions needed. Prometheus is one such famous tool.

- **How do I govern a microservices system?**

With lots of parallel service development going on, there is a primitive need to have a centralized governing policy. Not only do we need to take care of certifications and server audits, but also centralized concerns such as security, logging, scalability, and distributed concerns such as team ownership, sharing concerns between various services, code linters, service-specific concerns, and so on. In such a case, some standard guidelines can be made such as each team should provide a Docker configuration file that bundles the software right from getting dependencies to building it and producing a container that has the specifics of the service. The Docker image can then be run in any standard way, or using orchestration tools such as Amazon EC2, GCP, or Kubernates.

- **Should all the microservices be coded in the same language?**

The generic answer to this question is it is not a prerequisite. Microservices interact with each other via predefined protocols such as HTTP, Sockets, Thrift, RPC, and so on, which we will see in much detail later on. This means different services can be written in completely different technological stacks. The internal language implementation of the microservice is not important as the external outcome, that is, the endpoint and API. As long as the communication protocols are maintained, language implementation is not important, while it is an added advantage for not just having one language, but adding too many languages will also result in an added complexity of system developers to maintain language environment needs. The entire ecosystem should not be a wild jungle where you grow anything.

Cloud-based systems now have a standard set of guidelines. We will look at the famous twelve-factor applications and how microservices adhere to those guidelines.

Twelve-factor application of microservices

"Good code fails when you don't have a good process and a platform to help you. Good team fails when you don't have a good culture that embraces DevOps and microservices."

- Tim Spann

The **twelve-factor application** is a methodology for **Software as a Service (SaaS)** or web applications or software deployed in the cloud. It tells us about the characteristics of the output expected from such applications. It essentially is just outlining necessities for making well-structured and scalable cloud applications:

- **Codebase**: We maintain a single code base here for each microservice, with a configuration specific to their own environments, such as development, QA, and prod. Each microservice would have its own repository in a version control system such as Git, mercurial, and so on.
- **Dependencies**: All microservices will have their dependencies as part of the application bundle. In Node.js, there is `package.json`, which mentions all the development dependencies and overall dependencies. We can even have a private repository from where dependencies will be pulled.
- **Configs**: All configurations should be externalized, based on the server environment. There should be a separation of config from code. You can set environment variables in Node.js or use Docker compose to define other variables.
- **Backing services**: Any service consumed over the network such as database, I/O operations, messaging queries, SMTP, the cache will be exposed as microservices and using Docker compose and be independent of the application.
- **Build, release, and run**: We will use automated tools like Docker and Git in distributed systems. Using Docker we can isolate all the three phases using its push, pull, and run commands.
- **Processes**: Microservices designed would be stateless and would share nothing, hence enabling zero fault tolerance and easy scaling. Volumes will be used to persist data thus avoiding data loss.

- **Port binding**: Microservices should be autonomous and self-contained. Microservices should embed service listeners as part of service itself. For example— in Node.js application using HTTP module, service network exposing services for handling ports for all processes.
- **Concurrency**: Microservices will be scaled out via replication. Microservices are scaled out rather than scaled up. Microservices can be scaled or shrunk based on the flow of workload diversity. Concurrency will be dynamically maintained.
- **Disposability**: To maximize the robustness of application with fast startup and graceful shutdown. Various options include restart policies, orchestration using Docker swarm, reverse proxy, and load balancing with service containers.
- **Dev/prod parity**: Keep development/production/staging environments exactly alike. Using containerized microservices helps via *build once, run anywhere strategy*. The same image is deployed across various DevOps stage.
- **Logs**: Creating separate microservice for logs for making it centralized, to treat as event streams and send it to frameworks such as **elastic stack** (**ELK**).
- **Admin processes**: Admin or any management tasks should be packed as one of the processes, so they can be easily executed, monitored, and managed. This will include tasks like database migrations, one-time scripts, fixing bad data, and so on.

Microservices in the current world

Now, let's look at the pioneer implementers of microservices in the current world, the advantages they have got, and the roadmap ahead. The common objective of why these companies adopted microservices was getting rid of monolithic hell. Microservices even saw its adoption at the frontend. Companies such as **Zalando** use microservices principles to have composition at the UI level too.

Netflix

Netflix is one of the front-runners in microservice adoption. Netflix processes billions of viewing events per day. It needed a robust and scalable architecture to manage and process this data. Netflix used polyglot persistence to get the strength of each of the technological solutions they adopted. They used **Cassandra** for high volume and lower latency writes operations and a hand-made model with tuned configurations for medium volume write operations. They have **Redis** for high volume and lower latency reads at the cache level. Several frameworks that Netflix tailor-made are now open source and available for use:

Netflix Zuul	An edge server or the gatekeeper to the outside world. It doesn't allow unauthorized requests to pass through. It is the only point of contact for the outside world.
Netflix Ribbon	A load balancer that is used by service consumers to find services at runtime. If more than one instances of microservices are found, ribbon uses load balancing to evenly distribute the load.
Netflix Hystrix	A circuit breaker that is used to keep the system up and running. Hystrix breaks the connection for services that are going to fail eventually and only joins the connection when services are up again.
Netflix Eureka	Used for service discovery and registration. It allows services to register themselves at runtime.
Netflix Turbine	Monitoring tool to check the health of running microservices.

Just checking the stars on these repositories will give an idea of the rate of adoption of microservices using Netflix's tools.

Walmart

Walmart is one of the most popular companies on Black Friday. During Black Friday, it has more than 6 million page views per minute. **Walmart** adopted to microservices architecture to adopt to the world of 2020 to have 100% availability with reasonable costs. Migrating to microservices gave a huge uplift to the company. Conversion rates went up by 20%. They have zero downtime on Black Friday. They saved 40% of their computational power and got 20-50% cost savings overall.

Spotify

Spotify has 75 million active users per month with an average session length of 23 minutes. They adopted a microservice architecture and polyglot environment. Spotify is a company of 90 teams, 600 developers, and five offices across two continents, all working on the same product. This was a major factor in reducing dependencies as much as possible.

Zalando

Zalando implemented microservices at the frontend. They introduced fragments that served as separate services for the frontend. Fragments can be composed together at runtime as per the template definitions provided. Similar to Netflix, they have outsourced usage libraries:

Tailor	It's a layout service, which composes a page out of various fragments, as it does asynchronous and streams based fetching it has outstanding **time to the first byte (TTFB)**.
Skipper	HTTP router for communication, more of an HTTP interceptor, it has the ability to modify request and responses with filters.
Shaker	UI components library used for providing consistent user experience while developing fragments across multiple teams.
Quilt	Template storage and manager with REST API.
Innkeeper	Datastores for routes.
Tesselate	Server-side renderer and component tree builder.

It now serves more than 1500 fashion brands, generates more than $3.43 billion revenue, and developments are done in a team of more than 700 people.

In the next section, we will debunk microservices from the design point of view. We will see what components are involved in the microservices design and see widely prevalent microservices design patterns.

Microservice design aspects

While designing microservices, various important decisions need to be taken such as how will the microservices communicate with each other, how we will handle security, how we will do data management, and so on. Let's now look at those various aspects involved in the microservices design and understand various options available to it.

Communication between microservices

Let's understand this aspect with a real-world example to understand the problem. In the shopping cart application, we have our product microservices, inventory microservice, check out microservice, and user microservice. Now a user opts to buy a product; for the user, the product should be added to their cart, the amount paid, on successful payment, the checkout done, and inventory updated. Now if payment is successfully done, then only the checkout and inventory should be updated, hence the services need to communicate with each other. Let's now look at some of the mechanisms that microservices can use to communicate with each other or any of the external clients.

Remote Procedure Invocation (RPI)

Briefly speaking, remote procedure call is a protocol that anyone can use to access services from any other providers located remotely in the network, without the need of understanding the network details. The client uses the protocol of request and replies to make requests for services and it is one of the most feasible solutions to REST for big data search systems. It has one of the major advantages of serialization time. Some of the technologies providing RPI are **Apache Thrift** and **Google's gRPC**. gRPC is a widely adopted library and it has more than 23,000 downloads from Node.js per day. It has some awesome utilities such as pluggable authentication, tracing, load balancing, and health checking. It is used by Netflix, CoreOS, Cisco, and so on.

This pattern of communication has the following advantages:

- Request and reply are easy
- Simple to maintain as there is no middle broker
- Bidirectional streams with HTTP/2-based transportation methods
- Efficiently connecting polyglot services in microservices styled architectural ecosystems

This pattern has the following challenges and issues for consideration:

- The caller needs to know the locations of service instances, that is, maintain a client-side registry and server-side registry
- It only supports the request and reply model and has no support for other patterns such as notifications, async responses, the publish/subscribe pattern, publish async responses, streams, and so on

RPI uses binary rather than text to keep the payload very compact and efficient. These requests are multiplexed over a single TCP connection, which can allow multiple concurrent messages to be in flight without having to compromise for network consumption usage.

Messaging and message bus

This mode of communication is used when services have to handle the requests from various client interfaces. Services need to collaborate with each other to handle some specific operations, for which they need to use an inter-process communication protocol. Asynchronous messaging and message bus is one of them. Microservices communicate with each other by exchanging messages over various messaging channels. **Apache Kafka**, **RabbitMQ**, and **ActiveMQ**, **Kestrel** are some of the widely available message brokers that can be used for communication between microservices.

The message broker ultimately does the following set of functionalities:

- Route messages coming from various clients to different microservices destinations.
- Changes messages to desired transformations as per need.
- Ability to do message aggregations, segregate a message into multiple messages, and send them to the destination as per need and recompose them.
- Respond to errors or events.
- Provide content and routing using the publish-subscribe pattern.
- Using message bus as a means of communication between microservices has the following advantages:
    - The client is decoupled from the services; they don't need to discover any services. Loosely coupled architecture throughout.
    - Highly available as the message broker persists messages until the consumer is able to process them for operations.
    - It has support for a variety of communication patterns, including the widely used request/reply, notifications, async responses, publish-subscribe, and so on.

While this mode provides several advantages, it increases the complexity of adding a message broker that should be made highly available, as it can become a single point of failure. It also implies the need for the client to discover the location of the message broker, the single point of contact.

Protobufs

Protocol buffers or **protobufs** are a binary format created by Google. Google defines protobufs as a language and platform neutral extensive way of serializing structured data that can be used as one of the communication protocols. Protobufs also defines a set of some language rules that define the structure of messages. Some demonstrations effectively show that protobufs is six times faster than JSON. It is very easy to implement and it involves three major stages, which are creating message descriptors, message implementations, and parsing and serialization. Using protobufs in your microservices gives you the following advantages:

- Formats for protobufs are self-explaining—formal formats.
- It has RPC support; you can declare server RPC interfaces as part of protocol files.
- It has an option for structure validation. As it has larger datatype messages that are serialized on protobufs, it can be validated automatically by the code that is responsible for exchanging them.

While the protobuf pattern offers various advantages, it has some drawbacks, which are as follows:

- It is an upcoming pattern; hence you won't find many resources or detailed documentation for implementation of protobuf. If you just look for the protobuf tag on Stack Overflow, you will merely see a mere 10,000 questions.
- As it's binary format, it's non-readable when compared to JSON, which is simple to read and analyze on the other hand. The next generation of protobuf and flatbuffer is already available now.

Service discovery

The next obvious aspect to take care of is the method through which any client interface or any microservice will discover the network location of any service instance. Modern applications based on microservices run in virtualized or containerized environments where things change dynamically, including the number of instances of services and their location. Also, the set of service instances changes dynamically based on auto-scaling, upgrades, and so on. We need an elaborate a service discovery mechanism. Discussed ahead are widely used patterns.

Service registry for service-service communication

Different microservices and various client interfaces need to know the location of service instances so as to send requests. Usually, virtual machines or containers have a different or dynamic IP address, for example, an EC2 group when applied auto-scaling, it auto adjusts the number of instances based on load. Various options are available to maintain a registry anywhere such as client-side or server-side registrations. Clients or microservices look up to that registry to find other microservices for communication.

Let's take the real-life example of Netflix. Netflix Eureka is a service registry provider. It has various options for registering and querying available service instances. Using the POST API exposed an instance of service tells about its network location. It must be constantly updated every 30 seconds with the PUT API exposed. Any interface can use the GET API to get that instance and use it as per demand. Some of the widely available options are as follows:

- etcd: A key-value store used for shared configuration and service discovery. Projects such as Kubernates and cloud foundry are based on etcd as it can be highly available, key-value based, and consistent.
- consul: Yet another tool for service discovery. It has wide options such as exposed API endpoints that allow the client to register and discover services and perform health checks to determine service availability.
- ZooKeeper: Very widely used, highly available, and a high performant coordinated service used in distributed applications. Originally a subproject of Hadoop, Zookeeper is a widely used top-level project and it comes preconfigured with various frameworks.

Some systems have implicit in-built service registry, built in as a part of their framework. For example, Kubernates, Marathon, and AWS ELB.

Server-side discovery

All requests made to any of the services are routed via a router or load balancers that run in a location known to client interfaces. The router then queries a maintained registry and forwards the request based on the query response. An **AWS Elastic load balancer** is a classic example that has the ability to handle load balancing, handle internal or external traffic, and act as a service registry. EC2 instances are registered to ELB either via exposed API calls or either through auto-scaling. Other options include NGINX and NGINX Plus. There are available consul templates that ultimately generate the nginx.conf file from the consul service registry and can configure proxying as required.

Some of the major advantages of using server-side discovery are as follows:

- The client does not need to know the location of different microservices. They just need to know the location of the router and the service discovery logic is completely abstracted from the client so there is zero logic at the client end.
- Some environments provide this component functionality for free.

While these options have great advantages, there are some drawbacks too that need to be handled:

- It has more network hops, that is, one from the client service registry and another from the service registry microservice.
- If the load balancer is not provided by the environment, then it has to be set up and managed. If not properly handled, then it can be a single point of failure.
- The selected router or load balancer must support different communication protocols for modes of communication.

Client-side discovery

Under this mode of discovery, the client is responsible for handling the network location of available microservices and load balancing incoming requests across them. The client needs to query a service registry (a database of available services maintained on the client side). The client then selects service instances on the basis of an algorithm and then makes a request. Netflix uses this pattern extensively and has open sourced their tools Netflix OSS, Netflix Eureka, Netflix Ribbon, and Netflix Prana. Using this pattern has the following advantages:

- High performance and availability as there are fewer transition hops, that is, the client just has to invoke the registry and the registry will redirect to the microservice as per their needs.
- This pattern is fairly simple and highly resilient as besides the service registry there are no moving parts. As the client knows about available microservices, they can make intelligent decisions easily such as to use a hash, when to trigger auto-scaling, and so on.
- One significant drawback of using this mode of service discovery is implementation of client-side service discovery logic has to be done in every programming language of the framework that is used by the service clients. For example, Java, JavaScript, Scala, Node.js, Ruby, and so on.

Registration patterns – self-registration

While using this pattern, any microservice instance is responsible for registering and deregistering itself from the maintained service registry. To maintain health checks, a service instance sends heartbeat requests to prevent its registry from expiring. Netflix uses a similar approach and has outsourced their Eureka library, which handles all aspects of service registration and deregistration. It has its client in Java as well as Node.js. The Node.js client (`eureka-js-client`) has more than 12,000 downloads a month. The self-registration pattern has major benefits, such as any microservice instance would know its own state, hence it can implement or shift to other modes easily such as **Starting**, **Available**, and others.

However, it also has the following drawbacks:

- It couples the service tightly to the self-service registry, which forces us to enable the service registration code in each language we are using in the framework
- Any microservice that is in running mode, but is not able to handle requests, will often be unaware of which state to pursue, and will often end up forgetting to unregister from the registry

Data management

Another important question in microservice design aspect is the database architecture in a microservices application. We will see various options such as whether to maintain a private datastore, managing transactions, and making querying datastores easy in distributed systems. An initial thought can be going with a single database, but if we give it deep thought, we will soon see it as an unwise and unfitting solution because of tight coupling, different requirements, and runtime blocking by any of the services.

Database per service

In a distributed microservices architecture, different services have needs and usages of different storage requirements. The relational database is a perfect choice when it comes to maintaining relations and having complex queries. NoSQL databases such as MongoDB is the best choice when there is unstructured complex data. Some may require graph data and thus use *Neo4j* or *GraphQL*. The solution is to keep each of the microservices data private to that service and get it accessible only via APIs. Each microservice maintains its datastore and is a private part of that service implementation and hence it is not directly accessible by other services.

Some of the options you have while implementing this mode of data management are as follows:

- **Private tables/collections per service**: Each microservice has a set of defined tables or collections that can only be accessed by that service
- **Schema per service**: Each service has a schema that can only be accessed via the microservice it is bound to
- **Database per service**: Each microservice maintains its own database as per its needs and requirements

When thought of, maintaining a schema per service seems to be the most logical solution as it will have lower overhead and ownership can clearly be made visible. If some services have high usage and throughput and different usage, then maintaining a separate database is the logical option. A necessary step is to add barriers that will restrict any microservice from accessing data directly. Various options to add this barrier include assigning user IDs with restricted privileges or accessing control mechanisms such as grants. This pattern has the following advantages:

- Loosely coupled services that can stand on their own; changes to one service's datastore won't affect any other services.
- Each service has the liberty to select the datastore as required. Each microservice has the option of whether to go for relational or non-relational databases as per need. For example, any service that needs intensive search results on text may go for **Solr** or **Elasticsearch**, whereas any service where there is structured data may go for any SQL database.

This pattern has the following drawbacks and upcomings that need to be handled with care:

- Handling complex scenarios that involve transactions spanning across multiple services. The CAP theorem states that it is impossible to have more than two out of the following three guarantees—consistency, availability, and partitions in the distributed datastore, so transactions are generally avoided.
- Queries ranging across multiple databases are challenging and resource consuming.
- The complexity of managing multiple SQL and non-SQL datastores.

To overcome the drawbacks, the following patterns are used while maintaining a database per service:

- **Sagas**: A saga is defined as a batch sequence of local transactions. Each entry in the batch updates the specified database and moves on by publishing a message or triggering an event for the next entry in the batch to happen. If any entry in the batch fails locally or any business rule is violated, then the saga executes a series of compensating transactions that compensate or undo the changes that were made by the saga batch updates.
- **API Composition**: This pattern insists that the application should perform the join rather than the database. As an example, a service is dedicated to query composition. So, if we want to fetch monthly product distributions, then we first retrieve the products from the product service and then query the distribution service to return the distribution information of the retrieved products.
- **Command Query Responsibility Segregation (CQRS)**: The principle of this pattern is to have one or more evolving views, which usually have data coming from various services. Fundamentally, it splits the application into two parts—the command or the operating side and the query or the executor side. It is more of a publisher-subscriber pattern where the command side operates create/update/delete requests and emits events whenever the data changes. The executor side listens for those events and handles those queries by maintaining views that are kept up to date, based on the subscription of events that are emitted by the command or operating side.

Sharing concerns

The next big thing in distributed microservice architecture to handle is sharing concerns. How will general things such as API routing, security, logging, and configurations work? Let's look at those points one by one.

Externalized configuration

An application usually uses one or many infrastructures third-party services such as a service registry, message broker, server, cloud deployment platform, and so on. Any service must be able to run in multiple environments without any modifications. It should have the ability to pick up external configurations. This pattern is more of a guideline that advises us to externalize all the configurations, including database information, environment info, network location, and so on, that create a startup service that reads this information and prepares the application accordingly. There are various options available. Node.js provides setting environment variables; if you use Docker, then it has the `docker-compose.yml` file.

Observability

Revisiting the twelve-factor's required for an application, we observe that any application needs some centralized features, even if it's distributed. These centralized features help us to have proper monitoring and debugging in case of issues. Let's look at some of the common observability parameters to look out for.

Log aggregation

Each service instance will generate information about what it is doing in a standardized format, which contains logs at various levels such as errors, warning, info, debug, trace, fatal, and so on. The solution is to use a centralized logging service that collects logs from each service instance and stores them in some common place where the user can search and analyze the logs. This enables us to configure alerts for certain kinds of logs. Also, a centralized service will help to do audit logging, exception tracking, and API metrics. Available and widely used frameworks are **Elastic Stack** (Elasticsearch, Logstash, Kibana), **AWS CloudTrail**, and **AWS CloudWatch**.

Distributed tracing

The next big problem is to understand the behavior and application so as to troubleshoot problems when required. This pattern is more of a designing guideline that states to maintain a unique external request ID, which is maintained by a microservice. This external request ID needs to be passed to all services that are involved in handling that request and in all the log messages. Another guideline is to include the start time and end time of requests and operations performed when a microservice does the operation.

Based on the preceding design aspects, we will see common microservice design patterns and understand each pattern in depth. We'll see when to use a particular pattern, what the problems are that it solves, and what pitfalls to avoid while using that design pattern.

Microservice design patterns

As microservices evolve, so evolves its designing principles. Here are some of the common design patterns that help to design an efficient and scalable system. Some of the patterns are followed by Facebook, Netflix, Twitter, LinkedIn, and so on, which provide some of the most scalable architectures.

Asynchronous messaging microservice design pattern

One of the most important things to consider in a distributed system is **state**. Although highly powerful REST APIs, it has a very primitive flaw of being synchronous and thus blocking. This pattern is about achieving a non-blocking state and asynchronicity to maintain the same state across the whole application reliably, avoid data corruption, and allow a faster rate of change across the application:

- **Problem**: Speaking contextually, if we go with the principle of single responsibility, a model or an entity in the application can mean something different to different microservices. So, whenever any change occurs, we need to ensure that different models are in sync with those changes. This pattern helps to solve this issue with the help of asynchronous messaging. In order to ensure data integrity throughout, there is a need to replicate the state of key business data and business events between microservices or datastores.

- **Solution**: Since it's asynchronous communication, the client or the caller assumes that the message won't be received immediately, carries on and attaches a callback to the service. The callback is for when the response is received what further operation to be carried on. A lightweight message broker (not to be confused with orchestrators used in SOA) is preferably used. The message broker is dumb, that is, they are ignorant of the application state. They communicate to services handling events, but they never handle events. Some of the widely adopted examples include RabbitMQ, the Azure bus, and so on. Instagram's feed is powered by this simple RabbitMQ. Based on the complexity of the project, you can introduce either a single receiver or multiple receivers. While a single receiver is good, soon it can be the single point of failure. A better approach is going reactive and introducing the publish-subscribe pattern of communication. That way the communication from the sender will be available to subscriber microservices in one go. Practically, when we consider a routine scenario, an update in any of the models will trigger an event to all its subscribers, which may further trigger the change in their own models. To avoid this, event bus is generally introduced in such type of a pattern that can fulfill the role of inter micro service communication and act as the message broker. Some of the commonly available libraries are **AMQP**, **RabbitMQ**, **NserviceBus**, **MassTransit**, and so on for scalable architecture.

  Here is an example using AMQP: `https://gist.github.com/ parthghiya/114a6e19208d0adca7bda6744c6de23e`.

- **Take care of:** To successfully implement this design, the following aspects should be considered:
  - When you need high scalability, or your current domain is already a message-based domain, then preference should be given to message-based commands over HTTP.
  - Publishing events across microservices, as well as changing the state in the original microservices.
  - Make sure that events are communicated across; mimicking the event would be a very bad design pattern.
  - Maintain the position of the subscriber's consumer to scale up performance.
  - When to make a rest call and when to use a messaging call. As HTTP is a synchronous call, it should be used only when needed.

- **When to use:** This is one of the most commonly used patterns. Based on the following use cases, you can use this pattern or its variants as per your requirements:
    - When you want to use real-time streaming, use the *Event Firehouse* pattern, which has *KAFKA* as one of its key components.
    - When your complex system is orchestrated in various services, one of the variants of this system, RabbitMQ, is extremely helpful.
    - Often, instead of subscribing to services, directly subscribing to the datastore is advantageous. In such a case use, *GemFire* or *Apache GeoCode* following this pattern is helpful.

- **When not to use:** In the following scenarios, this pattern is less recommended:
    - When you have heavy database operations during event transmission, as database calls are synchronous
    - When your services are coupled
    - When you don't have standard ways defined to handle data conflict situations

Backend for frontends

The current world demands a mobile-first approach everywhere. The service may respond differently to mobile where it has to show little content, as it has very less content. On the web, it has to show huge content as lots of space is available. Scenarios may differ drastically based on the device. As for example in the mobile app, we may allow barcode scanner, but in desktop, it is not a wise option. This pattern addresses these issues and helps to effectively design microservices across multiple interfaces:

- **Problem**: With the advent of development of services supporting multiple interfaces, it becomes extremely painful to manage everything in one service. This constantly evolves change in any of the single interfaces; the need to keep services working in all interfaces can soon become a bottleneck and a pain to maintain.

- **Solution**: Rather than maintaining a general purpose API, design one backend per user experience or interface, better termed as a backend for frontend (**BFFs**). The BFF is tightly bound to a single interface or specific user experience and is maintained by their specific teams so as to easily adapt to new change. While implementing this pattern, one of the common concerns that occurs is maintaining the number of BFFs. A more generic solution would be separating concerns and having each BFF handle its own responsibility.

- **Take care of**: While implementing this design pattern, the following points should be taken care of as they are the most common pitfalls:

    - A fair consideration of the amount of BFFs to be maintained. A new BFF should only be created when concerns across a generally available service can be separated out for a specific interface.
    - A BFF should only contain client/interface-specific code to avoid code duplication.
    - Divide responsibilities across teams for maintaining BFFs.
    - This should not be confused with a **Shim**, a converter to the convert to interface-specific format required for that type of interface.

- **When to use**: This pattern is extremely useful in the following scenarios:

    - There are varying differences in a general-purpose backend service across multiple interfaces and there are multiple updates at any point in time in a single interface.
    - You want to optimize a single interface and not disturb the utility across other interfaces.
    - There are various teams, and implement an alternative language for a specific interface and you want to maintain it separately.

- **When not to use**: While this pattern does solve lots of issues, this pattern is not recommended in the following scenarios:

    - Do not use this pattern to handle generic parameter concerns such as authentication, security, or authorization. This would just increase latency.
    - If the cost of deploying an extra service is too high.
    - When interfaces make the same requests and there is not much difference between them.
    - When there is only one interface and support for multiple interfaces is not there, a BFF won't make much sense.

Gateway aggregation and offloading

Dump or move specialized, common services and functionalities to a gateway. This pattern can introduce simplicity by moving shared functionality into a single part. Shared functionality can include things such as the use of SSL certificates, authentication, and authorization. A gateway can further be used to join multiple requests into a single request. This pattern simplifies needs where a client has to make multiple calls to different microservices for some operation:

- **Problem**: Often, to perform a simple task, a client may need to make multiple HTTP calls to various different microservices. Too many calls to a server requires an increase in resources, memory, and threads, which adversely affects performance and scalability. Many features are commonly used across multiple services; an authentication service and a product checkout service are both going to use the log in the same way. This service requires configuration and maintenance. Also, these type of services need an extra set of eyes as they are essential. For example, token validation, HTTPS certificate, encryption, authorization, and authentication. With each deployment, it is difficult to manage that as it has to span across the whole system.

- **Solution:** The two major components in this design pattern are the gateway and gateway aggregator. The gateway aggregator should always be placed behind the gateway. Hence, single responsibility is achieved, with each component doing the operation they are meant to do.

- **Gateway:** It offloads some of the common operations such as certificate management, authentication, SSL termination, cache, protocol translation, and so on to one single place. It simplifies the development and abstracts all this logic in one place and speeds up development in a huge organization where not everyone has access to the gateway, only specialized teams work on it. It maintains consistency throughout the application. The gateway can ensure a minimum amount of logging and thus help out to find the faulty microservice. It's much like the facade pattern in object-oriented programming. It acts as the following:

  - Filter
  - Single entry point that exposes various microservices
  - Solution to a common operation such as authorization, authentication, central configuration, and so on, abstracting this logic into a single place
  - Router for traffic management and monitoring

Netflix uses a similar approach and they are able to handle more than 50,000 requests per hour and they open sourced **ZuuL**:

- **Gateway aggregator**: It receives the client request, then it decides to which different systems it has to dispatch the client request, gets the results, and then aggregates and sends them back to the client. For the client, it is just one request. Overall round trips between client and server are reduced.

 Here is an example for aggregator: `https://gist.github.com/parthghiya/3f1c3428b1cf3cc6d76ddd18b4521e03.js`

- **Take care of**: The following pitfalls should be properly handled in order to successfully implement this design pattern in microservices:
  - Do not introduce service coupling, that is, the gateway can exist independently, without other service consumers or service implementers.
  - Here, every microservice will be dependent on the gateway. Hence, the network latency should be as low as possible.
  - Make sure to have multiple instances of the gateway, as only a single instance of the gateway may introduce it as a single point of failure.
  - Each of the requests goes through the gateway. Hence, it should be ensured that gateway has efficient memory and adequate performance, and can be easily scaled to handle the load. Have one round of load testing to make sure that it is able to handle bulk load.
  - Introduce other design patterns such as bulkheads, retry, throttle, and timeout for efficient design.
  - The gateway should handle logic such as the number of retries, waiting for service until.
  - The cache layer should be handled, which can improve performance.
  - The gateway aggregator should be behind the gateway, as the request aggregator will have another. Combining them in a gateway will likely impact the gateway and its functionalities.

- While using the asynchronous approach, you will find yourself smacked by too many promises of callback hell. Go with the reactive approach, a more declarative style. Reactive programming is prevalent from Java to Node.js to Android. You can check out this link for reactive extensions across different links: `https://github.com/reactivex`.
- Business logic should not be there in the gateway.

- **When to use**: This pattern should be used in the following scenarios:
  - There are multiple microservices across and a client needs to communicate with multiple microservices.
  - Want to reduce the frequent network calls when the client is in lesser range network or cellular network. Breaking it in one request is efficient as then the frontend or the gateway will only have to cache one request.
  - When you want to encapsulate the internal structure or introduce an abstract layer to a large team present in your organization.

- **When not to use**: The following scenarios are when this pattern won't be a good fit:
  - When you just want to reduce the network calls. You cannot introduce a whole level of complexity for just that need.
  - The latency by the gateway is too much.
  - You don't have asynchronous options in the gateway. Your system makes too many synchronous calls for operations in the gateway. That would result in a blocking system.
  - Your application can't get rid of coupled services.

Proxy routing and throttling

When you have multiple microservices that you want to expose across a single endpoint and that single endpoint routes to service as per need. This application is helpful when you need to handle imminent transient failures and have a retry loop on a failed operation, thus improve the stability of the application. This pattern is also helpful when you want to handle the consumption of resources used by a microservice.

This pattern is used to meet the agreed SLAs and handle loads on resources and resource allocation consumption even when an increase in demand places loads on resources:

- **Problem**: When a client has to consume a multitude of microservices, challenges soon turn up such as client managing each endpoint and setting up separate endpoints. If you refactor any part of the code in any service then the client must also be updated as the client is directly in contact with the endpoint. Further, as these services are in the cloud, they have to be fault tolerant. Faults include temporary loss of connectivity or unavailability of services. These faults should be self-correcting. For example, a database service that is taking a large number of concurrent requests should throttle further requests until the memory load and resource utilization has decreased. On retrying the request, the operation is completed. The load on any application varies drastically on time period. For example, a social media chatting platform will have very less load during peak office hours and a shopping portal will have extreme load during festive season sales. For a system to perform efficiently it has to meet to agreed LSA, once it exceeds, subsequent requests needs to be stopped until load consumption has decreased.

- **Solution**: Place gateway layer in front of microservices. This layer includes the throttle component, as well as retry, once failed component. With the addition of this layer, the client needs only to interact with this gateway rather than interacting with each different microservice. It lets you abstract backend calls from the client and thus keeping the client end simple as the client only has to interact with the gateway. Any number of services can be added, without changing the client at any point in time. This pattern can also be used to handle versioning effectively. A new version of the microservice can be deployed parallelly and the gateway can route too, based on input parameters passed. New changes can be easily maintained by just a configuration change at the gateway level. This pattern can be used as an alternative strategy to auto-scaling. This layer should allow network requests only up to a certain limit and then throttle the request and retry once the resources have been released. This will help the system to maintain SLAs. The following points should be considered while implementing the throttle component:

- One of the parameters to consider for throttling is user requests or tenant requests. Assuming that a specific tenant or user triggers throttle, then it can be safely assumed that there's some issue with the caller.
- Throttling doesn't essentially mean to stop the requests. Lower quality resources if available can be given, for example, a mobile-friendly site, a lower quality video, and so on. Google does the same.
- Maintaining priority over microservices. Based on the priority they can be placed in the retry queue. As an ideal solution, three queues can be maintained—cancel, retry, and retry-after sometime.

- **Take care of**: Given here are some of the most common pitfalls that we can come across while successfully implementing this pattern:
  - The gateway can be a single point of failure. Proper steps have to be taken to ensure that it has fault tolerant capabilities during development. Also, it should be run in multiple instances.
  - Gateway should have proper memory and resource allocation otherwise it will introduce a bottleneck. Proper load testing should be done to ensure that failures are not cascaded.
  - Routing can be done based on IP, header, port, URL, request parameter, and so on.
  - The retry policy should be crafted very carefully based on the business requirements. It's okay in some places to have a please try again rather than having waiting periods and retrials. The retry policy may also affect the responsiveness of the application.
  - For effective application, this pattern should be combined with **Circuit Breaker Application**.
  - If service is idempotent, then and only then should it be retried. Trying retrial on other services may have unhealthy consequences. For example, if there is a payment service that waits for responses from other payment gateways, the retry component may think it fails and may send another request and the customer gets charged twice.
  - Different exceptions should handle the retry logic accordingly, based on the exceptions.
  - Retry logic should not disturb transaction management. The retry policy should be used accordingly.

- All failures that trigger a retry should be logged and handled properly for future scenarios.
- An important point to be considered is this is no replacement for exception handling. The first priority should be given to exceptions always, as they would not introduce an extra layer and add latency.
- Throttling should be added early in the system as it's difficult to add once the system is implemented; it should be carefully designed.
- Throttling should be performed quickly. It should be smart enough to detect an increase in activity and react accordingly by taking appropriate measures.
- Consideration between throttling and auto-scaling should be decided based on business requirements.
- The requests that are throttled should be effectively placed in a queue based on priority.

- **When to use:** This pattern is very handy in the following scenarios:
  - To ensure that agreed LSAs are maintained.
  - To avoid a single microservice consuming the majority of the pool of resources and avoid resource depletion by a single microservice.
  - To handle sudden bursts in consumption of microservices.
  - To handle transient and short-lived faults.

- **When not to use:** In the following scenarios, this pattern should not be used:
  - Throttling shouldn't be used as a means to handle exceptions.
  - When faults are long-lasting. If this pattern is applied in that case, it will severely affect the performance and responsiveness of the application.

Ambassador and sidecar pattern

This pattern is used when we want to segregate common connectivity features such as monitoring, logging, routing, security, authentication, authorization, and more. It creates helper services that act as ambassadors and sidecars that do the objective of sending requests on behalf of a service. It is just another proxy that is located outside of the process. Specialized teams can work on it and let other people not worry about it so as to provide encapsulation and isolation. It also allows the application to be composed of multiple frameworks and technologies.

The sidecar component in this pattern acts just like a sidecar attached to a motorcycle. It has the same life cycle as the parent microservice, retires the same time a parent microservice does, and it does essential peripheral tasks:

- **Solution:** Find a set of operations that are common throughout different microservices and place them inside their own container or process, thus providing the same interface for these common operations to all frameworks and platforms services in the whole system. Add an ambassador layer that acts as a proxy between applications and microservices. This ambassador can monitor performance metrics such as the amount of latency, the resource usage, and so on. Anything inside the ambassador can be maintained independently of the application. An ambassador can be deployed as a container, common process, daemon, or windows service. An ambassador and sidecar are not part of the microservice, but rather are connected to the microservice. Some of the common advantages of this pattern are as follows:

  - Language-independent development of the sidecar and ambassador, that is, you don't have to build a sidecar and ambassador for every language you have in your architecture.
  - Just part of the host, so it can access the same resources as any other microservice can.
  - Due to connection with microservices, there hardly is any latency Netflix uses a similar approach and they have open sourced their tool **Prana** (`https://github.com/Netflix/Prana`). Take a look at the following diagram:

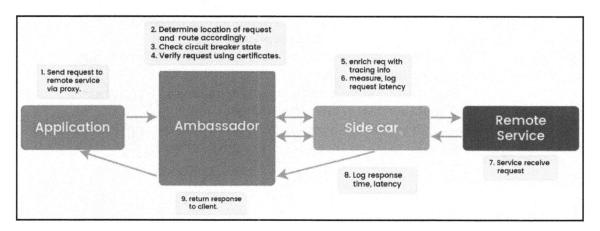

- **Take care of**: The following points should be taken care of as they are the most common pitfalls:
  - The ambassador can introduce some latency. Deep thought should be given on whether to use a proxy or expose common functionalities as the library.
  - Adding generalized functionalities in ambassador and sidecar is beneficial, but is it required for all scenarios? For example, consider the number of retries to a service, it might not be common for all use cases.
  - The language or framework in which ambassador and sidecar will be built, managed, and deployed strategy for it. The decision to create single or multiple instances of it based on need.
  - Flexibility to pass some parameters from service to ambassador and proxy and vice versa.
  - The deployment pattern: this is well suited when the ambassador and sidecar are deployed in containers.
  - The inter-micro service communication pattern should be such that it is framework agnostic or language agnostic. This would be beneficial in the long run.

- **When to use**: This pattern is extremely helpful in the following scenarios:
  - When there are multiple frameworks and languages involved and you need a common set of general features such as client connectivity, logging, and so on throughout the application. An ambassador and sidecar can be consumed by any service across the application.
  - Services are owned by different teams or different organizations.
  - You need independent services for handling this cross-cutting functionality and they can be maintained independently.
  - When your team is huge and you want specialized teams to handle, manage, and maintain core cross-cutting functionalities.
  - You need to support the latest connectivity options in a legacy application or an application that is difficult to change.
  - You want to monitor resource consumption across the application and cut off a microservice if its resource consumption is huge.

- **When not to use**: While this pattern does solve many issues, this pattern is not recommended in the following scenarios:
  - When network latency is utmost. Introducing a proxy layer would introduce some overhead that will create a slight delay, which may not be good for real-time scenarios.
  - When connectivity features cannot be generalized and require another level of integration and dependency with another service.
  - When creating a client library and distributing it to the microservices development team as a package.
  - For small applications where introducing an extra layer is actually an overhead.
  - When some services need to scale independently; if so, then the better alternative would be to deploy it separately and independently.

Anti-corruption microservice design pattern

Often, we need interoperability or coexistence between legacy and modern applications. This design provides an easy solution for this by introducing a facade between modern and legacy applications. This design pattern ensures that the design of an application is not hampered or blocked by legacy system dependencies:

- **Problem**: New systems or systems in the process of migration often need to communicate with the legacy system. The new system's model and technology would probably be different, considering that old systems are usually weak, but still, legacy resources may be needed for some operations. Often, these legacy systems suffer from poor design and poor schema designs. For interoperability, we may still need to support the old system. This pattern is about solving such corruption and still have a cleaner, neater, and easier to maintain microservice ecosystem.

- **Solution:** To avoid using legacy code or a legacy system, design a layer that does the following task: acts as the only layer for communicating with legacy code, which prevents accessing legacy code directly wherein different people may deal with them differently. The core concept is to separate out a legacy or the corrupt application by placing an ACL with the objective of not changing the legacy layer, and thus avoid compromising its approach or major technological change.

- The **anti-corruption layer** (**ACL**) should contain all the logic for translating as per new needs from the old model. This layer can be introduced as a separate service or translator component any place where needed. A general approach to organizing the design of the ACL is a combination of a facade, adapters, translators, and communicators to talk to systems. An ACL is used to prevent unexpected behavior of an external system from leaking in your existing context:

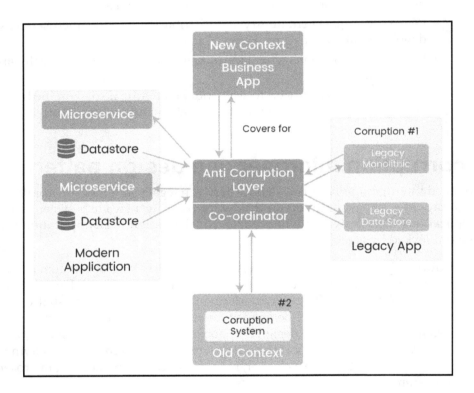

- **Take care of:** While effectively implementing this pattern, the following points should be considered as they are some of the major pitfalls:
    - The ACL should be properly scaled and given a better resources pool, as it will add latency to calls made between two systems.
    - Make sure that the corruption layer you introduce is actually an improvement and you don't introduce yet another layer of corruption.
    - The ACL adds an extra service; hence it must be effectively managed and maintained and scaled.

- Effectively decide the number of ACLs. There can be many reasons to introduce an ACL—a means to translate undesirable formats of the object in required formats means to communicate between different languages, and so on.

- Effective measures to make sure that transactions and data consistency are maintained between both systems and can be monitored.

- The duration of the ACL, will it be permanent, how will the communication be handled.

- While an ACL should successfully handle exceptions from the corruption layer, it should not completely, otherwise it would be very difficult to preserve any information about the original error.

- **When to use:** The anti-corruption pattern is highly recommended and extremely useful in the following scenarios:

  - There is a huge system up for refactoring from monolithic to microservices and there is a phase-by-phase migration planned instead of the big bang migration wherein the legacy system and new system need to coexist and communicate with each other.

  - If the system that you are undertaking is dealing with any data source whose model is undesirable or not in sync with the needed model, this pattern can be introduced and it will do the task of translating from undesirable formats to needed formats.

  - Whenever there is a need to link two bounded contexts, that is, a system is developed by someone else entirely and there is very little understanding of it, this pattern can be introduced as a link between systems.

- **When not to use:** This pattern is highly not recommended in the following scenarios:

  - There are no major differences between new and legacy systems. The new system can coexist without the legacy system.

  - You have lots of transactional operations and maintaining data consistency between the ACL and the corrupt layer adds too much latency. In such case, this pattern can be merged with other patterns.

  - Your organization doesn't have extra teams to maintain and scale the ACL as and when needed.

Bulkhead design pattern

Separate out different services in the microservices application into various pools such that if one of the services fails, the others will continue to function irrespective of failure. Create a different pool for each microservice to minimize the impact:

- **Problem**: This pattern takes inspiration from sectioned out parts of a ship's hull. If the hull of a ship is damaged, then only the damaged section would fill with water, which would prevent the ship from sinking. Let's say you are connecting to various microservices that are using a common thread pool. If one of the services starts showing delay, then all pool members will be too exhausted to wait for responses. Incrementally, a large number of requests coming from one service would deplete available resources. That's where this pattern suggests a dedicated pool for every single service.

- **Solution**: Separate service instances into different groups based on load and network usage. This allows you to isolate system failures and prevent depletion of resources in the connection pool. The essential advantages of this system are the prevention of propagating failures and ability to configure capacity of the resource pool. For higher priority services, you may assign higher pools.

> For example, given is a sample file from which we can see pool allocation for service shopping-management: `https://gist.github.com/parthghiya/be80246cc5792f796760a0d43af935db`.

- **Take care of**: Make sure to take care of the following points to make sure that a proper bulkhead design is implemented:
  - Define proper independent partitions in the application based on business and technical requirements.
  - Bulkheads can be introduced in forms of thread pools and processes. Decide which one is suitable for your application.
  - Isolation in the deployment of your microservices.

- **When to use:** The bulkhead pattern adds an advantage in the following scenarios:
    - The application is huge and you want to protect it from cascading or spreading failures
    - You can isolate critical services from standard services and you can allocate separate pools for them

- **When not to use:** This pattern is not advisable for the following scenarios:
    - When you don't have that much budget for maintaining separate overheads in terms of cost and management
    - The added level of complexity of maintaining separate pools is not necessary
    - Your resources usage is unexpected and you can't isolate your tenants and keep a limit on it as it is not acceptable when you would place several tenants in one partition

Circuit breaker

Services sometimes need to collaborate with each other when they need to handle requests. In such cases, there is a very high scenario that the other service is not available, is showing high latency, or is unusable. This pattern essentially solves this issue by introducing a breakage in the circuit that stops propagation in the whole architecture:

- **Problem**: In the microservices architecture when there is inter-services communication, a remote call needs to be invoked instead of an in-memory call. It may so happen that the remote call may fail or reach a timeout limit and hang without any response. Now in such cases when there are many callers, then all such locked threads that you can run out of resources and the whole system will become unresponsive.

- **Solution**: A very primitive idea for solving this issue is introducing a wrapper for a protected function call, it monitors for failures. Now this wrapper can be triggered via anything such as certain threshold in failures, database connection fails, and so on. All further calls will return with an error and stop catastrophic propagation. This will trip the circuit open, and while the circuit is open, it will avoid making the protected call. The implementation is done in the following three stages just as in an electric circuit. It is in three stages: **Closed State**, **Open State**, and **Half-Open State**, as explained in the following diagram:

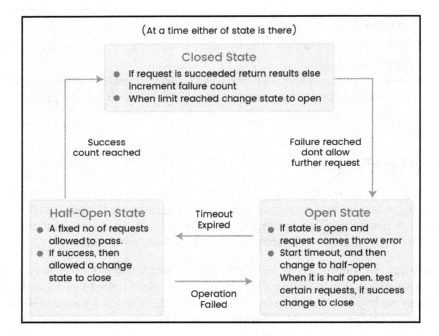

 Here is an example for implementation in Node.js: Hystrix is open sourced by Netflix https://gist.github.com/parthghiya/777c2b423c9c8faf0d427fd7a3eeb95b

- **Take care of**: The following needs to be taken care of when you want to apply the circuit breaker pattern:
    - Since you are invoking a remote call, and there may be many remote call invocation asynchronous and reactive principles for using future, promises, async, and await is must.
    - Maintain a queue of requests; when your queue is overcrowded, you can easily trip the circuit. Always monitor the circuit, as you will often need to activate it again for an efficient system. So, have a mechanism ready for reset and failure handlers.
    - You have a persistent storage and network cache such as **Memcache** or **Redis** to record availability.
    - Logging, exception handling, and relaying failed requests.

- **When to use**: In the following use cases, you can use the circuit breaker pattern:
    - When you don't want your resources to be depleted, that is, an action that is doomed to fail shouldn't be tried until it is fixed. You can use it to check the availability of external services.
    - When you can compromise a bit on performance, but want to gain high availability of the system and not deplete resources.

- **When not to use**: In the following scenarios, it is not advisable to introduce the circuit breaker pattern:
    - You don't have an efficient cache layer that monitors and maintains states of services for a given time for requests across the clustered nodes.
    - For handling in-memory structures or as the substitute for handling exceptions in business logic. This would add overhead to performance.

Strangler pattern

Today's world is one where technology is constantly evolving. What is written today, is just tomorrow's legacy code. This pattern is very helpful when it comes to the migration process. This pattern is about eventually migrating a legacy system by incrementally replacing particular parts of functionality with new microservices application and services. It eventually introduces a proxy that redirects either to the legacy or the new microservices, until the migration is complete and at the end, you can shut off the strangler or the proxy:

- **Problem**: With aging systems, new evolving development tools, and hosting options, the evolution of cloud and serverless platforms maintaining the current system gets extremely painful with the addition of new features and functionalities. Completely replacing a system can be a huge task, for which gradual migration needs to be done such that the old system is still handled for the part that hasn't been migrated yet. This pattern solves this very problem.
- **Solution**: The strangler solution resembles a vine that strangles a tree that it's wrapped over. Over time, the migrated application strangles the original application until you can shut off the monolithic application. Thus, the overall process is as follows:
    - **Reconstruct**: Construct a new application or site (in serverless or AWS cloud-based on modern principles). Incrementally reconstruct the functionalities in an agile manner.
    - **Coexist**: Leave the legacy application as it is. Introduce a facade that eventually acts as a proxy and decides where to route the request based on the current migration status. This facade can be introduced at web server level or programming level based on various parameters such as IP address, user agent, or cookies.
    - **Terminate**: Redirect everything to the modern migrated application and loosen off all the ties with the legacy application.

A sample gist of `.htaccess` that acts as a facade can be found at this link: `https://gist.github.com/parthghiya/a6935f65a262b1d4d0c8ac24149ce61d`.

The solution instructs us to create a facade or a proxy that has the ability to intercept the requests that are going to the backend legacy system. The facade or proxy then decides whether to route it to the legacy application or the new microservices. This is an incremental process, wherein both the systems can coexist. The end users won't even know when the migration process is complete. It gives the added advantage that if the adopted microservice approach doesn't work, there is a very simple way to change it.

- **Take care of**: The following points need to be taken care of for effectively applying the strangulation pattern:
  - The facade or the proxy needs to be updated with the migration.
  - The facade or the proxy shouldn't be a single point of failure or bottleneck.
  - When the migration is complete, facade will evolve as the adapter for legacy applications.
  - The new code written should be such that it can easily be intercepted, so in future, we can replace it in future migrations.

- **When to use**: The strangler application is extremely useful when it comes to replacing a legacy and monolithic application with microservices. The pattern is used in the following cases:
  - When you want to follow the test-driven on behavior-driven development, and run fast and comprehensive tests with the accessibility of code coverages and adapt CI/CD.
  - Your application can be contained bounded contexts within which a model applies in the region. As an example, in a shopping cart application, the product module would be one context.

- **When not to use**: This pattern may not be applicable in the following scenarios:
  - When you are not able to intercept the user agent request, or you are not able to introduce a facade in your architecture.
  - When you think of doing a page by page migration at a time or you are thinking of doing it all at once.
  - When your application is more frontend-driven; that's where you have to entirely change and rework the interacting framework based on the way the frontend is interacting with services, as you don't want to expose the various ways the user agent is interacting with services.

Summary

In this chapter, we debunked microservices to understand the evolution of microservices, the characteristics of microservices, and the advantages of microservices. We went through various design principles of microservices, the process of refactoring from monolithic applications to microservices, and the various microservice design patterns.

In the next chapter, we will start our microservice journey. We will go through all the setup required for our microservice journey. We will go through concepts related to Node.js and TypeScript, which are essential throughout the book. We will also create our first microservice, `Hello World`.

Gearing up for the Journey

2

After learning the theory about microservices, we will now move on to hands-on implementation. This chapter will lay the foundation for the journey ahead and will revisit Node.js and TypeScript concepts essential to the book. It will tell you about the trends and adoption rates of both languages. We will go through all the required installations, and we will prepare our development environment. We will test the development environment by implementing the customary `Hello World` microservice. In this chapter, we will focus on the following topics:

- **Setting up the primary development environment**: We will set up a primary environment with all the prerequisites needed. We will understand all aspects required for microservice development.

- **Primer to TypeScript**: In this section, we are going to walk through some of the major TypeScript topics that we are going to use throughout the book. We will justify usage of TypeScript as our language in Node.js, and understand how applications can be written in TypeScript and Node.js.

- **Primer to Node.js**: In this section, we will go through some advanced Node.js topics such as clustering in Node.js, the recently introduced async/await, and others. We will understand the Event Loop, and briefly look at Node streams and latest trends in Node.js.

- **Microservice implementation**: We will write a `Hello World` microservice that will use our development environment.

Setting up primary environment

In this section, we will set up our environment required for our journey ahead. You already installed Node.js and TypeScript globally. At the time of writing, the available version of Node.js was **9.2.0** and TypeScript was **2.6.2**.

Visual Studio Code (VS Code)

VS Code is one of the best available editors right now for TypeScript. By default, VS Code TypeScript displays warnings on incorrect code, which helps us to write better code. Linters, debugging, build issues, errors, and so on are provided out of the box by VS Code. It has supports for JSDoc, sourcemaps, setting different out-files for files that are generated, hiding derived JavaScript files, and so on. It has support for auto-imports, generating method skeletons directly just like Eclipse for Java developers. It also provides options for version control systems. Hence, it will be our primary choice as IDE. You can download it from `https://code.visualstudio.com/download`.

Installing it for Windows is the easiest thing, as it's an `.exe` file and all you have to do is select a path and follow the steps. Installing it on a Unix/Ubuntu machine involves downloading the `deb` file and then executing the following command lines:

```
sudo dpkg -i <file>.deb
sudo apt-get install -f # Install dependencies
```

Once VS Code is available, open extensions and download `https://marketplace.visualstudio.com/items?itemName=pmneo.tsimporter` and `https://marketplace.visualstudio.com/items?itemName=steoates.autoimport`. We will use the advantages of these extensions, which will be helpful for easy code management, prebuilt skeletons, and more.

PM2

It is the advanced processor manager for Node.js. Node.js, being single threaded, requires some add-on tools for server management such as restarting server, memory management, multiple process management, and so on. It has a built-in load balancer, and it allows you to keep the application running forever. It has zero downtime and other system admin options that has eased up life. It is also exposed as a module, so we can runtime trigger various options at any phase of Node.js applications. To install PM2, open up a Terminal and shoot the following command:

```
npm install pm2 -g
```

More detailed options and APIs can be found at `http://pm2.keymetrics.io/docs/usage/pm2-api/`.

NGINX

NGINX is one of the most popular web servers. It can be used as a load balancer, HTTP cache, reverse proxy, and shock absorber. It has a capacity for handling more than 10,000 simultaneous connections with a very low footprint (approximately 2.5 MB per 10,000 inactive `https://en.wikipedia.org/wiki/HTTP_persistent_connection`). It was specifically designed to overcome Apache. It can roughly handle four times more requests per second than Apache. NGINX can be used in various ways, such as the following:

- Deployed standalone
- As a frontend proxy for Apache acting as a network offload device
- Act as a shock absorber, providing servers from a sudden spike in traffic or slow internet connections

It is our perfect fit for microservice applications, as containerized microservice applications need a frontend that is able to conceal and deal with the complex and ever-changing nature of applications running behind it. It performs some major things such as forward HTTP requests to different applications, shock absorber protection, routing, consolidated logging, Gzip compression, zero downtime, caching, scalability, and fault tolerance. Hence, it is our ideal application delivery platform. Let's begin NGINX 101.

Download the latest version from this site, `http://nginx.org/en/download.html`, based on your operating system. At the time of writing, the mainline Version was **1.13.7**.

Once extracted, you can simply start NGINX as follows:

```
start nginx
```

To check whether NGINX is up or not you, can hit the following command in Windows:

```
tasklist /fi "imagename eq nginx.exe"
```

In the case of Linux, you can use the following command line:

```
ps waux | grep nginx
```

The following are other useful NGINX commands:

`nginx -s stop`	Fast shutdown
`nginx -s quit`	Graceful shutdown
`nginx -s reload`	Changing configuration, starting new worker processes with a new configuration, and graceful shutdown of old worker processes
`nginx -s reopen`	Re-opening log files

Docker

Docker is an open source platform for developing, shipping, and running applications with the major advantage of separating your application from your infrastructure so you can adapt to major changes easily and quickly. Docker promotes the philosophy of containers. A **container** is a runnable instance of any configured image. A container is totally isolated from the other containers and the host machine. This very much resembles our microservice philosophy. We will see Docker in much more detail when we come to the deployment part. Let's install Docker on our system.

Docker for Windows requires Windows 10 Pro edition and Hyper-V. So as a generally available alternative, we will go for Linux. Windows users can download Oracle VM VirtualBox, download any Linux image, and then follow the same process. Follow along with the steps given here: `https://docs.docker.com/engine/installation/linux/docker-ce/ubuntu/`.

To check the installation, hit the following command:

```
sudo docker run hello-world
```

You should see output like the following:

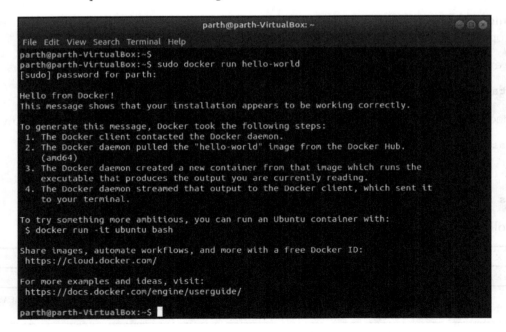

Docker installation

Primer to TypeScript

TypeScript originated from shortcomings in JavaScript development with the advent of using JavaScript for large-scale applications. TypeScript introduced a JavaScript compiler with presets of syntactical language extensions, class-based programming, and ways to convert extensions into regular JavaScript. TypeScript became extremely popular as it introduced type safety in JavaScript, which happens to be one of the most flexible languages ever. This enables JavaScript to be a more object-oriented and compile safe language. TypeScript is more of a superset of ES standards, which enables developers to write cleaner, easy-to-refactor, and upgradable code. In this section, we will go through various primary topics of TypeScript, which are essential for our journey ahead. TypeScript is JavaScript with type annotations. TypeScript has a transpiler and type checker, which throws an error if there is a mismatch in types, and converts TypeScript code to JavaScript code. We will look at the following topics briefly, which will essentially help us to write Node.js in TypeScript:

- Understanding `tsconfig.json`
- Understanding types
- Debugging TypeScript in Node.js

Understanding tsconfig.json

Adding a `tsconfig.json` file is an indication of having a directory that is of a TypeScript project, and a configuration file is needed to compile the TypeScript into JavaScript. You compile the TypeScript into JavaScript by using the `tsc` command. Invoking it, the compiler searches for configurations loaded in `tsconfig.json`. You can specify compilation for a complete project (from the current directory to the parent directory) or you can specify `tsc` for a particular project. You can find all possible options using the following command:

```
tsc --help
```

Let's have a look at what the command does:

```
C:\Users\parth.ghiya.KADC
>tsc --help
Version 2.8.1
Syntax:    tsc [options] [file ...]

Examples: tsc hello.ts
          tsc --outFile file.js file.ts
          tsc @args.txt

Options:
 -h, --help                              Print this message.
 --all                                   Show all compiler options.
 -v, --version                           Print the compiler's version.
 --init                                  Initializes a TypeScript project and creates a tsconfig.json file.
```

The tsc help command

At the time of writing, the version of TypeScript is **2.6.2** and all context would be made from the same version. If you do not have the updated version, run the following commands:

```
npm uninstall typescript -g
npm install typescript@latest -g
```

Let's now look into the sample `tsconfig.json` file and all options that are available:

```json
{
    "compilerOptions":{
        "target":"es6",
        "moduleResolution":"node",
        "module":"commonjs",
        "declaration":false,
        "noLib":false,
        "emitDecoratorMetadata":true,
        "experimentalDecorators":true,
        "sourceMap":true,
        "pretty":true,
        "allowUnreachableCode":true,
        "allowUnusedLabels":true,
        "noImplicitAny":true,
        "noImplicitReturns":false,
        "noImplicitUseStrict":false,
        "outDir":"dist/",
        "baseUrl":"src/",
        "listFiles":false,
        "noEmitHelpers":true
    },
    "include":[
        "src/**/*"
    ],
```

```
    "exclude":[
        "node_modules"
    ],
    "compileOnSave":false
}
```

Let's now dissect this file and understand the most common options used.

compilerOptions

All settings required to compile the project are mentioned here. A detailed list of all the compiler options, along with default values, can be found at this site: `https://www.typescriptlang.org/docs/handbook/compiler-options.html`. If we don't specify this option, then the default values will be picked up. This is the file from where we instruct TypeScript on how to handle various things such as various decorators, supporting JSX files, and transpiling pure JavaScript files. The following are some of the most commonly used options, which we can understand with respect to the preceding sample code:

`noImplicitAny`	This tells the `tsc` compiler to shout if it finds variable declarations that have declarations which accept any types, but the explicit type definition for any type is missing.
`experimentalDecorators`	This option enables using decorators in TypeScript projects. ES has not yet introduced decorators, so they are disabled by default. A decorator is any declaration that can be attached to class declarations, method, accessors, properties, or parameters. Using decorators simplifies programming.
`emitDecoratorMetaData`	TypeScript supports emitting certain types of metadata for any declarations that have decorators. To enable this option, it must be set to true in `tsconfig.json`.
`watch`	This option is more like `livereload`; whenever any of the source file is changed, then the compiling process is re-triggered to generate the transpiled files again.
`reflect-metadata`	It preserves the type information in an object's metadata.
`module`	It is the output module type. Node.js uses CommonJS, so that is why there are CommonJS in modules.
`target`	The output presets we are targeting; Node.js uses ES6, so we use ES6.

`moduleResolution`	This option will tell TypeScript which resolution strategy to use. Node.js users require a module strategy, so TypeScript then uses this behavior to resolve these dependencies.
`sourceMap`	This tells TypeScript to generate the sourcemaps, which can be easily used to debug TypeScript just like we debug JavaScript.
`outDir`	The location in which the transpiled files should be kept.
`baseUrl` **and** `paths`	Instructing TypeScript where it can find the type files. We basically tell TypeScript that for every (*) found in the .ts file, it needs to look in the file location <base_url> + src/types/*.

include and exclude

Here, we define our project context. It basically takes an array of global patterns that need to be included in the compilation path. You can include or exclude an array of global patterns that adds or removes files to the transpilation process. Note that this is not the final value; there are property files that take an array of filenames and they override include and exclude.

extends

If we want to extend any of the base configurations, then we use this option and specify the file path that it has to extend. You can find the complete schema of `tsconfig.json` at `http://json.schemastore.org/tsconfig`.

Understanding types

TypeScript needs to span across other JavaScript libraries too if we want to efficiently and globally use TypeScript. TypeScript uses the `.d.ts` files to provide types of JavaScript libraries that were not written in ES6 or TypeScript. Once the `.d.ts` file is defined, it becomes very easy to see the return types and provide easy type checking. The TypeScript community is very active and it provides types for most files: `https://github.com/DefinitelyTyped/DefinitelyTyped/tree/master/types`.

Revisiting our `tsconfig.json` file, we have specified the option `noImplicitAny: true` and we need a mandatory `*.d.ts` file for any of the libraries we use. If we set that option to false, `tsc` will not give any errors, but that's not a recommended practice at all. Having an `index.d.ts` file for every library we use is one of the standard practices. We'll look at various topics such as how to install types, what if types are not available, how to generate types, and what the general processes for types are.

Installing types from DefinitelyTyped

Types from any library would be a `dev` dependency and all you have to do is install it from `npm`. The following command installs express types:

```
npm install --save-dev @types/express
```

This command downloads the express type to the `@types` folder, and TypeScript looks in the `@types` folder to resolve mappings for that type. As we only need it during development time, we have added the `--save-dev` option.

Writing your own types

Many times we may need to write our own `.d.ts` file in order to efficiently use TypeScript. We will look at how we can generate our own typing and instruct TypeScript from where to find the types. We will use the automated tool and learn ways to manually write our own `.d.ts` file, then tell TypeScript where to find a location of custom types.

Using the dts-gen tool

This is an open sourced utility provided by Microsoft. We will use it to generate our typings for any project. Shoot up a Terminal as Admin or use `sudo su -` and enter the following:

```
npm install -g dts-gen
```

For all global modules, we will use the command prompt as Admin for Windows, and for Linux/Mac we will use the root user or `sudo su -`.

We will use one globally available module and generate its typing. Install `lusca` and generate its typing using the following command:

```
dts-gen -m lusca
```

You should see output such as `Wrote 83 Lines to lusca.d.ts`, and when you check, you can see all method declarations there, just like an interface.

Writing your own *.d.ts file

When you are writing your own `*.d.ts` file, the stakes are very high. Let's create our own `*.d.ts` file for any module. Say we want to write a module for `my-custom-library`:

1. Create one blank file called `my-custom-library.d.ts` and write the following inside it:

   ```
   declare module my-library
   ```

   This will silence the compiler and won't throw any errors.

2. Next, you need to define all the methods there and what the return type expected out of each method is. You can find several templates here: `http://www.typescriptlang.org/docs/handbook/declaration-files/templates.html`. Here, we need to define the available methods and what they are returning. For example, take a look at the following code snippet:

   ```
   declare function myFunction1(a: string): string;
   declare function myFunction2(a: number): number;
   ```

Debugging

The next big important question would how to debug a Node.js application return in TypeScript. Debugging JavaScript was easy, and to give the same experience TypeScript has a feature called **sourcemaps**. When sourcemaps are enabled in TypeScript, it allows us to drop breakpoints in TypeScript code, which will be paused when the equivalent line of JavaScript is hit. The sole purpose of sourcemaps is to map the generated source to the original source that generated it. We will briefly see debugging a Node.js, and TypeScript application in our editor VS Code.

Primarily, we need to enable sourcemaps. First of all, we need to ensure that TypeScript has sourcemap generation enabled. Go to your `tsconfig.json` file and write the following content:

```
"compilerOptions":{
    "sourceMap": true
}
```

Now when you transpile your project, next to every JavaScript file you generate you will see a `.js.map` file.

The next thing is to configure VS Code for debugging. Go create a folder, `.vscode`, and add a file named `launch.json`. This is very similar to using `node-inspector`. We will debug the `node-clusters` project, which you can find in the source code. Open that project in VS Code; if it doesn't have a `dist` folder then generate a distribution by executing the `tsc` command at the main level, which will create the `dist` folder.

Next, create a folder named `.vscode` and inside it create a `launch.json` file with the following configurations:

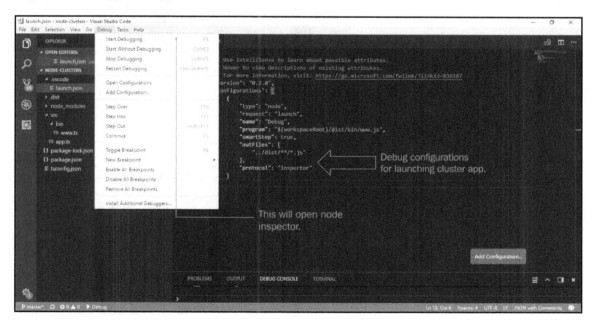

VS Code debugging

When you click on **Start Debugging**, the following screen appears. Look at the screen, which has a detailed description of debugging points:

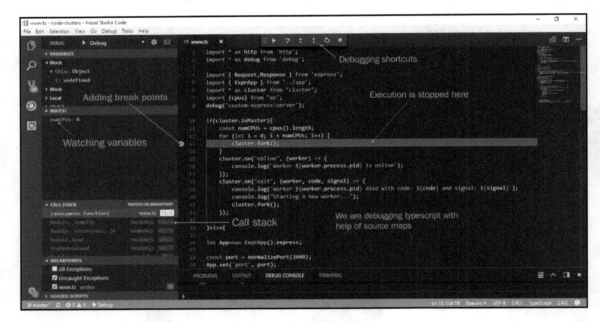

VS debugger

Primer to Node.js

Node.js has evolved over the years and has now become the go-to technology for anyone who wants to embrace microservices. Node.js was created to solve the massive I/O scaling problem, which when applied to our microservice design will result in a match made in heaven. The package manager for Node.js has more modules than Maven, RubyGems, and NuGet, which can be used directly and save lots of productive hours. Characteristics such as an asynchronous nature, event-driven I/O, and non-blocking mode make it one of the best solutions for creating high-end, efficient performance, real-time applications. When applied to microservices, it will be able to handle an extreme amount of load with low response times and low infrastructure. Let's look at one of the success stories of Node.js and microservices.

PayPal, seeing the trending Node.js, decided to go with Node.js in their accounts overview page. They were bewildered by the following results:

- Node.js application development was developed at twice the rate of Java development and with fewer people
- The code had 33% fewer **Lines of Code** (**LOC**) and 40% fewer files
- A single core Node.js application handled double the requests per second when compared to five core Java application setups

Netflix, GoDaddy, Walmart, and many more have similar stories.

Let's look at some of the primary and useful concepts essential for Node.js development that we will use throughout our journey. We will see various topics such as the Event Loop, how to achieve clustering, async fundamentals, and more.

Event Loop

Due to the single-threaded design of Node.js, it is considered to be one of the most complicated architectures. Being completely event-driven, understanding Event Loop is key to mastering Node.js. Node.js is designed as an event-based platform, meaning anything that occurs in Node.js is just a reaction to an event. Any operation done in Node.js passes through a series of callbacks. The complete logic is abstracted from developers and is handled by a library called `libuv`. We will gain a thorough understanding of the Event Loop in this section including how it works, common misconceptions, its various phases, and more.

The following are some of the common myths about Event Loop and a brief on the actual workings:

- **Myth#1—Event Loop works in a different thread than the use code**: There are two threads maintained, one parent thread where the user-related code or user-related operations run, and another where the event looping code runs. Any time an operation is executed, the parent thread passes over the work to the child thread, and once the child thread operation is completed, it pings the main thread to execute the callback:
  - **Fact**: Node.js is single-threaded and everything runs inside the single thread. Event Loop maintains the execution of the callback.

- **Myth#2—Thread pool handles asynchronous events**: All asynchronous operations, such as callbacks to data returned by a database, reading filestream data, and WebSockets streams, are off loaded from a thread pool maintained by libuv:
    - **Fact**: The libuv library indeed creates a thread pool with four threads to pass on the asynchronous work, but today's operating systems already provide such interfaces. So as a golden rule, libuv will use those asynchronous interfaces rather than the thread pool. The thread pool will only be used as the last alternative.
- **Myth#3—Event Loop, like a CPU, maintains a stack or queue of operations**: The Event Loop goes through a maintained queue of asynchronous tasks maintained via the *FIFO rule*, and executes the defined callbacks maintained in a queue:
    - **Fact**: While there are queue-like structures involved in libuv, the callbacks are not processed through a stack. The Event Loop is more of a phase executioner with tasks processed in a round-robin manner.

Understanding Event Loop

Now that we have ruled out basic misconceptions regarding Event Loop in Node.js, let's look at the workings of Event Loop in detail and all the phases that are in the Event Loop phase execution cycle. Node.js processes everything occurring in the environment in the following phases:

- **Timers**: This is the phase where all the setTimeout() and setInterval() callbacks are executed. This phase will run early because it has to be executed in the time interval specified in the calling functions. When the timer is scheduled, then as long as the timer is active the Node.js Event Loop will continue to run.
- **I/O callbacks**: Most common callbacks are executed here except timers, close connection events, setImmediate(). An I/O request can be blocking as well as non-blocking. It executes more things such as connection error, failed to connect to a database, and so on.
- **Poll**: This phase executes the scripts for timers when the threshold has elapsed. It processes events maintained in the poll queue. If the poll queue is not empty, the Event Loop will iterate through the entire queue synchronously until the queue empties out or the system hard peak size is reached. If the poll queue is empty, the Event Loop continues with the next phase—it checks and executes those timers. If there are no timers, the poll queue is free; it waits for the next callback and executes it immediately.

- **Check**: When the poll phase is idle, the check phase is executed. Scripts that have been queued with `setImmediate()` will be executed now. `setImmediate()` is a special timer that has use of the `libuv` API and it schedules callbacks to be executed after the poll phase. It is designed in such a way that it executes after the poll phase.

- **Close callbacks**: When any handle, socket, or connection is closed abruptly, the close event is emitted in this phase, such as `socket.destroy()`, connection `close()`, that is, all on (`close`) event callbacks are processed here. Not technically parts of the Event Loop, but two other major phases are `nextTickQueue` and other micro tasks queue. The `nextTickQueue` processes after the current operation gets completed, regardless of the phase of Event Loop. It is fired immediately, in the same phase it was called, and is independent from all phases. The `nextTick` function can contain any tasks and they are just invoked as follows:

```
process.nextTick(() => {
  console.log('next Tick')
})
```

The next important part is the micro and the macro tasks. `NextTickQueue` has higher priority over micro and macro tasks. Any task that is in `nextTickQueue` will be executed first. Micro tasks include functions such as resolved promise callbacks. Some examples of micro tasks can be `promise.resolve`, `Object.resolve`. An interesting point to note here is native promises only come under micro tasks. If we use libraries such as `q` or `bluebird`, we will see them getting resolved first.

Node.js clusters and multithreading

Any Node.js instance runs in a single thread. If any error occurs, the thread breaks, the server stops, and you need to restart the server. To take advantage of all the cores available in a system, Node.js provides an option to launch a cluster of Node.js processes so that the load is evenly distributed. There are many tools available that do the same thing. We will look at a basic example and then learn about automated tools such as **PM2**. Let's get started:

1. The first step is to create an express server. We will need `express`, `debug`, `body-parser`, and `cookie-parser`. Open up a Terminal and hit the following:

```
npm install body-parser cookie-parser debug express typescript
--save
```

2. Next, we download the types for these modules:

```
npm install @types/debug @types/node @types/body-parser
@types/express
```

3. Then, we create our `app.ts` and `www.ts` files. Construct your `app.ts` file as follows:

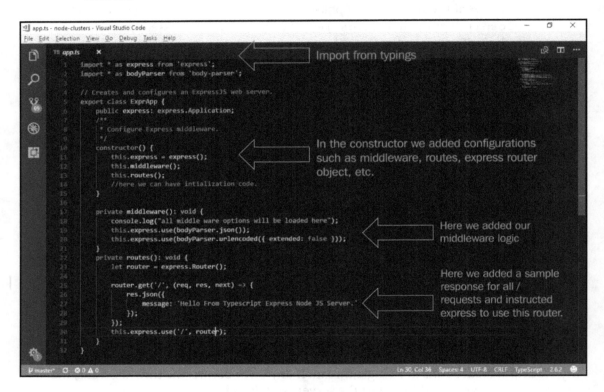

Express the TypeScript way

4. For `www.ts`, we will use the `cluster` module and create workers available as a number of cores. Our logic would be divided as follows:

```
import * as cluster from "cluster";
import { cpus } from "os";
if (cluster.isMaster) {
  /* create multiple workers here cpus().length will give me
number of   cores available
  */
  cluster.on("online", (worker) => { /*logic when worker
```

```
becomes online*/ });
    cluster.on("exit", (worker) => { /*logic when worker becomes
online*/ });
} else {
    //our app intialization logic
}
```

5. Now when we transpile the source and run `www.js`, we will see multiple workers online.

 Complete files can be found at `node-clusters/src/bin/www.ts`. Go and run the application. You should see multiple workers online now.

An alternative approach is to use *PM2* (`https://www.npmjs.com/package/pm2`). PM2 has various options for `livereload`, reload with zero downtime, and starting mode in clusters. Some sample commands available in PM2 are as follows:

`pm2 start www.js -i 4`	Start four instances of an application in cluster mode. It will load balance requests to each node.
`pm2 reload www.js`	Zero downtime needed for reloading `www.js` with changes.
`pm2 scale www.js 10`	Scaling clustered apps to 10 processes.

Async/await

As JavaScript is asynchronous in nature, it becomes very difficult to maintain the execution of tasks once a process is completed. What once started with callbacks soon turned to promises, async module, generators and yield, and async and await. Let's start with async/await 101:

- Async/await is one of the modern ways to write asynchronous code
- Built on top of promises, it cannot be used with plain callbacks or Node promises
- Async/await is non-blocking code even though it appears synchronous, which is its main power
- Based on `node-fibers`, it is lightweight and is TypeScript friendly as typings are embedded

Let's now see a practical implementation of async/await. What once started as huge callback hell and nested chains of `.then()` can simply be reduced to the following:

```
let asyncReq1=await
axios.get('https://jsonplaceholder.typicode.com/posts/1');
console.log(asyncReq1.data);
let asyncReq2=await
axios.get('https://jsonplaceholder.typicode.com/posts/1');
console.log(asyncReq2.data);
```

We will now look into two common async/await design patterns.

Retrying failed requests

Often, we add back safe or retry requests in our system to make sure that if the service returns errors, we can retry the service if it is down for some time. In this sample, we have used an async/await pattern efficiently as an exponential retry parameter, that is, retry after 1, 2, 4, 8, and 16 seconds. A working example can be found in `retry_failed_req.ts` in a source code:

```
wait(timeout: number){
  return new Promise((resolve) => {
    setTimeout(() => {
      resolve()
    }, timeout)
  })
 }
async requestWithRetry(url: string){
  const MAX_RETRIES = 10;
  for (let i = 0; i <= MAX_RETRIES; i++) {
    try { return await axios.get(url); }
    catch (err) {
      const timeout = Math.pow(2, i);
      console.log('Waiting', timeout, 'ms');
      await this.wait(timeout);
      console.log('Retrying', err.message, i);
    }
  }
 }
```

You will see output like the following:

```
PS C:\Users\parth.ghiya.KADC\Desktop\tsms chapter2\handing-asynchronous-nature> node .\dist\retry_failed_req.js
Waiting 1 ms
Retrying connect ECONNREFUSED 127.0.0.1:8081 0
Waiting 2 ms
Retrying connect ECONNREFUSED 127.0.0.1:8081 1
Waiting 4 ms
Retrying connect ECONNREFUSED 127.0.0.1:8081 2
Waiting 8 ms
Retrying connect ECONNREFUSED 127.0.0.1:8081 3
Waiting 16 ms
Retrying connect ECONNREFUSED 127.0.0.1:8081 4
Waiting 32 ms
Retrying connect ECONNREFUSED 127.0.0.1:8081 5
Waiting 64 ms
Retrying connect ECONNREFUSED 127.0.0.1:8081 6
```

Retrying request exponentially

Multiple requests in parallel

Executing multiple parallel requests becomes a piece of cake with async/await. Here, we can execute several asynchronous tasks at once, and use their values in different places. The complete source code can be found at `multiple_parallel.ts` in `src`:

```
async function executeParallelAsyncTasks() {
  const [valueA, valueB, valueC] = await
    Promise.all([
            await axios.get('https://jsonplaceholder.typicode.com/posts/1')
            await
axios.get('https://jsonplaceholder.typicode.com/posts/2'),
            await
axios.get('https://jsonplaceholder.typicode.com/posts/3')])
            console.log("first response is ", valueA.data);
            console.log(" second response is ", valueB.data);
            console.log("third response is ", valueC.data);
    }
```

Streams

Briefly, a **stream** is an abstract interface for streaming data continuously in Node.js. A stream can be a sequence of data coming over time from a source and running to a destination. The source can be anything—a database of 50 million records, a file of size 4.5 GB, some HTTP call, and so on. Streams are not available all at once; they don't fit in memory, they just come some chunks at a time. Streams are not only for handling large files or a huge amount of data, but also they give us a good option of composability through piping and chaining. Streams are one of the ways to do reactive programming, which we will look at in more detail in the next chapter. There are four streams available in Node.js:

- **Readable stream**: The streams from which data can be read only; that is, here data can only be consumed. Examples of readable streams can be HTTP responses on the client, `zlib` streams, and `fs` read streams. Data at any stage in this stream will either be in a flowing state or paused state. On any readable stream, various events can be attached such as data, error, end, and readable.
- **Writable stream**: Streams to which data can be written. For example, `fs.createWriteStream()`.
- **Duplex stream**: Streams that are both readable and writable. For example, `net.socket` or a TCP socket.
- **Transform stream**: A transform stream is basically a duplex stream that can be used to transform data while it is being written or read. For example, `zlib.createGzip` is one of the streams to compress a lot of data using gzip.

Now, let's understand the workings of a stream via an example. We will create a custom `Transform` stream and extend the `Transform` class, thus seeing read, write, and transform operations all at once. Here, the output of the transform stream will be computed from its input:

- **Problem**: We have a user's information and we want to hide sensitive parts such as email address, phone number, and so on.
- **Solution**: We will create one transform stream. The transform stream will read data and transform it by removing sensitive information. So, let's start coding. Create one empty project with `npm init`, add one folder, `src`, and the `tsconfig.json` file of the earlier section. Now, we will add Node.js typings from `DefinitelyTyped`. Open up a Terminal and type the following:

```
npm install @types/node --only=dev
```

Now, we will write our custom filter transform stream. Create a `filter_stream.ts` file and inside it, let's write the transform logic:

```
import { Transform } from "stream";
export class FilterTransform extends Transform {
  private filterProps: Array<String>;
  constructor(filterprops: Array<String>, options?: any) {
    if (!options) options = {};
    options.objectMode = true;
    super(options);
    this.filterProps = filterprops;
  }
  _transform(chunk: any, encoding?: string, callback?: Function) {
    let filteredKeys = Object.keys(chunk).filter((key) => {
      return this.filterProps.indexOf(key) == -1;
    });
    let filteredObj = filteredKeys.reduce((accum: any, key: any) => {
    accum[key] = chunk[key];
      return accum;
    }, {})
    this.push(filteredObj);
    callback();
  }
  _flush(cb: Function) {
    console.log("this method is called at the end of all transformations");
  }
}
```

What did we just do?

- We created a custom transform and exported it, so it can be used anywhere in other files.
- Options are not mandatory in a constructor if they aren't passed; we create the default options.
- By default, streams expect buffer/string values. There is an `objectMode` flag that we have to set in the stream so it can accept any JavaScript object, which we did in the constructor.
- We overrode the transform method to suit it to our needs. In the transform method, we removed those keys that are passed out in filter options and created a filtered object.

Next, we will create an object of filter stream, to test out our results. Create a file called `stream_test.ts` parallelly to `filter_stream.ts` and add the following contents:

```
import { FilterTransform } from "./filter_stream";
//we create object of our custom transformation & pass phone and email as
sensitive properties
let filter = new FilterTransform(['phone', 'email']);
//create a readable stream that reads the transformed objects.
filter.on('readable', function () { console.log("Transformation:-",
filter.read()); });
//create a writable stream that writes data to get it transformed
filter.write({ name: 'Parth', phone: 'xxxxx-xxxxx', email:
'ghiya.parth@gmail.com', id: 1 });
filter.write({ name: 'Dhruvil', phone: 'xxxxx-xxxxx', email:
'dhruvil.thaker@gmail.com', id: 2 });
filter.write({ name: 'Dhaval', phone: 'xxxxx-xxxxx', email:
'dhaval.marthak@gmail.com', id: 3 });
filter.write({ name: 'Shruti', phone: 'xxxxx-xxxxx', email:
'shruti.patel@gmail.com', id: 4 });
filter.end();
```

Open up your `package.json` file and add `"start":"tsc && node .\\dist\\stream_test.js"` in your `scripts` tag. Now when you run `npm start`, you will be able to see the transformed output.

 Note that if you are on Linux/macOS, replace \\ with //.

Writing your first Hello World microservice

Let's start by writing our first microservice. Based on the previous topics, we will construct our first microservice with best practices and the widely used `node_modules`. We will use:

CORS (`https://www.npmjs.com/package/cors`)	Adds CORS headers, so that cross applications can access it.
Routing Controllers (`https://www.npmjs.com/package/routing-controllers`)	Beautiful decorators provided in this module, which help us to write our API's and routes easily.
Winston (`https://www.npmjs.com/package/winston`)	Perfect logging module with many advanced features.

So, open up a Terminal and create one Node project with a default `package.json`. Follow these steps. The full source code for reference is available in the `first-microservice` folder in the extracted source:

1. First of all, we will download the preceding dependencies and basic express dependencies. Enter the following command lines:

   ```
   npm install body-parser config cookie-parser cors debug express
   reflect-metadata rimraf routing-controllers typescript winston --
   save
   ```

2. Download the types of necessary modules as follows:

   ```
   npm install @types/cors @types/config @types/debug @types/node
   @types/body-parser @types/express @types/winston --only=dev
   ```

3. Now, we will create our application structure, as shown in the following screenshot:

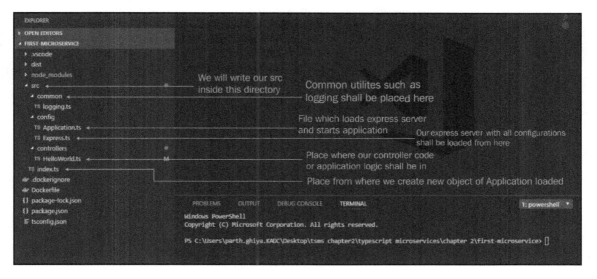

Folder structure

4. So, let's create our express file and configure it using the `routing_controllers` module. Create one express config class and instruct it to use our directory controllers as the source from where it can find the routes:

```
export class ExpressConfig {
  app: express.Express;
  constructor() {
    this.app = express();
    this.app.use(cors());
    this.app.use(bodyParser.json());
    this.app.use(bodyParser.urlencoded({ extended: false }));
    this.setUpControllers();
  }
  setUpControllers() {
    const controllersPath = path.resolve('dist',
'controllers');
    /*useExpressServer has lots of options, can be viewed at
node_modules\routing-
controllers\RoutingControllersOptions.d.ts*/
    useExpressServer(this.app, {
      controllers: [controllersPath + "/*.js"]
    }
    );
  }
}
```

5. Now, let's write our application startup logic inside `application.ts`:

```
export class Application {
  server: any; express: ExpressConfig;
  constructor() {
  this.express = new ExpressConfig();
    const port = 3000; this.server =
      this.express.app.listen(port, () => {
        logger.info(`Server Started! Express:
http://localhost:${port}`);
      });
  }
}
```

6. The next step is to write our controller and to return JSON:

```
@Controller('/hello-world')
export class HelloWorld {
  constructor() { }
  @Get('/')
  async get(): Promise<any> {
```

```
        return { "msg": "This is first Typescript Microservice" }
    }
}
```

7. The next step is to create a new object of our `Application` file inside `index.ts`:

```
'use strict';
/* reflect-metadata shim is required, requirement of routing-
controllers module.*/
import 'reflect-metadata';
import { Application } from './config/Application';
export default new Application();
```

8. You are all done; compile your TypeScript and start a transpiled version of `index.ts`. When you hit `localhost:3000/hello-world`, you will see JSON output—`{"msg":"This is first Typescript Microservice"}`.

9. To add the automation of all the tasks while starting a server, we define scripts in our `package.json`. The first script is to always clean before transpiling:

```
"clean":"node ./node_modules/rimraf/bin.js dist",
```

The next script is for building TypeScript using the `typescript` version available inside the `node` modules:

```
"build":"node ./node_modules/typescript/bin/tsc"
```

The final one basically instructs it to clean, build, and start the server by executing `index.js`:

```
"start": "npm run clean && npm run build && node
./dist/index.js".
```

10. The next step is to create a Docker build. Create one `Docker` file and let's write the Docker image script:

```
#LATEST NODE Version -which node version u will use.
FROM node:9.2.0
# Create app directory
RUN mkdir -p /usr/src/app
WORKDIR /usr/src/app
#install depedencies
COPY package.json /usr/src/app
RUN npm install
#bundle app src
COPY . /usr/src/app
CMD [ "npm" , "start" ]
```

11. We will learn about Docker in more detail in future chapters. Now, go ahead and enter the following command:

```
sudo docker build -t firstypescriptms .
```

 Don't forget the dot at the end of the command while building the image. A dot indicates that we are using Dockerfile in the local directory.

Your Docker image will be built. You will see output like the following:

```
parth@parth-VirtualBox:~/Desktop/typescript-microservices/chapter 2/first-microservice$ sudo docker build -t firstypescriptms .
Sending build context to Docker daemon  58.88kB
Step 1/7 : FROM node:9.2.0
9.2.0: Pulling from library/node
85b1f47fba49: Pull complete
ba6bd283713a: Pull complete
817c8cd48a09: Pull complete
47cc0ed96dc3: Pull complete
8888adcbd08b: Pull complete
6f2de60646b9: Pull complete
9dd205971dc0: Pull complete
5859715a4691: Pull complete
Digest: sha256:7c9099e0f68242387d7755eaa54c287e16cedd3cca423444ca773794f5f1e423
Status: Downloaded newer image for node:9.2.0
 ---> c1d02ac1d9b4
Step 2/7 : RUN mkdir -p /usr/src/app
 ---> Running in 8f83b0563ceb
 ---> fa3bffe08b51
Removing intermediate container 8f83b0563ceb
Step 3/7 : WORKDIR /usr/src/app
 ---> d17282a4ca91
Removing intermediate container f0bf27df96ad
Step 4/7 : COPY package.json /usr/src/app
 ---> ff984e30dbaf
Step 5/7 : RUN npm install
 ---> Running in 284c3be59ee7
npm notice created a lockfile as package-lock.json. You should commit this file.
added 96 packages in 58.729s
npm WARN clusters@1.0.0 No repository field.

 ---> 065af12205c4
Removing intermediate container 284c3be59ee7
Step 6/7 : COPY . /usr/src/app
 ---> 2caaf9e51845
Step 7/7 : CMD npm start
 ---> Running in 5231188dff05
 ---> 2d08409ff56c
Removing intermediate container 5231188dff05
Successfully built 2d08409ff56c
Successfully tagged firstypescriptms:latest
parth@parth-VirtualBox:~/Desktop/typescript-microservices/chapter 2/first-microservice$
```

Docker create image

12. You can use the `sudo docker images` command to check the image, which you can later use anywhere. To run the image, just use the following command line:

```
sudo docker run -p 8080:3000 -d firstypescriptms:latest
```

13. After that, you can hit `localhost:8080/hello-world` to check the output.

 While we just exposed the REST API, for the outer world it's just another service on port `8080`; the inner implementation is abstracted from the consumer. This is one of the major differences between REST API and microservices. Anything within the container can change at any time.

Summary

In this chapter, we had a primary introduction to some of the most fundamental concepts of Node.js and TypeScript that are essential for making scalable applications suitable for enterprise needs. We set up our primary environment and learned about Docker, PM2, and NGINX. At the end, we created our traditional `Hello World` microservice the TypeScript way in Node.js.

In the next chapter, we are going to learn the fundamentals of reactive programming, the advantages of reactive programming, and how you can do reactive programming in Node.js. We will see various operators available in reactive programming, which shorten and streamline our day-to-day development. We will see a combination of traditional SOA-based orchestration and reactive processes, and go through various situations to see which approach fits where.

3
Exploring Reactive Programming

Until now, we described our application as a mixture of very famous industry buzz words, such as asynchronous, real-time, loosely coupled, scalable, distributed, message-driven, concurrent, non-blocking, fault tolerant, low latency, and high throughput. In this chapter, we'll go one step further and understand reactive programming, which brings together all of these characteristics. We will see and understand the Reactive Manifesto—a set of principles that when collectively applied, will bring all of the preceding advantages. We will understand some key aspects of a reactive microservice, what it should be, and what are the key advantages of reactive programming. We will look at what problems reactive programming solves, different styles of reactive programming, and more.

In this chapter, we will focus on the following:

- Introduction to reactive programming
- Reactive Manifesto
- Reactive microservice—major building blocks and concerns
- When to react and when not to react (orchestrate)—introduction to hybrid approaches
- Being reactive in Node.js

Introduction to reactive programming

If we want a view of reactive programming from 50,000 above ground level, it can briefly be termed as:

When input x in any function changes, output y automatically updates in the corresponding response without the need to manually invoke it. In short, the sole purpose is to continuously respond to external inputs whenever prompted by output worlds.

Reactive programming is achieved through utilities such as map, filter, reduce, subscribe, unsubscribe, streams. Reactive programming focuses more on events and message-driven patterns rather than manually fiddling with huge implementation details.

Let's take a practical day-to-day example to understand reactive programming. We all have used Excel since the beginning of our IT lives. Now, let's say you write one formula based on a cell value. Now, whenever the cell value is changed, all corresponding results based on that value will reflect the change automatically. That's called being **reactive**.

Briefly understanding reactive programming when combined to deal with various data flows, the reactive programming can be advanced data flows with the ability to handle the following things:

- Event streams, streams we can tap into and subscribe, and then use subscription output as a data source.
- Having streams gives us the ability to manipulate streams, create new streams from original ones, and apply transformations as and when needed.
- Transformations should work independently in a distributed system. A specific transformation can be the merge of several streams received from various places.

Functional reactive programming is the variant of reactive programming that we are going to use. Briefly stated, our functional reactive microservice should have the following two fundamental properties:

- **Signifying or denotative**: Each function, service, or type is precise, simple, single, responsible, and implementation-independent.
- **Continuous time**: Programming should keep in mind time-varying values. Variables in functional reactive programming have a value for a very short time. It should provide us transformation flexibility, efficiency, modularity, single responsibility.

The following are the characteristics of functional reactive programming:

- **Dynamic**: Knows how to react to time or to handle various input changes
- **Handle time variations**: When reacting values change continuously, handle appropriate changes
- **Efficient**: When there is a change in input value, have a minimum amount of processing as and when required
- **Aware of historic transitions**: Maintain state changes locally and not globally

Now that we briefly know about reactive programming, let's look into what advantages we get while adopting reactive programming. The next section talks about and gives us very strong reasons for why you should drop everything and start reactive programming.

Why should I consider adopting reactive programming?

Now that we have unveiled the mystery of reactive programming, the next big question is why we should care about reactive programming and what advantages we can get while doing reactive programming. In this section, we'll see major benefits of reactive programming and how easily code can be managed to introduce major new functionalities at any point in time:

- Easy to interpret or tap into any functions compared to callbacks or middleware.
- Handle errors and memory management easily, without any centralized configurations. A single subscription can have an error function in which you can easily dispose of the resources.
- Efficiently handle time-related complexities. Sometimes, we are bound by rate limiting constraints in calling some external APIs such as the Google Cloud Vision API. Reactive programming has immense use cases in such situations.
- Go to market rate is faster. When correctively implemented, reactive programming drastically reduces old school code to a very few lines of code.
- Easy-to-handle throttleable input streams, that is, my input stream is dynamic. It can increase or decrease as per demand.

Now that we have gone through some of the major advantages of reactive programming, in the next section we will talk about the outcome of reactive programming, a reactive system. We will see a set of standards defined in the Reactive Manifesto.

Reactive Manifesto

A reactive system is meant to be more loosely coupled, flexible, easy to migrate, and easily scalable on demand. These qualities make it easy to develop, gracefully handle faults, and react to errors. Errors are met with elegance rather than claustrophobic disasters. Reactive systems are effective and instantly respond, giving effective and interactive feedback to users. In order to summarize all the traits of a reactive system, the **Reactive Manifesto** was introduced. In this section, we'll look at the Reactive Manifesto and all the criteria needed. Now, let's look at what the Reactive Manifesto states.

Responsive systems

As part of responsive criteria, reactive systems always need to be responsive. They need to provide and respond to the user in a timely manner. This improves user experience, and we can handle errors in a better way. Any failure in the service should not propagate to the system, as it can cause a series of errors. A response is an essential thing. A failed service should provide a response even if it is degraded.

Resilient to errors

Systems should be resilient to all errors. Resiliency should be such that errors are handled gracefully and not crash the entire system. A resilient architecture can be achieved by the following:

- Replication in order to make sure that there's a replica in case the main node goes down. This avoids single points of failure. In order to make sure that components or services should delegate services between them in such a way that single responsibility is handled.
- Ensuring containment and isolation in the system so that the component is contained in its boundaries. It should prevent cascading errors. The client of a component is not burdened with handling its own failures.

Elastic scalable

This is usually used to reference a system's capability to handle varying loads by increasing or decreasing the number of resources utilized in time. Reactive systems should be able to react to a point-in-time load and take actions on the available resources accordingly to provide a cost-effective solution, that is, or scaling down when resources are not required, scaling up but only to that percentage of resources that is needed in order to keep the cost of infrastructure under a preset value. The system should be able to shard or replicate components and distribute inputs among them. A system should have the ability to spawn new instances for downstream and upstream services for client service requests as and when needed. There should be an efficient service discovery process to aid elastic scaling.

Message-driven

Asynchronous message passing is the base of reactive systems. This helps us to establish boundaries between components and parallelly ensure loose coupling, isolation, and location transparency. If a particular component is not available now, the system should delegate failures as messages. This pattern helps us to enable load management, elasticity, and flow control by controlling the message queues in the system with the option of applying back pressure as and when needed. Non-blocking communication leads to less system overhead. There are many tools available for message passing such as **Apache Kafka, Rabbit MQ, Amazon Simple Queue Service, ActiveMQ, Akka**, and so on. Different modules of the code interact with each other via message passing. Thinking deeply about the Reactive Manifesto, microservices just seems to be an extension of the Reactive Manifesto.

Major building blocks and concerns

Continuing on our reactive journey, we will now talk about major building blocks of reactive programming (functional reactive programming to be precise) and what concerns a reactive microservice should actually handle. The following is a list of major building blocks of reactive programming and what they all handle. A reactive microservice should be designed on similar principles. These building blocks will allow us to make sure that a microservice is isolated, has a single responsibility, can pass a message asynchronously, and is mobile.

Observable streams

An oservable streams is nothing but an array that is built over time. Instead of being stored in memory, items arrive asynchronously over time. Observables can be subscribed to, and events emitted by them can be listened to and reacted upon. Every reactive microservice should be able to deal with native observable streams of events. An observable allows you to emit values to the subscriber by calling the `next()` function in the series:

- **Hot and cold observables**: Observables are further classified into hot and cold, based on the producer of the subscription. If it needs to be created more than once, it is called a **hot observable**, whereas if it needs to be created only once, it is called a **cold observable**. Simply stated, hot observables usually *multicast*, while cold observables usually *unicast*. Taking a live example, when you open up any video on YouTube, each subscriber will see the same sequence, from start to end that's basically a cold observable. However, when you open a live stream, you only can view the most recent view and see further on. This is a hot observable, where only a reference to the producer/subscriber is there and the producer is not created from the beginning of each subscription.
- **Subjects**: A subject is just an observable that can call the `next()` method by itself in order to emit new values on demand. Subjects allow you to broadcast values from a common point while limiting the subscription to only one occurrence. A single shared subscription is created. A subject can be termed both an observer and as observable. It can act as a proxy for a group of subscribers. Subjects are used for implementing observables for general purpose utilities such as caching, buffering, logs, and so on.

Subscription

While an observable is an array that fills over time, a **subscription** is a `for` loop that iterates over that array, which happens over time. A subscription provides easy to use and easy to dispose of methods, so there are no memory loading issues. On disposing of a subscription, an observable will stop listening to particular subscriptions.

emit and map

When an observable throws out a value, there is a subscriber that listens to the value thrown by the observable. **emit** and **map** allow you to listen to this value and manipulate it as per your needs. For example, it can be used to convert a response of an HTTP observable to JSON. To further add-on to the chain, the `flatMap` operator is provided, which creates a new stream from the functions return value it receives.

Operator

When an observable emits values, they are not always in the form that we desire. Operators come in handy, as they help us to alter the way in which observables emit values. Operators can be used in the following stages:

- While creating an observable sequence
- Converting events or some asynchronous patterns to observable sequences
- Dealing with multiple observable sequences to combine them into single observables
- Sharing side effects of an observable
- Doing some mathematical transformations on observable sequences
- Time-based operations such as throttling
- Handling exceptions
- Filtering values emitted by the observable sequence
- Grouping and windowing values emitted

Backpressure strategy

Up to now, we have played with observables and observers. We imitated our problem using streams of data (observables), transferred it to our desired output (using operators), and threw out some values or some side effects (observers). Now, a case can also occur where an observable is throwing out data faster than what the observer can process. This eventually leads to loss of data, which is called the **backpressure problem**. To handle back pressure, either we need to accept a loss of data or we need to buffer the observable stream and process it in chunks when losing data is not an option. Different strategies are available in both of the options:

When losing is an option	When losing isn't an option
Debouncing: Emit data only after timespan has passed.	**Buffer**: Set an amount of time or max number of events to buffer.
Pausing: Pause source stream for some time.	**BufferedPause**: Buffer whatever is emitted by the source stream.
	Controlled Streams: This is a push-pull strategy with the producer pushing events, and the consumer pulling only as much as it can process.

Currying functions

Currying is a process of evaluating function arguments one by one, at the end of each evaluation producing a new function with one argument less. Currying is useful when arguments of a function need to be evaluated at different places. Using the currying process, one argument may be evaluated at some component, then it can be passed to any other place, and then the result can be passed to another component until all the arguments are evaluated. This seems very similar to our microservices analogy. We will use currying later on when we have service dependencies.

When to react and when not to react (orchestrate)

Now, we are at a stage where we are well acquainted with the core concepts of microservices. The next question that we often interact with is regarding the implementation of microservices, and how they will interact with each other. The most common question is when to use orchestration, when to react, and is it possible to use a hybrid approach. In this section, we will understand each of the approaches, its pros and cons, and look at practical examples for the use of each approach. Let's start with orchestration.

Orchestration

Orchestration is more of a **Service Oriented Architecture (SOA)** approach where we handle interaction between various services in an SOA. When we say orchestration, we maintain one controller that is the orchestrator or the main coordinator of all the service interactions. This typically follows more of a request/response-type pattern where a mode of communication can be anything. For example, we can have one orchestrator in our shopping microservices that does the following tasks synchronously—first, take customer orders, then check the product, prepare a bill, and after successful payment, update the product inventory.

Benefits

It provides a systematic way to handle the flow of the programming, where you can actually control the manner in which requests are made. For example, you can ensure that request B can be successfully invoked only after request A completes.

Disadvantages

While the orchestration pattern may look beneficial, there are several trade-offs involved in this pattern, such as:

- There is a tight dependency on the system. Say if one of the initial services is down, then the next services in the chain will never be called. The system can soon become a bottleneck as several single points of failure would be there.
- Synchronous behavior would be introduced in the system. The total end to end time taken would be the sum of the time taken to process all of the individual services.

Reactive approach

Microservices are meant to coexist on their own. They are not meant to be dependent on each other. A **reactive approach** tends to solve some of the challenges of an orchestration approach. Instead of having a controlling orchestrator that takes care of the logic for which steps to happen at what stage, a reactive pattern promotes the service knowing the logic to be built in and executed ahead of time. The services know what to react to and how to deal with it ahead of time. The communication mode for services are dumb pipes and they don't have any logic inside them. Being asynchronous in nature, it removes the waiting part of the orchestration process. Services can produce events and keep on processing. Producing and consuming services are decoupled, so the producer doesn't need to know whether the consumer is up or not. There can be multiple patterns in this approach where producers may want to receive an acknowledgment from consumers. The centralized event stream takes care of all these things in a reactive approach.

Benefits

The reactive approach has lots of advantages and it overcomes lots of traditional problems:

- Parallel or asynchronous execution gives faster end to end processing. Asynchronous processing essentially won't prevent resource blocking while serving a request.
- Having a centralized event stream or a dumb communication pipe as a mode of communication has the advantage of easily adding or removing any service at any point in time.

- Control of the system is distributed. There is no longer a single point of failure in the system as the orchestrator.
- When this approach is clubbed with several other approaches, then various benefits can be achieved.
- When this approach is clubbed with event sourcing, all the events are stored and it enables event replay. So even if some service is down, the event store can still replay that event when the service is online again and the service can check up on updates.
- Another advantage is **Command Query Responsibility Segregation (CQRS)**. As seen in `Chapter 1`, *Debunking Microservices*, we can apply this pattern to separate out the read and write activities. Hence, any of the services can be scaled out independently. This is extremely helpful in situations where applications are either read or write heavy.

Disadvantages

While this approach does solve most of the complexities, it introduces a few trade-offs:

- Asynchronous programming can sometimes be painful to handle. It can't be figured out by just looking at the code. A thorough understanding of Event Loop as shown in `Chapter 2`, *Gearing up for the Journey*, is must to understand the actual workflow in *async coding*.
- Complexity and centralized code are now shifted in individual services. The flow control is now broken up and distributed across all the services. This may introduce redundant code in the system.

Like everything, a one-size-fits-all approach doesn't work here. Several hybrid approaches have come along, which take advantage of both processes. Let's now take a look at some hybrid approaches. A hybrid approach can add a lot of value.

React outside, orchestrate inside

The first hybrid patterns promote reactive patterns between different microservices and orchestration inside a service. Let's consider an example to understand this. Consider our shopping microservices example. Whenever someone buys a product, we will check inventory, calculate price, process payment, check out payment, add recommendation products, and so on. Each of these microservices would be different. Here, we can have a reactive approach between product inventory service, payment service, and recommendation products, and an orchestration approach between checkout service, process payment, and dispatch product. A collective service produces an event based on the outcome of all these three services, which can then be produced. There are several advantages and value additions, such as:

- Most of the services are decoupled. Orchestration only comes into the picture whenever it is required. The overall flow of the application is distributed.
- Having asynchronous events and an event-based approach ensures no single point of failure. If events are missed out by services, then events can be replayed whenever the service is available online.

While there are several advantages, there are some trade-offs introduced:

- If services are coupled, then they can soon become a single point of failure. They cannot be scaled independently.
- Synchronous processing can cause system blocking and resources would be occupied until the request is fully completed.

Reactive coordinator to drive the flow

The second approach introduces something more like a reactive orchestrator to drive the flow between various services. It uses more of a command-based and event-based approach to control the overall flow of the entire ecosystem. Commands indicate things that need to be done and events are outcomes of the commands that are done. The reactive coordinator takes in requests and produces commands, then pushes them to the event stream. Various microservices that are already set up for the commands consume those commands, do some processing, and then throw out an event when the command is successfully done and executed. The reactive coordinator consumes those events and reacts to the events as programmed and as and when necessary. This approach has several value additions, such as:

- Services are decoupled; even though there seems to be a coupling between the coordinator and services, the reactive approach and centralized event stream takes care of most of the previous drawbacks.
- An event stream or centralized event bus ensures asynchronous programming between microservices. Events can be replayed on demand. There are no single points of failure.
- Overall flow can be centralized in one place in the reactive coordinator. All such centralized logic can be kept there and there won't be any duplicated code anywhere.

While there are lots of benefits, there is the following trade-off introduced by this approach—the coordinator needs to be taken care of. If the coordinator goes down, the entire system can be impacted. The coordinator needs to know what commands are needed in order to react or perform a preset of actions.

Synopsis

After going through all the approaches, pure reactive, pure orchestration, and two different hybrid approaches, we will now go through various use cases in which we can apply the preceding four approaches. We will now learn which approach fits where.

When a pure reactive approach is a perfect fit

In the following scenarios, a purely reactive approach is a perfect fit:

- When most of the processing in your application can be done asynchronously. When you can have parallel processing in your application, the reactive architecture pattern is a great fit for processing application needs.
- Decentralizing the application flow in each service is manageable and it doesn't become a pain in the neck. For monitoring and auditing, centralized views can be generated using correlation IDs (**UUID, GUID, CUID**).
- When the application needs to be deployed quickly and speed to market is a top-most goal. When microservices are combined with a reactive approach, it helps to increase decoupling, minimize dependencies, handle temporary shutoff situations, and thus help to get products get faster to market.

When pure orchestration is a perfect fit

In the following scenarios, a pure orchestration approach is a perfect fit:

- When your application's needs are not fulfilled by parallel processing. All the steps have to be done with sequential processing and there are zero opportunities for parallel processing.
- If the application needs demand centralized flow control. Various domains such as **banking** and **ERP** have needs where viewing the end to end flow in one place is a high priority. If there are 100 services, each with their own flow of control, then maintaining a centralized flow may soon become a bottleneck in distribution.

When react outside, orchestrate inside is a perfect fit

In the following scenarios, a hybrid approach, more specifically react outside, orchestrate inside, is a perfect fit:

- Most of your processing can be done asynchronously. Your services can communicate with each other via an event stream and you can have parallel processing in the system, that is, you can pass data via event streams or commands based on your system. For example, whenever payment is successfully credited, then one microservice to show related products and one microservice to dispatch orders to the seller.

- Decentralizing flow in each microservice is easily manageable and there is not duplicated code everywhere.
- Speed to market is the main priority.
- Sequential steps don't apply within the system and they apply within the service. As long as sequential steps don't apply across the system.

When introducing a reactive coordinator is the perfect fit

In the following scenarios, introducing a reactive coordinator is the perfect solution:

- Based on the data being processed, the flow of the application can change. The flow could have several hundred microservices and application demands temporary shut-ins and as soon as the application gets back online events can be replayed.
- There are several asynchronous processing blocks that need to be processed synchronously in the system.
- It allows easy service discovery. Services can easily be scaled at any time. Moving the entire service can be easily done.

Based on your overall needs, you can decide on any one of the strategies in your microservice architecture.

Being reactive in Node.js

Now that we have gone through the concepts of reactive programming and advantages of reactive programming in microservices, let's now look at some practical implementations of reactive programming in Node.js. In this section, we will understand the building blocks of reactive programming by seeing implementations of reactive programming in Node.js.

Rx.js

This is one of the most trending libraries and it is actively maintained. This library is available for most programming languages in different forms such as **RxJava**, **RxJS**, **Rx.Net**, **RxScala**, **RxClojure**, and so on. At the time of writing, it had more than 40 lakh downloads in the last month. Besides this, a huge amount of documentation and online support is available for this. We will be using this library most of the time, except when the need arises. You can check this out at: `http://reactivex.io/`. At the time of writing, the stable version of Rx.js was **5.5.6**. Rx.js has lots of operators. We can use the Rx.js operators for various things such as combining various things, applying conditions as and when needed, creating new observables from promises or events, error handling, filtering data, having a publisher-subscriber pattern, transforming data, request-response utilities, and so on. Let's have a quick hands on. In order to install RxJS, we need to install the Rx package and Node-Rx bindings. Open up a Terminal and shoot `npm install rx node-rx --save`. We will need one more module as this library has to support our Node.js as a build system. Hit this command in the Terminal—`npm install @reactivex/rxjs --save`. Throughout the chapter, we will be using our `Hello World` microservices skeleton, which we just created in `Chapter 2`, *Gearing up for the Journey*, and continuing further with this. The following are various options that we are going to see in the demo:

`forkjoin`	When we have a group of observables and we want only the last value. This cannot be used if one of the observable never completes.
`combineAll`	It just flattens/combines an observable of observables by waiting for an outer observable to complete and then automatically applying `combineLatest`.
`race`	The observable whose value is emitted first will be used.
`retry`	Retries an observable sequence a specific number of times should an error occur.
`debounce`	Ignores emitted values that take less than a specified time. Example, if we set debounce to one second, then any values that are emitted before one second will be ignored.
`throttle`	Emits a value only when a duration determined by the provided function has passed.

The following example throttles values until two seconds:

```
const source = Rx.Observable.interval(1000);
const example2 = source.throttle(val => Rx.Observable.interval(2000));
const subscribe2 = example2.subscribe(val => console.log(val));
```

The following example will trigger a race condition on observables:

```
let example3=Rx.Observable.race(
 Rx.Observable.interval(2000)
            .mapTo("i am first obs"),
  Rx.Observable.of(1000)
            .mapTo("i am second"),
 Rx.Observable.interval(1500)
            .mapTo("i am third")
  )
let subscribe3=example3.
                    subscribe(val=>console.log(val));
```

You can follow along with the source at `using_rxjs` in a source folder. An example of all the operators in the preceding table can be found at `rx_combinations.ts`, `rx_error_handing.ts`, and `rx_filtering.ts`. A full list of API's can be found at `http://reactivex.io/rxjs/`.

Bacon.js

Bacon.js is a small, compact functional reactive programming library. When integrated with Node.js, you can easily turn your spaghetti code into clean, declarative code. It has more than 29,000 downloads a month. At the time of writing, the version available was **1.0.0**. Let's have a quick hands on. In order to install Bacon.js, we need to install Bacon.js and its typings. Open up a Terminal and shoot `npm install baconjs --save` and `npm install @types/baconjs --only=dev`. Now, let's see one basic example where we will see how clean the code looks. We have one JSON object where some products are mapped with a number 1 for `mobile`, 2 for `tv`, and so on. We create one service to return the product name and if the product is not there, it should return `Not found`. The following is the service code:

```
baconService(productId: number){
    return Bacon.constant(this.productMap[productId])
}
```

The following is the controller code:

```
@Get('/:productId')
async get(@Req() req: Request,@Res() res: Response,@Param("productId")
productId: number) {
  let resp: any;
  this.baconService.baconService(productId)
    .flatMap((x) => {
      return x == null || undefined ? "No Product Found" : x;
```

```
    })
    .onValue((o: string) => {
      resp = o;
    })
  return resp;
}
```

You can follow along with the source code at `using_baconjs` in the source folder. A full list of APIs can be found at `https://baconjs.github.io/api.html`.

HighLand.js

This is more of a generic functional library and it is built on top of Node.js streams, thus allowing it to handle asynchronous and synchronous code. One of the best features of **HighLand.js** is the way it handles backpressure. It has a built-in feature for pausing and buffering, that is, when the client is not able to handle any more data, the stream will be paused until it's ready, and if the source can't be paused then it will maintain a temporary buffer until normal operations can be resumed. Time to get our hands dirty with a practical example. Let's deviate from the express theme and focus on a file-reading theme. We will see the power of Node.js I/O operations with parallel executions that can take place. Shoot up a Terminal and hit `npm install highland --save`.

Going with our previous skeleton, create `index.ts` with the following code, which basically reads three files and prints their contents:

```
import * as highland from "highland";
import { Stream } from "stream";
import * as fs from "fs";

var readFile = highland.wrapCallback(fs.readFile);
console.log("started at", new Date());

var filenames = highland(['file1.txt', 'file2.txt', 'file3.txt']);
filenames
  .map(readFile)
  .parallel(10) //reads up to 10 times at a time
  .errors((err: any, rethrow: any) => {
    console.log(err);
    rethrow();
  })
  .each((x: Stream) => {
    console.log("---");
    console.log(x.toString());
    console.log("---");
```

```
});
console.log("finished at", new Date());
```

Transpile the file, keep three `.txt` files parallel to `package.json`, and run the `node` file. The contents will be read. You can follow along with the project at `using_highlandjs` in the `src` folder of the source code. A full list of APIs is available at `http://highlandjs.org/`
.

Key takeaways

Now that we have seen all three libraries, we will summarize the following key points and salient features:

	Rx.js	Bacon.js	Highland.js
Documentation	Well documented, very mature APIs along with lots of options, has extensions in other languages.	Fewer examples for Node.js, great API docs, native support for Node.js.	Very little documentation and fewer helper methods, evolving footprint.
Backpressure	Implemented.	Not supported.	Best implementation.
Community	Used by big companies such as Netflix, and Microsoft. Has similar concepts in all other languages, more like Java, learning curve.	Smaller than Rx.js, reduced learning curve compared to Rx.js.	Least active community, have to dig right into the code base.
Licenses	Apache 2.0	MIT	Apache 2.0

Summary

In this chapter, we learned about the Reactive Manifesto. We clubbed reactive principles and applied them in microservices. We learned how to apply reactive programming in Node.js. We learned about possible approaches to design the microservice architecture, saw its advantages and disadvantages, and saw some practical scenarios to find out in which situations we can apply those patterns. We saw orchestration processes, reaction processes, and two special cases of hybrid approaches.

In the next chapter, we will begin developing our shopping cart microservices. We will design our microservice architecture, write some microservices, and deploy them. We will see how to organize our code into the proper structure.

Beginning Your Microservice Journey

4

Microservices are one of the most tangible solutions in an enterprise to make quick, effective, and scalable applications. However, if they are not properly designed or understood, incorrect implementations and interpretations can lead to disastrous or irrecoverable failures. This chapter will begin our microservices journey by getting our hands dirty and diving deep into practical implementations.

The chapter will start with a description of shopping microservices, which we are going to develop throughout our journey. We will learn how to slice and dice a system into a connected set of microservices. We will design the overall architecture of our shopping cart microservices, define separation layers, add cache levels, and more.

This chapter will cover the following topics:

- Overview of shopping cart microservices
- Architecture design of shopping cart microservices
- Implementation plan for shopping cart microservices
- Schema design and database selection
- Microservice predevelopment aspects
- Developing some microservices for the shopping cart
- Microservice design best practices

Overview of shopping cart microservices

The most important aspect while working on a new system is its design. A poor initial design is always a leading cause of more challenges ahead. Rather than moaning later, solving errors, or applying patches to cover up a poor design, it is always wise not to rush through the design process, spend enough time, and have a flexible fool-proof design. This can only be achieved by understanding the requirements clearly. In this section, we will give a brief overview of shopping cart microservices; the problem we need to solve via microservices; and an overview of the business process, functional view, and deployment and design views.

Business process overview

The use case for our scenario is pretty straightforward. The following process diagram shows the end-to-end shopping process that we need to convert to microservices. The user adds an item to the cart, the inventory is updated, the user pays for the item, and then is able to check out. There are several validations involved, based on business rules. For example, if the user's payment fails, then they should not be able to check out; if the inventory is not available, then the item should not be added to the cart and so on. Take a look at the following diagram:

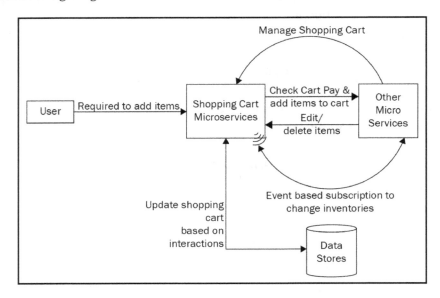

Business process overview

Functional view

Each business capability and its sub-capabilities are shown in a row, which essentially constitutes the shopping cart microservices. Some sub-capabilities are involved in more than one business capability and hence we need to manage some cross-cutting concerns. For example, an inventory service is used both as a separate process and when a person checks out a product. The following diagram shows the functional view of the shopping cart microservices:

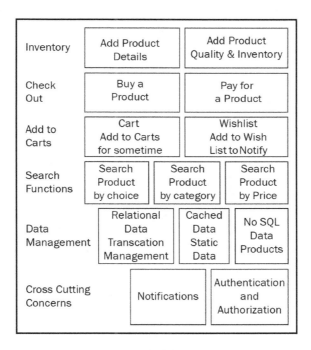

Functional view

The diagram combines the business capabilities into one picture. For example, the inventory service states there are two sub-functions—add product details and add product quantity and inventory items. That summarizes the inventory service's objectives. Creating a functional view for our system gives us a clear understanding of all the business processes and related things involved in them.

Deployment view

The requirement for deployment is pretty straightforward. Based on demand, we need to add new services to support various business capabilities on the fly. Say, for example, right now the payment medium is **PayPal**, but it may happen in the future that we also need to support some local payment options, such as bank wallets. At that time, we should easily be able to add new microservices without disrupting the entire ecosystem. The following diagram shows the deployment view. Right now, there are two nodes (one master and one slave), but based on demand, the number of nodes may increase or decrease based on the business capabilities, a spike in traffic, and other requirements:

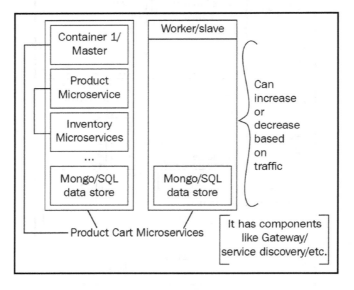

Deployment view

In this section, we got a brief overview of our shopping cart microservice system. We understood its functional, business process, and deployment views. In the next section, we will see the architecture design of the shopping cart microservices.

Architecture design of our system

In this section, we will look at the architectural aspects involved in distributed microservices. We will look at our overall architecture diagram, which we are going to make throughout the book, and look at aspects such as separating concerns, how to apply reactive patterns, and the microservice efficiency model. So, let's get started.

Now that we know our business requirements, let's design our architecture. Based on our knowledge of microservices and other concepts from `Chapter 1`, *Debunking Microservices*, we have the final overall diagram, as shown here:

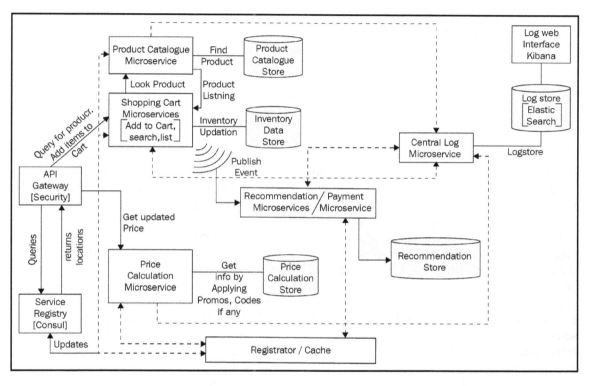

Microservice architecture

 We will study components such as API Gateway, service registry, and discovery in much more detail in later chapters. Here, they are just mentioned as part of the overall view.

Let's understand the key components in the preceding diagram to get a better idea of our architecture.

Different microservices

If we understood our business requirements correctly, we will come up with the following business capabilities:

- Product catalog
- Price catalog
- Discounts
- Invoice
- Payment
- Inventory

Based on our business capabilities and single responsibility, we divided our microservices briefly into various smaller applications. In our design, we ensured that each business capability is implemented by a single microservice and we don't overload a microservice with more than one microservice. We briefly divided our entire system into various microservices, such as a shopping cart microservice, products microservice, payment microservice, consumer microservice, cache microservice, price calculations and suggestions microservice, and so on. The overall granular flow can be seen in the preceding diagram. Another important thing to notice is that each microservice has its separate data store. Different business capabilities have different needs. For example, when a person checks out a product, if the transaction failed, then all transactions such as adding a product to a customer's purchase item, deducting quantity from a product inventory, and so on should be rolled back. In this case, we need relational databases that can handle transactions, whereas in the case of products, our metadata constantly changes. Some products may have more features than other products. In such cases, having a fixed relational schema is not wise and we can go for NoSQL data stores.

At the time of writing this book, MongoDB 4.0 had not yet been introduced. It provides the following transactional plus NoSQL benefits in one.

Cache microservice

The next component that we are going to see is centralized cache storage. This microservice directly interacts with all microservices and we may use this service to cache our responses when needed. Often it may happen that a service goes down, and we may still preserve the application by showing cached data (things such as product information and metadata rarely change; we may cache them for a certain interval of time, thus preventing an extra database hop). Having a cache increases the performance and availability of the system, which ultimately leads to cost optimization. It provides a blazing fast user experience. As microservices are constantly moving, often they may not be reached. In such cases, it is always advantageous to have a cached response when reaching out to availability zones fails.

Service registry and discovery

At the start of the diagram, we included the service registry. This is a dynamic database maintained on the startup and shutdown events of all microservices. Services subscribe to the registry and listen for updates to know whether the service has gone down or not. The entire process is done through the service registry and discovery. The registrator updates the registry whenever a service goes down or goes up. This registry is cached on all clients who subscribe to the registry, so whenever a service needs to be interacted with, an address is fetched from this registry. We will look in detail at this process in Chapter 6, *Service Registry and Discovery*.

Registrator

The next component that we are going to look at, which is available alongside the cache, is the **Registrator** (http://gliderlabs.github.io/registrator/latest/). The Registrator is a third-party service registration tool that basically watches for startup and shutdown events of microservices and, based on the output of those events, dynamically updates the centralized service registry. Different services can then directly communicate with the registry to get updated locations of services. The Registrator ensures that registration and deregistration code is not duplicated across systems. We will look at this in more detail in Chapter 6, *Service Registry and Discovery*, where we integrate the Registrator with the consul.

Logger

One of the important aspects of any application is the logs. Analyzing any problem becomes very easy when appropriate logs are used. Hence, here we have a centralized logger microservice that is based on the famous Elastic framework. Logstash watches for log files and transforms them into appropriate JSON before pushing to Elasticsearch. We can visualize the logs through the Kibana dashboard. Each microservice will have its unique UUID or some log pattern configured. We will look at this in much more detail in Chapter 9, *Deployment, Logging, and Monitoring*.

Gateway

This is the most important part and the starting point of our microservices. It is the central point where we will handle cross-cutting concerns, such as authentication, authorization, transformation, and so on. While creating different microservices on various servers, we usually abstract the information of hosts and ports from the client. The client just makes a request to the gateway and the gateway takes care of the rest by interacting with the service registry and load balancer and redirecting the request to the appropriate service. This is the most important part in a microservice and it should be made highly available.

After going through the architecture diagram, now let's understand some aspects related to the architecture that we will use later.

Design aspects involved

Before actually coding, we need to understand the *how* and *why*. Let's say if I have to cut down a tree (PS: I am a nature lover and I don't support this), instead of directly chopping it down, I would rather first sharpen the axe. We are going to do the same, sharpen our axe first. In this section, we are going to look at various aspects involved in designing microservices. We will look at what models of communication to go through, what is included in microservices, and what areas to take care of in order to achieve efficient microservice development.

Microservice efficiency model

Based on the various needs and requirements, we have defined a microservice efficiency model. Any proper implementation of microservices must adhere to it and provide a standard set of functionalities, as follows:

- Communication over HTTP and HTTP listeners
- Message or socket listeners
- Storage capabilities
- Proper business/technical capabilities definitions
- Service endpoint definitions and communication protocols
- Service contacts
- Security services
- Service documentation through tools such as Swagger

In the following diagram, we have summarized our microservice efficiency model:

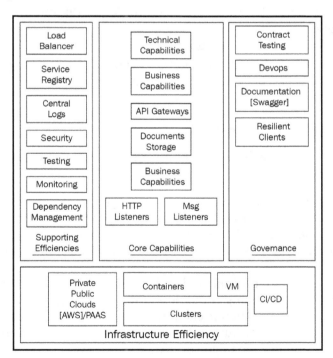

Microservice efficiency model

Let's now look at each of the four sections of the preceding diagram.

Core functionalities

Core functionalities are part of the microservice itself. They include the following functionalities:

- **Technical capabilities**: Any technical functionalities needed, such as interacting with the service registry, sending out events to an event queue, processing events, and so on, are involved here.
- **Business capabilities**: Microservices written to achieve a business capability or fulfill a business requirement.
- **HTTP listeners**: A part of the technical capability; here we define APIs for external consumers. While starting the server, an HTTP listener is started, eliminating any other needs.
- **Message listeners**: A part of event-based communication where the sender doesn't worry whether the message listeners are implemented.
- **API Gateway**: One point of communication for the end client. The API Gateway is the single place for handling any core concerns.
- **Document storage or data storage**: Our data layer for the application. Based on our needs, we may use any of the available data stores.

Supporting efficiencies

These are solutions to help in achieving core microservice implementation. They include the following components:

- **Load balancer**: An application load balancer to redirect based on changes in the server topology. It handles dynamic services going up or down.
  Service registry: A runtime environment for services if they go up or down to publish to. It maintains the active log of all services along with the available instances.
  Central logs: A core centralized logging solution to observe logs all places, rather than individually opening containers and seeking logs there.
  Security: Checking authentic client requests through common available mechanisms, such as OAuth, token-based, IP-based, and so on.
  Testing: Testing out the microservices and essentials, such as inter-microservice communication, scalability, and so on.

Infrastructure role

The following are the infrastructure expectations needed for efficient microservice implementation:

- **Server layer**: An efficient mechanism to choose for deploying our microservice. Well-known options include Amazon EC2 instance, Red Hat OpenShift, or serverless.
- **Container**: Dockerizing the application, so it can run easily on any OS without much fuss about installation.
- **CI/CD**: A process to maintain easy deployment cycles.
- **Clustering**: Server load balancers to handle the load or spike in applications as required.

Governance

Processes and reference information to ease up our overall life cycle in application development include the following:

- **Contract testing**: Testing out microservice expectations and actual outputs to make sure frequent changes don't break anything
- **Scalablity**: Spawning new instances and removing those instances on demand to handle spikes in load
- **Documentation**: Generating documentation to easily understand what someone is actually doing

In the next section, we will carve out an implementation plan for our microservice development.

Implementation plan for shopping cart microservices

One of the key challenges in microservice development is fixing the scope of a microservice:

- If a microservice is too big, you end up in monolithic hell and get stuck in a huge turnaround time, with difficulty adding new features and implementing bug fixes

- If a microservice is too small, either we end up with tight coupling among services or too much code duplication and resource consumption
- If a microservice size is right, but the bounded context isn't fixed, such as services sharing a database, it leads to higher coupling and dependencies

In this section, we are going to devise an implementation plan for our shopping cart microservices. We will formulate a general workflow or plan and design our system according to the plan. We will also see what to do when our scope is not clear, and how to proceed in such cases to ultimately reach our microservices goal. We will look at how to potentially avoid the aforementioned loop holes.

What to do when the scope is not clear

Until now, we have designed our architectural plan based on scoping microservices, but that was when our requirements were pretty clear. We knew exactly what we had to make. But in most cases, you won't have a similar scenario. You will either be migrating from a monolithic system to microservices or you will be engulfed in constantly changing requirements or business capabilities that are still evolving, or it may be that the complexities of technical capabilities could not be estimated at the primer stage, making it difficult for you to scope the microservices. The following section is for such scenarios where you can perform the following steps:

1. **Dream big and start big**: Deciding the scope of microservices is always a huge task, as it defines the overall bounded context. If that is not decided clearly, we ultimately get stuck in monolithic hell. However, if the scope is narrowed down too much, it has its disadvantages too. You will suffer difficulties, as you will end up with data duplication between two microservices, unclear responsibility, and difficulty deploying services independently. Carving out microservices from existing microservices is much easier than managing too narrowly carved microservices.

2. **Separate out microservices from existing microservices**: Once you feel that a microservice is too big, you will need to start separating out the service. First of all, the scope needs to be decided for both the existing and new microservice based on business and technical capabilities. Anything pertaining to a new microservice goes into its own module. Then any communication between the existing modules is moved to common interfaces, such as HTTP API/event-based communication, and so on. Microservices can be planned for later development too; when in doubt, always create a separate module, so we can easily move it out.

3. **Identify technical capabilities**: A technical capability is anything that supports other microservices, such as listening to events emitted by event queues, registering to the service registry, and so on. Keeping the technical capability inside the same microservice can be a huge risk as it will soon lead to tight coupling and the same technical capability might be implemented by lots of other services too.

4. **Adherence standards for microservices based on business and technical capabilities**: Microservices adhere to fixed standards—self-sufficiency, resiliency, transparency, automation, and distribution. Each of the points can briefly be stated as:

   - A microservice serves a single business capability (modularity is the key thing).
   - A microservice can be easily deployed individually. Each service would have its own build script and CI/CD pipeline. The common point would be the API Gateway and service registry.
   - You can easily find out the owners of microservices. They would be distributed and each team can own one microservice.
   - A microservice can be replaced without much hassle. We will have common registration options via the service registry and discovery. Each of our services can be accessed via HTTP.

By following these steps, you will ultimately reach the microservice level, where each service will be serving a single business capability.

Schema design and database selection

The main part of any application is its database selection. In this section, we will look at how to design our database for microservices, whether to keep it separate, to keep it shared, and which database to go to—SQL or NoSQL? We will look at how to categorize data stores based on data types and business capabilities. There are lots of options available. Microservices support polyglot persistence. The approach of selecting a particular data store based on business capabilities and needs is termed polyglot persistence. The following points discuss which database to refer to based on use cases:

- We can leverage Apache Cassandra to support tabular data, such as inventory data. It has options such as distributed consistency and lightweight transactions to support ACID transactions.
- We can leverage Redis to support cache data where the data model is simply a key-value pair. Read operations in Redis are super fast.

- We can leverage MongoDB to support product data stored in unstructured form with the ability to index on any particular field. A document-oriented database such as MongoDB has powerful options, such as an index in specific attributes to search faster.
- We can leverage GraphQL to support complex relationships. GraphQL is extremely useful for many-to-many relationships, for example, our shopping cart recommendation system. Facebook uses GraphQL.
- We can use relational databases to support legacy systems or systems that require maintaining structured relational data. We use relational data where data doesn't change frequently.

In this section, we will look into these points in detail and understand things such as how should the data layer be in a microservice. Then, we will look into types of databases and understand their advantages, disadvantages, and use cases. So, let's get started.

How to segregate data between microservices

The hardest thing about microservices is our data. Each microservice should maintain data by owning their individual database. Data must not be shared via a database. This rule helps us to eliminate a common case that leads to tight coupling between different microservices. If two microservices share the same database layer, and if the second service doesn't know about the first service changing the database schema, it will fail. Due to this, service owners need to be constantly in touch and this differs from our microservice path.

Some of the questions that may come to our mind are how will the database stay in the microservice world? Will the services be sharing databases? If yes, then what would be the repercussions of shared data? Let's answer these questions. We all know the phrase, *with ownership comes responsibility*. Similarly, if a service owns a data store, then it is solely responsible for keeping it up to date. Also, for optimal performance, the data that a microservice needs should be nearby or local, preferably within the microservice container itself, as microservices need to often interact with it. So far, we have learned about two principles for how to segregate data:

- Data should be divided so that each microservice (fulfilling a certain business capability) should easily ensure that the database is up to date and not allow any other services direct access.
- Data relevant to that microservice should be in a nearby vicinity. Keeping it far away increases database costs plus network costs.

One of the general processes for segregating data is to build up a domain model comprising entities, objects, and aggregates. Let's say we have the following use cases—allowing a customer to search for a product, allowing a customer to buy a particular type of product, and allowing a customer to buy the product. We have three functionalities—search, buy, and inventory. Each functionality has its own needs and so the product database is stored in the product catalog service, the inventory is stored differently, and the search service queries the product catalog service, and these results are cached.

In this section, we will look at these rules in detail with an example, which will help us to decide where to keep a data layer and how it should be divided to give us maximum advantage.

Postulate 1 – data ownership should be regulated via business capabilities

One of the major ideas for deciding where data belongs in a microservice system is deciding on the basis of business capabilities. A microservice is just a service fulfilling a business capability that cannot be possible without having a data store. A business capability defines the contained region of the microservice. Everything that belongs to handling that capability should reside inside the microservice. For example, only one microservice should have a customer's personal details, comprising a delivery address, and email address. Another microservice can have a customer's purchase history and a third microservice can have customer preferences. The microservice responsible for the business capability is responsible for storing the data and keeping it up to date.

Postulate 2 – replicate the database for speed and robustness

The second factor at play when selecting where a piece of data should be stored in a microservice system is decided based on the scope or locality. There's a big change if the data store is in the vicinity of a microservice or far off, even though we are talking about the same data. A microservice can query its own database for data or a microservice can query another microservice for that same data. The latter, of course, will come with cons and tight dependencies. Looking in the local neighborhood is much faster than looking at different cities. Once you have decided on the scope of the data, you will realize that microservices need to talk to one another very often.

This kind of microservice often creates a very tight dependency, meaning we are stuck to the same old monolithic stuff. To loosen this, coupling a caching database or maintaining a cache store often comes in handy. You can cache responses as they are, or you can add a read model to expire cache after a certain time interval. The microservice that owns the local data should be in the best position to decide when a particular piece of code becomes invalid based on the business capability. HTTP cache headers should be used to control caching. Managing a cache is simply controlling the cache-control header. For example, the line `cache-control: private, max-age:3600` caches the response for 3,600 seconds.

In the next section, we will look into how to select the best database based on the following criteria:

- How is my data? Is it a bunch of tables, a document, a key-value pair, or a graph?
- How much is my data write and read frequency? Do my write requests come randomly or are they evenly distributed in time? Is there a read-all-at-once scenario?
- Are there more write operations or are there more read operations?

How to choose a data store for your microservice

One of the most fundamental questions that pop up while designing microservices is *how does one choose the correct data store?* We will be talking about this in much more detail in the *Service state* section in `Chapter 7`, *Service State and Interservice Communication*, but here, let's get our fundamentals right.

The first and foremost step in selecting any ideal data store is to find out the nature of our microservice data. Based on the nature of the data, we can briefly define the following categories:

- **Ephemeral or short-lived data**: A cache server is a classic example of short-lived data. It is a temporary store whose objective is to enhance the user experience by serving information in real time, thus avoiding frequent database calls. This is especially important where most of the operations are read intensive. Also, this store has no extra durability or security concerns as it does not have a master copy of the data. However, that being said, this should not be treated lightly as it has to be highly available. Failures can cause poor user experience and subsequently crash the main database as it won't be able to handle such frequent calls. Examples of such data stores include Redis, Elasticsearch, and so on.

- **Transient or momentary data**: Data such as logs and messages usually come in bulk volume and frequency. Ingestion services process this information before passing it to the appropriate destinations. Such data stores need high frequency writes. Features such as time series data or JSON format are added advantages. The support requirements for transient data are higher as it is mostly used in event-based communications.

- **Operational or functional data**: Operational data focuses on any information that is gathered from user sessions, such as user profiles, user shopping cart, wish lists, and so on. Being the primary data store, this kind of microservice provides better user experience with real-time feedback. For business continuity, this kinds of data must be retained. Here the durability, consistency, and availability requirements are very high. We can have any kind of data store as per our needs, providing any of the following structures—JSON, graph, key-value, relational, and so on.

- **Transactional data**: Data gathered from a series of processes or transactions, such as payment processing, order management, must be stored in a database that supports ACID controls to avoid disasters (we will mostly use relational databases for transactional data). At the time of writing of this book, MongoDB 4.0, supporting transactional data, was still not available. Once generally available NoSQL data stores can be used even for transaction management.

Design of product microservices

Based on our requirements, we can categorize data into the following various segments:

Microservice	Data store type
Caching	Ephemeral (example: ELK)
User comments, ratings, feedback, and product top sellers	Transient
Product catalog	Operational
Product search engine	Operational
Order processing	Transactional
Order fulfillment	Transactional

For our product catalog database, we will proceed with the following design.

In the current chapter, we are going to go with the product catalog service, which requires us to use an operational data store. We will go with MongoDB. A product will have at least the following items—variant, price, hierarchy, vendor, feedback email, configurations, description, and so on. Instead of getting everything in a single document, we will use the following schema design:

```
{"desc":[{"lang":"en","val":"TypescriptMicroservicesByParthGhiya."}],"name"
:"TypescriptMicroservices","category":"Microservices","brand":"PACKT","ship
ping":{"dimensions":{"height":"13.0","length":"1.8","width":"26.8"},"weight
":"1.75"},"attrs":[{"name":"microservices","value":"exampleorientedbook"},{
"name":"Author","value":"ParthGhiya"},{"name":"language","value":"Node.js"}
,{"name":"month","value":"April"}],"feedbackEmail":"ghiya.parth@gmail.com",
"ownerId":"parthghiya","description":"thisistestdescription"}
```

Some of the advantages of this schema design are as follows:

- It is easy to have a faceted search which returns results in quick milliseconds
- Each index will end with _id, making it useful for pagination
- Efficient sorting can be done on various attributes

Microservice predevelopment aspects

In this section, we are going to look at some common development aspects that we will follow throughout the book. We will understand some common aspects, such as which HTTP message code to use, how to set up logging, which kinds of logging to keep, how to use PM2 options, and how to trace a request or attach a unique identifier to a microservice. So, let's get started.

HTTP code

HTTP code dominates standard API communication and are one of the general standards across any general-purpose API. It resolves common issues for any request that is made to the server, whether it is successful, whether it is producing a server error, and so on. HTTP resolves every single request with HTTP code with ranges that indicate the nature of the code. HTTP codes are standards (http://www.w3.org/Protocols/rfc2616/rfc2616-sec10. html) based on various code and response actions are taken accordingly, so the concept of not reinventing the wheel essentially applies here. In this section, we will look at some of the standard code ranges along with their meanings.

1xx – informational

The **1xx** code provides primitive functionalities, such as operations happening in the background, switching protocols, or the state of the initial request. For example, 100 Continue indicates that the server has received request headers and is now awaiting the request body, 101 Switching Protocols indicates that the client has requested a protocol change from the server and the request has been approved, and 102 indicates that the operation is happening in the background and will take time to complete.

2xx – success

This is to indicate that a certain level of success has been achieved with information success code used in HTTP requests. It packages several responses into specific code. For example, 200 Ok means that nothing went wrong and a GET or POST request was successful. 201 Created means that a GET or POST request has been fulfilled and a new resource has been created for the client. 202 Accepted means that a request has been accepted and is now being processed. 204 No Content means that there is no content coming back from the server (very similar to 200). 206 Partial Content is usually used for paginated responses indicating there is more data to follow.

3xx – redirections

The **3xx** range is all about the status of the resource or the endpoint. It indicates what additional actions must be taken to complete that request as the server is still accepting communication, but the endpoint contacted is not the correct point of entry in the system. The most common codes used are 301 Moved Permanently, which indicates that future requests must be handled by different URIs, 302 Found, which indicates a temporary redirect is needed for some reason, 303 See other, which tells browsers to see another page, and 308 Permanent Redirect, which indicates a permanent redirection for that resource (this is the same as 301, but does not allow the HTTP method to change).

4xx – client errors

This range of codes is the most well known due to the traditional 404 Not found error, which is a well-known placeholder for URLs that are not properly formed. This range of codes indicates that there is something wrong with the request. Other well-known codes include 400 Bad Request (a request that is syntactically incorrect), 401 Unauthorized (lack of authentication from the client), and 403 Forbidden (the user does not have privileges). Another common code is 429 Too Many Requests, which is used for rate-limiting requests to indicate that traffic from the particular client is rejected.

5xx – server errors

This range of codes indicates that there has been a processing error on the server or there is something wrong in the server. Whenever a **5xx** code is issued, it states that there is some sort of problem in the server that cannot be fixed by the client and has to be handled accordingly. Some of the widely used codes are 500 Internal Server Error (this indicates that an error has occurred in the server's software and no information is disclosed), 501 Not Implemented (this indicates an endpoint that is not yet implemented, but is still being requested for), and 503 Service Unavailable (this states that the server is down for some reason and is not able to process any more requests). On receiving 503, appropriate actions must be taken to start the server again.

Why HTTP code is vital in microservices?

Microservices are fully distributed and constantly moving. Therefore, without any standard means of communication, we won't be able to trigger the corresponding fail-safe measure. For instance, if we implement the circuit breaker pattern, the circuit should know that whenever it receives the **5xx** series of code, it should keep the circuit open as the server is unavailable. Similarly, if it received 429, then it should block the request from that particular client. The complete microservice ecosystem includes proxies, caches, RPCs, and other services for which HTTP is the common language. Based on the aforementioned code, they can take appropriate action accordingly.

In the next section, we will learn about logging aspects and how to handle logging in microservices.

Auditing via logs

Until now, we have heard that microservices are distributed and services are constantly in flux. We need to keep track of all the services and the output that they throw. Using `console.log()` is a very bad practice as we won't be able to keep track of all the services because `console.log()` doesn't have a fixed format. Also, we need a stack trace whenever there is an error to debug the possible problem. To have distributed logging, we will use the `winston` module (`https://github.com/winstonjs/winston`). It has various options, such as log levels, log formats, and so on. For each microservice, we will be passing a unique microservice ID, which will identify it when we aggregate the logs. For aggregation, we will use the famous ELK Stack, described in `Chapter 9`, *Deployment, Logging, and Monitoring*. The following are various kinds of log, sorted in priority order, which are generally used:

- **Fatal/emergency (0)**: This is the most catastrophic level, used when the system won't be able to recover or function normally. This forces things like shutdown or some other heinous errors.
- **Alert (1)**: Upon receiving this severe log, actions must be taken immediately to prevent system shutdowns. The critical difference here is that the system is still usable.
- **Critical(2)**: Here, action needs not be taken immediately. This level includes situations such as failure to connect to a socket, failure to get the latest chat message, and so on.
- **Error(3)**: This is a problem that should be investigated. The Sys Admin has to be notified about it, but we don't need to drag him out of bed as this is not an emergency. It is generally used to track overall quality.
- **Warning(4)**: This level is used when there might be an error or there might not be an error. Warning conditions are close to errors but they are not errors. They indicate potentially harmful situations or events that might possibly lead to an error.
- **Notice(5)**: This level is a normal log, but with some significant conditions. As an example, you may get messages such as **Caught SIGBUS attempting to dump core in ....**
- **Info(6)**: This level is used for unnoticeable information, such as the server has been running for *x* hours and interesting runtime events. These logs are immediately visible on the console, as the purpose of these logs is to be conservative. These logs should be kept to the minimum.
- **Debug(7)**: This is used for detailed information on the flow through the system. It includes messages used for the sake of debugging, for example, something like **Opening file...** or **Getting products for productId 47.**

Logs need to be enabled. If you enable fatal logs, then all logs will be seen. If you enable info logs, then only info and debug logs will be seen. Logs for all levels have their custom method in Winston and we can add our own format.

PM2 process manager

Node.js is single threaded, meaning any use of a JavaScript `throw` statement will raise an exception that must be handled using the `try...catch` statements. Otherwise, the Node.js process will exit immediately, making it unavailable to process any further requests. As Node.js runs on single process uncaught exceptions, it needs to be handled carefully. If not, it will crash and bring down the whole application. So, the golden rule in Node.js is *if any exception bubbles out to the top without being handled, our application dies*.

PM2 is a process manager designed to keep our service alive forever. It is a production process manager with a built-in load balancer and is the perfect candidate for microservices. PM2 comes in quite handy as it allows us to declare the behavior of each microservice with a simple JSON format. PM2 is an advanced task runner with built-in monitoring and zero downtime utilities. Scaling a PM2 command is just a matter of typing the number of instances we want to spawn up or down. Starting a new process with PM2 will initiate a fork mode of the process and let the load balancer handle the rest. PM2 acts as a round robin between the main process and the process workers so that we can cope with the extra load at the same time. Some of the standard deployment features provided by PM2 are as follows:

`pm2 start <process_name>`	Starts a process in fork mode with auto-restart when the server goes down
`pm2 stop <process_name>`	Stops the PM2 process
`pm2 restart <process_name>`	Restarts a process with updated code
`pm2 reload <process_name>`	Reloads PM2 process with zero downtime
`pm2 start <process_name> -i max`	Starts a PM2 process in the max number of fork modes; that is, it will spawn the max number of instances based on the number of CPUs available
`pm2 monit`	Monitors a PM2 process
`pm2 start ecosystem.config.js --env staging`	Starts a process, taking configurations from `ecosystem.config.js`

PM2 can also be used as a deployment tool or an advanced means for CI/CD. All you need to do is define your deployment script in the `ecosystem.config.js` file, as follows:

```
"deploy": {
    "production": {
        "key": "/path/to/key.pem", // path to the private key to
authenticate
        "user": "<server-user>", // user used to authenticate, if its AWS
than ec2-user
        "host": "<server-ip>", // where to connect
        "ref": "origin/master",
        "repo": "<git-repo-link>",
        "path": "<place-where-to-check-out>",
        "post-deploy": "pm2 startOrRestart ecosystem.config.js --env
production"
    },
}
```

Then, all we have to do is hit the following command:

```
pm2 deploy ecosystem.config.js production
```

This command acts as a local deployment tool. Adding things such as path, PEM file key, and so on are steps where we can connect to the server. Once connected to the server using the specified user, the PM2 process starts and we can run our application. The latest Git repository will be cloned and then PM2 will start the `dist/Index.js` file in the **forever** option.

Tracing requests

Tracing request origins is very important, as sometimes we need to reconstruct the entire journey of the customer in our system. It provides useful information on the system, such as sources of latency. It also enables developers to observe how an individual request is being handled by searching across all aggregated logs with some unique microservice ID, or to find out the overall journey of the user by passing in a time frame. The following is a sample log generated through Winston:

```
{ level: 'info', serviceId: 'hello world microservice' ,
  message: 'What time is the testing at?',
  label: 'right meow!', timestamp: '2017-09-30T03:57:26.875Z' }
```

All important data can be seen from the log. We will be using the ELK Stack for our log. ELK has huge advantages, as it combines the power of the following three tools—**Logstash** (configured to read logs or register events from a myriad of sources and send log events to multiple sources), **Kibana** (a configurable web dashboard that is used to query Elasticsearch for log information and present it to the user), and **Elasticsearch** (a search server based on Lucene, used to collect logs, parse them, and store them for later purposes, providing a RESTful service and schema-free JSON documents). It has the following advantages:

- Each instance of **Winston** is configured with ELK. Thus, our log service is externalized and the storing of our logs is centralized. Hence, there is a single data source where requests can be traced.
- Due to the auto-schema definition and proper format of Winston, we have log-structured data. For example, if I want to query all the logs from 4:40 to 4.43, I am just an Elasticsearch query away as I know that all my logs have a time component at a fixed level in JSON.
- Winston log formats take care of creating and passing a correlational identifier across all the requests. Therefore, server-specific logs, if required, can be traced easily by querying that specific parameter.
- Our logs are searchable through Elasticsearch. Elasticsearch provides Kibana as well as REST APIs, which can be called upon to look at any point in time through all the data in the data source. A lucene-based implementation helps to fetch results faster.
- The logging level can be changed on the fly in Winston. We can have various log levels and based on the priority of logs, the lower level of logs may or may not be seen. This is pretty helpful in solving production-level issues.

In this section, we looked at logging and how it solves such problems as understanding customer behavior (how much time a customer spends on the page, how much time an action on each page took, what are some of the possible problems, and so on). In the next section, we will start developing shopping cart microservices.

Developing some microservices for a shopping cart

In this section, we will develop some microservices for a shopping cart, uniquely identified by their business capabilities. So, let's get a quick overview of our current problems before getting our hands dirty. The shopping cart monolithic was going well, but with the advent of digitalization, there was a huge increase in transaction volumes—300-500 times compared the original estimates. The end to end architecture was reviewed and it had the following limitations, based on which the microservice architecture was introduced:

- **Firmness and sturdiness**: The firmness of the system was greatly impacted due to errors and stuck threads, which forced the Node.js application server to not accept any new transactions and do a forceful restart. Memory allocation issues and database lock threads were major problems. Certain resource-intensive operations were impacting the entire application and the resource allocation pool was always consumed.

- **Deployment outages**: Due to adding more and more capabilities, the server outage window increased largely because of the server startup time. The large size of `node_modules` turned out to be the primary culprit. Since the entire application was packaged as a monolith, the entire application demanded to install the `node` modules again and again and then start our node-HTTP server.

- **Sharpness**: The complexity of code increased exponentially over time and so did the distribution of work. A tight coupling dependency was created among the teams. As a result, changes were harder to implement and deploy. Impact analysis became too complex to perform. As a result, it was like *fix one bug, 13 others come up*. Such complexity rose to a situation where the `node_modules` size was over 1 GB. Such complications eventually stopped **continuous integration (CI)** and unit test casing. Eventually, the quality of the product deteriorated.

Such situations and problems demanded an evolutionary approach. Such situations demanded a microservices development approach. In this section, we will look at the microservice setup approach, which will give us various advantages, such as selective service scaling, technological independence (easy migration to new technologies), containing faults, and so on.

Itinerary

Let's quickly go through the itinerary that we are going to perform in this exercise:

- **Development setup and prerequisite modules**: In this section, we will summarize the development tools and npm modules that we will use in the project. We will look at such prerequisites as application properties, custom middleware, dependency injection, and so on.
- **Application directory configurations**: We will analyze the structure that we will use in other microservices and understand all the files that we will need and where to write the logic.
- **Configuration files**: We will have a look at all the configuration files through which we can specify various settings, such as database hostname, port URL, and so on.
- **Processing data**: We will briefly summarize code patterns and how they can support optimal developer output and make the developer's life easier.
- **Ready to serve**: We will analyze package.json and Docker files and see how we can use these two files to make our microservice ready to serve any service requests.

So, let's get started with our itinerary.

Development setup and prerequisite modules

In this section, we will look at several aspects that we need to take care of while developing and creating our **Development Sandbox**. We will get an overview of all the node modules that we will use and the core aspects that each node module will satisfy. So, it's time to get our hands dirty.

 Note: We saw how to write custom types in Chapter 2, *Gearing up for the Journey*, for any node module that is not written in ES6. We will leverage this for any module whose types are not available in the DefinitelyTyped repository.

Repository pattern

In this section, we will understand the repository pattern, which gives us the power to have our code in a single place. TypeScript introduced generics (just like the feature in Java), which we are going to utilize to the full extent in our microservices. The repository pattern is one of the most widely used patterns to create an enterprise-level application. It enables us to directly work with data in the application by creating a new layer for database operations and business logic.

Combining generics and the repository pattern opens up countless advantages. Working with the JavaScript application, we need to deal with problems such as code sharing between applications and going modular. The generic repository pattern solves this by giving us the power to write an abstraction of data when we have one abstract class with generics (or many depending on the business capability) and reuse the implementation layer independent of the data model, passing only the types to someone's classes. When we talk about the repository pattern, it is a repository where we can keep all the operations of the database (CRUD) in one locality for any generic business entity. When you need to do the operation in the database, your application calls the repository methods, thus enabling transparency for whoever calls. Combining this with generics leads to one abstraction, one base class that has all the common methods. Our `EntityRepository` only extends the base class with all the implementations of the database operations.

 This pattern follows the open/closed principle, where the base class is open for extension but closed for modification.

It has various advantages, as follows:

- It can be used as an extensibility measure where you just need to write one class for all common operations, such as CRUDs, when all other entities should have similar operations
- Business logic can be unit tested without touching the data access logic
- The database layer can be reused
- Database access code is centrally managed in order to implement any database access policies and, like caching, it is a walk in the park

Configuring application properties

As per the twelve-factor standards (recall the, *Twelve-factor app of microservices*, section in Chapter 1, *Debunking Microservices*), one code base should suffice for multiple environments, such as QA, dev, production, and so on. Ensure that we have the application properties file in our application, where we can specify the environment name and environment-related stuff. Config (https://www.npmjs.com/package/config) is one such module, which helps you in organizing all configurations. This module just reads configurations files in the ./config directory (it should be at the same level as package.json).

Salient features of config are as follows:

- It can support formats such as YAML, YML, JSON, CSV, XML.
- It can create one directory config parallel to package.json and inside it create one file, default.ext (here, .ext can be any of the aforementioned formats).
- To read from config files, just use the following lines of code:

```
import * as config from 'config';
const port = config.get('express.port');
```

- It has support for various config files, where a hierarchy is maintained for supporting various environments.
- It even has support for multiple node instances; the perfect fit for microservices.

Custom health module

Sometimes, adding new modules to the application causes the application to go out of order. We need custom health modules to actually keep watch on the service and alert us that the service is out of order (service discovery does exactly this, which we will look at in Chapter 6, *Service Registry and Discovery*). We will be using express-ping (https://www.npmjs.com/package/express-ping) to find out the health of our node. By introducing this module in our middleware, we can expose a simple API that will tell us about its internal health to both operators and other applications.

Salient features of express-ping are as follows:

- It is a zero configuration module, where just injecting this in the middleware will expose a health endpoint.

- To use this module, simply use the following lines of code:

```
import * as health from 'express-ping';
this.app.use(health.ping());
```

- Adding just the previous LOCs will expose a `<url>/health` endpoint that we can use for health check purposes.We can add authorized access or even use middleware for our exposed `/ping` API, which is just plain old express:

```
app.get('/ping', basicAuth('username', 'password'));
app.use(health.ping('/ping'));
```

- This endpoint can be used anywhere just to check the health of the application.

Dependency injection and inversion of control

In this section, we will see how to use basic principles such as dependency injection and inversion of control. Coming from a Java background, I tend to use these principles in any application in order to make my development process smoother. Luckily, we have the exact modules matching our requirements. We will use `inversify` (`https://www.npmjs.com/package/inversify`) as the inversion of control container and `typedi` (`https://www.npmjs.com/package/typedi`) for dependency injection.

Inversify

Inversion of control (IOC) is about getting freedom, more flexibility, and less dependency on others. Say you are using a desktop computer, you are enslaved (or let's say controlled). You have to sit before a screen and look at it, using the keyboard to type and mouse to navigate. Badly written software can enslave you similarly. If you replace your desktop with a laptop, then you have inverted control. You can easily take it and move around. So, now you can control where you are with your computer rather than the computer controlling it. IOC in software is very similar. Traditionally speaking, IOC is a design principle in which custom-written portions of the computer program receive the flow of control from a generic framework.We have `inversifyJS` available as an `npm` module. As per their official docs:

InversifyJS is a lightweight inversion of control container for TypeScript and JavaScript applications. An IOC container will use a class constructor to identify and inject its dependencies. It has a friendly API and encourages the usage of best OOP and IoC practices adhering to SOLID principles.

Typedi

Dependency injection is a means by which classes, components, and services specify which libraries they depend on. By simply injecting dependencies into a microservice, the service is empowered with the ability to reference dependencies directly, rather than looking them up in a service registry or using a service locator. The power to encapsulate any service, discover it, and distribute load is an extremely valuable addition to microservices. **Typedi** is a dependency injection tool for JavaScript and TypeScript. Using Typedi is very easy. All you do is create a container and start using dependency injection principles on that container. Typedi provides various annotations, such as `@Service`, `@Inject`, and more. You can even create your own custom decorators.

TypeORM

Inspired by frameworks such as hibernate and doctrine, the Entity Framework **TypeORM** (`https://www.npmjs.com/package/typeorm`) is an ORM framework supporting active record and data mapper patterns, unlike all other JavaScript ORMs. This enables us to write high quality, loosely coupled, scalable, and maintainable applications in the most productive way ever. It has the following advantages:

- Uses multiple database connections
- Works with multiple database types
- Query caching
- Hooks, such as subscribers and listeners
- Written in TypeScript
- Supports both the Data Mapper and Active Record patterns
- Replication
- Connection pooling
- Streaming raw results (reactive programming)
- Eager and lazy relations
- Supports SQL as well as NoSQL databases

Application directory configurations

The directory structure of this application focuses on our architectural approach based on separation of concerns. Each folder structure will have files specifically pertaining to the name of the folder. In the following screenshot, you can see the overall structure and detailed structure:

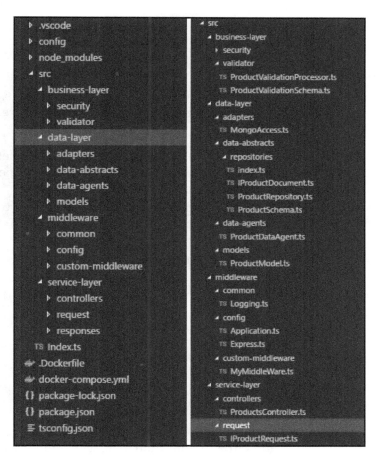

Configuration structure

In the preceding screenshot, you can see two folder structures. The first one is the high-level and overall folder structure highlighting important folders, whereas the second one is a detailed expanded view of the `src` folder. The folder structure follows the *separation of concerns* approach to eliminate code duplication and share singleton services between controllers.

In computer science, **separation of concerns (SoC)** is a design principle for dividing a computer program into distinct sections or capabilities so that each section addresses a separate concern and is independent of the other. A concern is a set of information that affects the code of any application.

Let's understand our folder structure and the files it contains, and what concern the folder actually addresses.

src/data-layer

This folder is responsible for the overall organization of the data, its storage, and accessibility methods. Model definitions and iridium files can be found here. It has the following folders:

- **Adapters**: This implements the setup of MongoDB connection methods for connecting to the MongoDB database and adding events on connected, error, open, disconnected, reconnected, and forced exit methods
- **Data-abstracts**: This has both the schemas representing the structure of each MongoDB collection and the documents representing each set of data in the collection
- **Data-agents**: This has the query transactions against the data store for each MongoDB collection
- **Model**: This has a TypeScript class representation of the data portrayed by the MongoDB document

src/business-layer

This folder has the implementation of business logic and other resources that are needed by the service layer or the middleware layer, as follows:

- **Security**: If we want some security or tokens at a particular microservice level, this is where we will add our authentication logic (generally, we don't write the authentication layer at the individual service level). Rather, we write it at the API Gateway level, which we will see in Chapter 5, *Understanding API Gateway*. Here, we will write code for the service registration/deregistration, verification, internal security, microservices communicating with the service registry, the API Gateway, and so on.

- **Validators**: This will have schema and processing logic for validating data sent with API requests. We will write our class-validator (`https://www.npmjs.com/package/class-validator`) schema here, together with some custom validation functions.

src/service-layer

This folder includes the processes for establishing API endpoints in the form of routes, which will handle all responses to data requests. It has the following folders:

- `controllers`: This serves as a primer for processing any data requests associated with routes. The custom `controllers` are featured by npm module `routing-controllers` (`https://www.npmjs.com/package/routing-controllers`) using in-built decorators, such as `@Get`, `@Put`, `@Delete`, `@Param`, and so on. These functions implement basic GET, POST, DELETE, and PUT methods for transacting with the database via the RESTful API. We can even have socket initialization code and more. We will use dependency injection to inject some services which will be used here.
- `request`: This has TypeScript interfaces defining and showing the attributes that constitute each of the different kinds of request in the controller.
- `response`: This has TypeScript interfaces defining and showing the attributes that constitute each of the different kinds of response in the controller.

src/middleware

This contains resources that have any server configuration, as well as a certain place to store any utility processes that can be shared across any application. We can have centralized configurations, such as `logger`, `cache`, `elk`, and so on:

- `common`: This has an instantiation of the logger module, which can be shared across the entire application. This module is based on `winston` (`https://www.npmjs.com/package/winston`).
- `config`: This has vendor-specific implementations. We will have express configuration and express middleware defined here, as well as all the important configurations for organizing the REST API endpoints.
- `custom-middleware`: This folder will have all our custom-written middleware, which we can utilize in any controller class or any particular method.

In the next section, we will look at some of the configuration files that configure and define the application and determine how it will run. For example, the port on which it will run, the port the database is connected to, the modules installed, the transpilation configuration, and so on.

Configuration files

Let's look at some of the configuration files that we will use throughout the project, and use them to govern the project in different environments or as per the use case:

- `default.json`: Node.js has an excellent module, `node-config`. You can find the `config` file in the `config` folder parallel to `package.json`. Here, you can have multiple configuration files that can be picked up based on environments. For example, `default.json` would be loaded first, followed by `{deployment}.json`, and so on. Here is a sample file:

```
{
    "express": {
        "port": 8081,
        "debug": 5858,
        "host": "products-service"
    }
}
```

- `src/Index.ts`: This initializes our application, by making a new object of the application defined in the `middleware/config/application`. It imports reflected metadata that initializes our dependency injection container.
- `package.json`: This serves as the manifest file in all of the Node.js application. It delineates the external libraries required for building the application in two sections, `dependencies` and `devDependencies`. This provides a `scripts` tag that has external commands for building, running, and packaging the module.
- `tsconfig.json`: This provides options for TypeScript when it performs the task of transpiling to JavaScript. For example, if we have `sourceMaps:true`, we will be able to debug TypeScript code via generated sourcemaps.

- `src/data-layer/adapters/MongoAccess.ts`: This will have a connection to the MongoDB database and various event handlers attached to various events of MongoDB, such as `open`, `connected`, `error`, `disconnected`, `reconnected`, and so on:

```
export class MongooseAccess {
  static mongooseInstance: any;
  static mongooseConnection: Mongoose.Connection;
  constructor() {
    MongooseAccess.connect();
  }
  static connect(): Mongoose.Connection {
    if (this.mongooseInstance) {
      return this.mongooseInstance;
    }
    let connectionString =
config.get('mongo.urlClient').toString();
    this.mongooseConnection = Mongoose.connection;
    this.mongooseConnection.once('open', () => {
      logger.info('Connect to an mongodb is opened.');
    });
    //other events
  }
```

- `src/middleware/config/Express.ts`: This is where our express middleware resides. We will attach standard configurations, such as `helmet`, `bodyparser`, `cookieparser`, `cors origin`, and so on, and set up our `controllers` folder with the following:

```
setUpControllers(){
  const controllersPath =
      path.resolve('dist', 'service-layer/controllers');
  useContainer(Container);
  useExpressServer(this.app,
    {
      controllers: [controllersPath + "/*.js"],
      cors: true
    }
  );
}
```

Processing data

As with most web servers that accept and process requests from clients, we have a very similar thing here. We just have granularized things at a macro level. The overall flow of the process is shown in the following diagram:

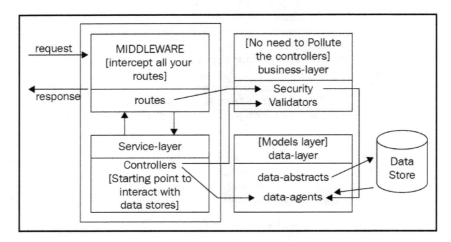

Processing data

Let's understand the process by taking any of the sample endpoints through each of the sections in the preceding diagram. You can find the whole sample in
`chapter-4/products-catalog` service:

1. An API request to put a specific product based on the attributes of the product is sent to the server, `http://localhost:8081/products/add-update-product`:

   ```
   body: {//various product attributes}
   ```

2. The registered controllers with the `/products` path capture the request based on the URI `/products/`. If a middleware is registered in `Express.ts`, it will get triggered first; otherwise, the controller method gets called. Registering a middleware is simple. Create a middleware class with the following code:

   ```
   import { ExpressMiddlewareInterface } from "routing-
   controllers";
   export class MyMiddleware implements ExpressMiddlewareInterface
   {
   ```

```
use(request: any, response: any, next?: (err?: any) => any):
any {
    console.log("custom middleware gets called, here we can do
anything.");
    next();
  }
}
```

3. To use this middleware in any controller, just make use of the `@UseBefore` and `@UseAfter` decorators on top of any method/controller.

4. Since we want to execute some core logic (such as picking the response from the cache or logging), the `middleware` function gets executed first. This resides in `middleware/custom-middleware/MyMiddleWare.ts`. Using the `async` capabilities of Node.js, the method will do what is necessary and then proceed on to the next request with `next()`.

5. In the custom middleware, we can have various checks; for example, we may want to expose the APIs only if there is a valid `ownerId` or only to authorized sellers. If the request does not have a valid `ownerId`, the request will no longer progress through the rest of the application, and we can throw an error indicating authenticity or an invalid `productId`. However, if the `ownerId` is valid, then the request will continue to progress through the routes. This is the role of `MyMiddleWare.ts`. The next part will go through the controllers.

6. The next part is the `@JsonControllers` defined by the decorators provided by routing controllers. We define our routing controller and post API for adding and updating a product:

```
@JsonController('/products')
@UseBefore(MyMiddleware)
export class ProductsController {
  constructor() { }

  @Put('/add-update-product')
  async addUpdateProduct( @Body() request:
IProductCreateRequest,
    @Req() req: any, @Res() res: any): Promise<any> {
    //API Logic for adding updating product
  }
}
```

This will create a PUT request for API `<host:url>/products/add-update-product`. The `@Body` annotation will convert a cast of the request body to `IProductCreateRequest` (`src/service-layer/request/IProductRequest.ts`) in the variable request (as seen in the argument of the `addIpdateProduct` method), which will be available throughout the method. The `request` and `responses` folder contains the transformation of a various `request` and `response` objects.

7. The first part of the controller is to validate the request. The validation and security logic will be inside the `src/business-layer` folder. Inside the `validator` folder, we will have `ProductValidationSchema.ts` and `ProductValidatorProcessor.ts`. Inside `ProductValidationSchema.ts`, add the validation schema rules (various validation messages through which we want to identify whether a request is correct or has junk data) using the `class-validator` (https://www.npmjs.com/package/class-validator) inbuilt decorators, (`@MinLength`, `@MaxLength`, `@IsEmail`, and so on):

```
export class ProductValidationSchema {
  @Length(5, 50)
  name: string;

  @MinLength(2, { message: "Title is too Short" })

  @MaxLength(500, { message: "Title is too long" })
  description: string;

  @Length(2, 15)
  category: string;

  @IsEmail()
  feedbackEmail: string;
  //add other attributes.
}
```

8. Next, we will use these messages to validate our request object. In `ProductValidationProcessor.ts`, create a validator method that returns a consolidated array of messages:

```
async function validateProductRequest(productReqObj: any):
Promise<any> {
  let validProductData = new
ProductValidationSchema(productReqObj);
  let validationResults = await validate(validProductData);
  let constraints = []
```

```
    if (validationResults && validationResults.length > 0) {
      forEach(validationResults,
        (item) => {
          constraints.push(pick(item, 'constraints',
'property'));
        });
    }
    return constraints;
}
```

9. In `ProductsController.ts`, call the method. If there are errors in the request, the request will stop there and won't propagate to the rest of the API. If the response is valid, then it will pass through the data agent to push the data to MongoDB:

```
let validationErrors: any[] = await
validateProductRequest(request);
logger.info("total Validation Errors for product:-",
validationErrors.length);
if (validationErrors.length > 0) {
  throw {
    thrown: true,
    status: 401,
    message: 'Incorrect Input',
    data: validationErrors
  }
}
let result = await
this.productDataAgent.createNewProduct(request);
```

10. When the request is valid, the controller, `ProductController.ts`, calls the `ProductDataAgent.ts` method, `createNewProduct(..)`, in the data layer in order to put the data into MongoDB. Further more, based on the Mongoose schema definition, it will automatically maintain a duplication check entry:

```
@Put('/add-update-product')
async addUpdateProduct(@Body() request: IProductCreateRequest,
                       @Req() req: any, @Res() res: any):
Promise < any > {
  let validationErrors: any[] = await
validateProductRequest(request);
  logger.info("total Validation Errors for product:-",
validationErrors.length);
  if(validationErrors.length> 0) {
    throw {
      thrown: true,
      status: 401,
```

```
                 message: 'Incorrect Input',
                 data: validationErrors
            }
        }
        let result = await
    this.productDataAgent.createNewProduct(request);
        if(result.id) {
            let newProduct = new ProductModel(result);
            let newProductResult = Object.assign({ product:
    newProduct.getClientProductModel() });
            return res.json(<IProductResponse>(newProductResult));
        }else{
            throw result;
        }
    }
```

Controllers in the service layer not only provide access to the data layer through data agents used for negotiating queries against the data store, but they also provide an entry point of access to the business layer to process other business rules, such as validating product input. The `ProductDataAgent.ts` method returns the object returned by MongoDB. It also has other methods, such as `deleteProduct`, `findAllProducts`, `findProductByCategory`, and so on.

11. After completing the transaction with the data store in `ProductDataAgent.ts`, a promise in the form of a vanilla object is returned to `ProductController.ts`, indicating a failure or success. When a successful product is added to a database, the object inserted along with MongoDB's `ObjectID()` is returned. The data associated with the product is constructed as `ProductModel` and will be resolved as an `IProductResponse` to `ProductController.ts`:

```
async createNewProduct(product: any): Promise < any > {
  let newProduct = <IProductDocument>(product);
  if(newProduct.id) {
    let productObj = await ProductRepo.findOne({ productId: newProduct.id
});
    if (productObj && productObj.ownerId != newProduct.ownerId) {
      return { thrown: true, success: false, status: 403, message: "you are
not the owner of Product" }
    }
  }
  let addUpdateProduct = await ProductRepo.create(newProduct);
  console.log(addUpdateProduct);
  if(addUpdateProduct.errors) {
    return { thrown: true, success: false, status: 422, message: "db is
currently unable to process request" }
  }
```

```
    return addUpdateProduct;
}
```

> If some mishap occurs in the processing of the query in `ProductDataAgent.ts`, such as a broken connection to the data store, a result in the form of an error message will be returned. A similar error response will be thrown if an object with the same name already exists.

This completes the example of how data flows through the application. Based on many backend applications and cross-cutting factors, this is designed in order to have a smooth flow and eliminate redundant code.

Similarly, this project will have other APIs, as follows:

- GET request to get all products
- GET request to get products by ID
- GET request to get products by product type
- DELETE request to delete a single product

Ready to serve (package.json and Docker)

In this section, we will look at how to write scripts in `package.json` and then automate the whole thing using Docker.

package.json

Now that we know how data flows, let's understand how to make it ready to serve. Install TypeScript and `rimraf` as dependencies and add the following inside the `scripts` tag:

```
"scripts": {
  "start": "npm run clean && npm run build && node ./dist/index.js",
  "clean": "node ./node_modules/rimraf/bin.js dist",
  "build": "node ./node_modules/typescript/bin/tsc"
},
```

To run the entire process, execute the following command:

```
npm run start
```

This will first delete the `dist` folder if it exists, and then, based on the `src` folder, it will transpile the folder and generate the `dist` folder. Once the `dist` is generated, we can run our server with `node ./dist/Index.js` and `npm run start` in combination.

In a later chapter, we will do more things here, including test coverage and generating the swagger documentation. Our build script should cover the following things:

- Generate documentation via `swagger-gen`
- Invoke `Express.ts`, which will have all routes configured along with middleware and dependency injection
- The `tsc` command will transpile the TypeScript files into JavaScript files using the `"outputDirectory":"./dist"` attribute in `tsconfig.json` to identify where the JavaScript files should be placed
- SwaggerUI will generate the documentation, which will be available on the web

Now, to test the API, create a product JSON of the following order and hit a POST request with the following payload:

```
{"desc":[{"lang":"en","val":"TypescriptMicroservicesByParthGhiya."}],"name"
:"TypescriptMicroservices","category":"Microservices","brand":"PACKT","ship
ping":{"dimensions":{"height":"13.0","length":"1.8","width":"26.8"},"weight
":"1.75"},"attrs":[{"name":"microservices","value":"exampleorientedbook"},{
"name":"Author","value":"ParthGhiya"},{"name":"language","value":"Node.js"}
,{"name":"month","value":"April"}],"feedbackEmail":"ghiya.parth@gmail.com",
"ownerId":"parthghiya","description":"thisistestdescription"}
```

You will see a successful response with **ResponseCode: 200 and MongoDB's ObjectId**. It will look something like this: **"id": "5acac73b8bd4f146bcff9667"**.

This is the general approach to how we are going to write our microservice. It shows us more behavior on separation of control, how it can be achieved using TypeScript, and some enterprise design patterns. Thin controllers that lie in the service layer rely on references to the business layer and data layer for implementing the process with which we can eliminate redundant code and enable the sharing of services between controllers. Similarly, you can write countless services based on the same approach. Say you want to write a payment microservice, you can use the `typeorm` module for SQL operations and have the same code structure.

Docker

Now that our application is up and running, let's containerize it, so we can push our image to anyone. Containers such as Docker help us to package an entire application including the libraries, dependencies, environment, and anything else needed by the application to run. Containers are helpful as they isolate the application from the infrastructure so we can easily run it on different platforms without the need to worry about the system on which we are running.

Our objectives are as follows:

1. Spin up a working version of our product catalog microservice, Mongo microservice, just by running `docker-compose up`
2. The Docker workflow should be what we are using the Node.js workflow that includes transpiling, and serving the `dist` folder
3. Use data containers for initializing MongoDB

So, let's get started. We will create our `container` file and write starting scripts inside it by performing the following steps. You can find the source in the `Chapter 4/products-catalog -with-docker` folder:

1. First, create the `.dockerignore` file to ignore things that we don't want in our built container:

   ```
   Dockerfile
   Dockerfile.dev
   ./node_modules
   ./dist
   ```

2. Now, we will write our `Dockerfile`. An image is made up of a set of layers and instructions that we define in our `Dockerfile`. We will initialize our Node.js application code here:

   ```
   #LATEST NODE Version —which node version u will use.
   FROM node:9.2.0
   # Create app directory
   RUN mkdir -p /usr/src/app
   WORKDIR /usr/src/app
   #install dependencies
   COPY package.json /usr/src/app
   RUN npm install
   #bundle app src
   COPY . /usr/src/app
   #3000 is the port which we want to expose for outside container
   ```

```
world.
EXPOSE 3000
CMD [ "npm" , "start" ]
```

3. We are done with the Node.js part. Now, we need to configure our MongoDB. We will use `docker compose`, a tool for running multiple container applications, which will spin up our application and run it. Let's add a `docker-compose.yml` file for adding our MongoDB:

```yaml
version: "2"
services:
  app:
    container_name: app
    build: ./
  restart: always
    ports:
      - "3000:8081"
    links:
      - mongo
  mongo:
    container_name: mongo
    image: mongo
    volumes:
      - ./data:/data/db
    ports:
      - "27017:27017"
```

Running multiple containers inside a single container is not possible as such. We would be leveraging the Docker Compose up tool (https://docs.docker.com/compose/overview/),which can be downloaded by running `sudo curl -L https://github.com/docker/compose/releases/download/1.21.0/docker-compose-$(uname -s)-$(uname -m) -o/usr/local/bin/docker-compose`. We will look at `docker compose` in Chapter 9, *Deployment, Logging, and Monitoring*.

Breaking up this file shows us the following:

*   We have a service called `app`, which adds a container for the product-catalog service.
*   We instruct Docker to restart the container automatically if it fails.

- To build the app service (our TypeScript Node.js application), we need to tell the location of our `Dockerfile` where it can find build instructions. The `build ./` command tells Docker that the `Dockerfile` is at the same level as `docker-compose.yml`.
- We map the host and the container port (here we have kept both the same).
- We have added another service, Mongo, which pulls the standard Mongo image from the Docker Hub registry.
- Next, we define a data directory by mounting `/data/db` and the local data directory `/data`.
- This will have an advantage similar to when we start a new container. Docker compose will use the volume of previous containers and thus ensure there is no data loss.
- Finally, we link the app container to the Mongo container.
- Port `3000:8081` is basically telling us that the Node.js service exposed to the outside container world can be accessed at port `3000`, whereas internally the application runs on port `8081`.

4. Now, just open up a terminal at the parent level and hit the following command:

```
docker-compose up
```

This will spin up two containers and aggregate the logs of both containers. We have now successfully Dockerized our application.

5. Running `docker-compose up` will give you an error that it can't connect to MongoDB. What could we have done wrong? We are running multiple containers via the `docker-compose` option. Mongo runs inside its own container; hence, it is not accessible via `localhost:27017`. We need to change our connection URL to point it to the Docker service rather than the localhost. Change the following line in `default.json` from:

```
"mongo":{"urlClient": "mongodb://127.0.0.1:27017/products"}, to
"mongo":{"urlClient": "mongodb://mongo:27017/products"}
```

6. Now, run `docker-compose` up and you will be able to successfully get the service up and running.

By dockerizing our microservice, we have completed the development and build cycle. In the next section, we will quickly recap what we have done so far, before moving on to the next topic, *Microservice best practices*.

Synopsis

In this section, we will have a quick look at some of the modules that we used and describe their purpose:

routing-controllers	Has various options and is based on ES6. It has lots of decorators, such as @GET, @POST, and @PUT, which help us to design configuration-free services.
config	Config module from which we can write various files based on different environments, thus helping us to adhere to the twelve-factor app.
typedi	Used as a dependency injection container. We can then use it to inject services (@Service) into any controller.
winston	Used for the logging module.
typeORM	Module written in TypeScript for dealing with relational databases.
mongoose	Popular Mongoose ORM module for dealing with MongoDB.
cors	To enable CORS support for our microservices.
class-validator	Used to validate any input requests based on our configured rules.

Similarly, based on this folder structure and modules, we can create any number of microservices supporting any databases. Now that we have a clear understanding of how to design a microservice, in the next section we will look at some microservice design best practices.

Microservice design best practices

Now that we have developed some microservices, it's time to learn about some patterns and some design decisions involved around them. To get a broader perspective, we will look at what a microservice should handle and what it shouldn't. A number of factors need to be considered while designing microservices, keeping best practices in mind. Microservices are solely designed on the principle of single responsibility. We need to define boundaries and contain our microservices. The following sections cover all the factors and design principles that need to be considered for efficiently developing microservices.

Setting up proper microservice scope

One of the most important decisions relating to designing microservices is the microservice size. Size and scope can have a huge impact on microservice design. While comparing to traditional approaches, we can say there should be one REST endpoint per any container or any component that performs a single responsibility. Our microservices should be domain-driven, where each service is bound to the specific context in that domain and will be dealing with a specific business capability. A business capability can be defined as something or anything that is being done to contribute to achieving business goals. In our shopping cart microservice system, payment, adding to the cart, recommending a product, and dispatching a product are different business capabilities. Each different business capability should be implemented by a separate microservice. If we go with this model, we will end up in our microservices list with a product catalog service, price catalog service, invoice service, payment service, and so on. Each of the technical capabilities, if any, should be bundled as separate microservices. Technical capabilities don't directly contribute to achieving business goals, but rather serve as a simplification to support other services. An example includes the integration service. The main points that we should adhere to can be summarized as:

- Microservices should be responsible for a single capability (be it technical or business)
- Microservices should be individually deployable and scalable
- Microservices should be easily maintainable by a small team and should be replaceable at any point in time

Self-governing functions

Another important factor while scoping microservices is deciding when to pull out the function. If the function is self-sustaining, that is, it has very few dependencies on external functions, it processes a given output and gives out some output. It can then be taken as a microservice boundary and kept as a separate microservice. Common examples are caching, encryption, authorization, authentication, and so on. Our shopping cart has numerous such examples. For example, it can be a central log service, or a price calculation microservice that takes in various inputs, such as product name, customer discounts, and so on, and then calculates the price of the product after applying promotional discounts, if any.

Polyglot architecture

One of the key requirements that gave birth to microservices is support for a polyglot architecture. Various business capabilities need different treatment. The principle of "one rule applies everywhere" doesn't work anymore. Different technologies, architectures, and approaches are needed to handle all business and technological capabilities. When we are scoping microservices, this is another key factor to take care of. For example, in our shopping microservice system, a product search microservice doesn't need relational databases, but adding to the cart and the payment service need ACID compliance, as handling transactions there is a very niche requirement.

Size of independent deployable component

A distributed microservice ecosystem will take full advantage of currently increasing CI/CD processes for automation. Automating various steps, such as integration, delivery, deployment, unit testing, scaling, and code coverage and then creating a deployable unit makes life easier. If we include too many things in a single microservices container, it will pose some huge challenge, as there are a lot of processes involved, such as installing dependencies, automatic file copying or downloading the source from Git, building, deploying, and then starting up. With increasing complexity in the microservice, the size of the microservice will increase, which soon increases the trouble in managing it. A well-designed microservice makes sure that deployment units remain manageable.

Distributing and scaling services whenever required

While designing microservices, it is important to breakup microservices based on various parameters, such as in-depth analysis of which business capabilities are most sought after, a division of services based on ownership, loosely coupled architecture, and so on. Microservices designed with this division are effective in the long run as we can easily scale out any service on demand and isolate our failure points. In our product microservices, approximately 60% of the requests would be search based. In this case, our search microservice container has to run separately so it can scale separately when needed. Elasticsearch or Redis can be introduced on top of this microservice, which would give better response times. This will have various advantages, such as cost reduction, effective use of resources, business benefits, cost optimizations, and so on.

Being Agile

With dynamically changing requirements, the Agile methodology of development has been adopted everywhere. One of the important considerations in scoping out microservices is developing in such a way that each team can develop different parts of the pie. Each of the team builds different microservices and then we construct the full pie. For example, in our shopping cart microservices, we can have one recommendation service that specifically targets an audience based on their preferences and history. This can be developed keeping users' tracking history, browser history, and more in mind, which can result in a complex algorithm. This is why it will be developed as a separate microservice, which can be handled by separate teams.

Single business capability handler

Drifting away a bit from the traditional single responsibility principle, a single microservice should handle a single business capability or technical capability. One microservice should not perform multiple responsibilities. Based on the pattern of design, a business capability can be divided into more than one microservice. For example, in our shopping cart microservices in inventory management, we may introduce a CQRS pattern to achieve some quality attributes, where our reads and writes would be spread across different service containers. When each service is mapped to a bounded context, handling a single business capability, it is much easier to manage them. Each service may exist as separate products, targeting a specific community. They should be reusable, easily deployable, and so on.

Adapting to shifting needs

Microservices should be designed so that they can be easily detached from the system with the minimum amount of rewrites. This enables us to easily add experimental features. For example, in our shopping cart microservices, we may add a product ranking service based on the feedback received. If the service doesn't work out or the business capability is not achieved, this service can be thrown out or easily replaced with another service. Scoping microservices here plays an important role, as a minimum viable product can be made and then, on top of it, features can be added or removed as per the requirements.

Handling dependencies and coupling

Another important factor in scoping out services is dependencies and the coupling a service introduces. Dependencies in microservices have to be evaluated to make sure that tight coupling is not introduced in the system. To avoid a high-coupled system, decompose the system into business/technical/functional capabilities and create a functional dependency tree. Having too many request-response calls, cyclical dependencies, and so on are some of the factors that may break a microservice. Another important aspect in designing robust microservices is to have event-driven architecture; that is, instead of waiting for a response, a microservice should react upon receiving an event.

Deciding the number of endpoints in a microservice

While this may seem an important point in consideration for designing microservices, it is not at all a design consideration. A microservice container may host one or many endpoints. A more important consideration is bounding the microservice. Based on the business or technical capabilities, there may be only one endpoint, whereas in many cases there could be more than one endpoint in a microservice. For example, going back to our shopping cart services for our inventory management where we introduced a CQRS pattern, we have separate read and write services, each containing single endpoints. Another example can be a polyglot architecture, where we have multiple endpoints in order to have communication between various microservices. We usually break services into containers based on our deployment and scaling needs. For our checkout service, all services are connected and use the same relational database. In this case, there is no need to separate out these into different microservices.

Communication styles between microservices

Another important factor to be considered while designing microservices is the communication style between microservices. There can be a synchronous mode (sending requests, receiving responses) or an asynchronous mode of communication (fire and forget). Both modes have their own pros and cons and have their specific use cases where they can be used. In order to have a scalable microservice, a combination of both approaches is needed. Apart from this, nowadays "being real-time" is the new trend. Socket-based communication promotes real-time communication. Yet another way of dividing communication styles is based on the number of receivers. For a single receiver, we have a command-based pattern (CQRS, as seen in earlier chapters). For more than one receiver, we have an event-driven architecture that is based on the principle of the publish and subscribe pattern, where in-service buses are used.

Specifying and testing the microservices contract

A contract can be defined as a set of agreements (protocol, request body, address, and so on) between the consumer and the provider, which helps to smooth the interactions that take place between them. Microservices should be designed so that they can be independently deployed, without any dependencies on one another. To achieve this complete independence, each microservice should have well written, versioned, and defined contracts, which all its clients (other microservices) must adhere to. Introducing breaking changes at any time might be a problem as clients may require previous versions of the contract. Only after appropriate communication should a contract be put out of service or turned down. Some best practices include deploying new versions side by side and including versioning in your API. For example, `/product-service/v1`, then `/product-service/v2`. Using **consumer-driven contracts** (**CDCs**) is one of the modern ways to test microservices, as compared to integration tests. Further, in this book, we will be using Pact JS to test our contracts (`Chapter 8`, *Testing, Debugging, and Documenting*).

Number of microservices in a container

Containerizing your microservice is one of the most recommended ways for deploying microservices. Containers provide agility in your system and it streamlines the development and testing experience. Containers are portable across any infrastructure and can be easily deployed on AWS too. Deciding on the number of microservices that a container can contain is vital and is dependent upon various factors such as container capacity, memory, selective scaling, resource requirements, traffic volume per service, and so on. Based on these facts, we can decide whether deployments can be brought together or not. Even if services are brought together, it has to be ensured that these services are run independently and they are not sharing anything. Selective scaling is also one of the crucial factors in deciding on the number of microservices in a container. It should be such that deployments are self-managed, an example being AWS Lambda. The following are the available patterns and the limitations of each of the patterns:

- **Service instance per virtual machine**: Here, you package each service as a virtual machine image (traditional approach), such as an Amazon EC2 EMI. Here, each service is a separate VM that is launched in a separate VM image:
    - **Limitations**:
        - Less efficient resource utilization
        - You pay for entire VM; therefore, if you are not utilizing the entire VM, you are paying charges for nothing
        - Deploying a new version on a service is very slow
        - Managing multiple VMs soon becomes a huge pain and a time-consuming activity
- **Service instance per container**: Here, each service runs on its own container. Containers are one portable virtualization technique. They have their own root filesystem and portable namespaces. You can limit their CPU resources and memory.
    - **Limitations**:
        - A container is not as mature as a VM
        - Handling spikes in the load is an extra added task
        - Monitoring the VM infrastructure and container infrastructure is again an added task

- **Serverless**: One of the latest "worry free trends" is the serverless architecture, where you package a microservice, package it as a ZIP, and deploy it to serverless platforms, such as AWS Lambda. You are just billed for each request based on the time taken and memory consumed. For example, a Lambda function is stateless.
  - **Limitations:**
    - This approach is not feasible for long-term running services. An example can be where a service is dependent on another service or a third-party broker.
    - Requests must complete in less than 300 seconds.
    - Services must be stateless, as each separate instance is run for each request.
    - Services must start quickly or else they will be timed out.
    - Services must be run in one of the supported languages. For example, AWS Lambda supports Java, Node.js, and Python.

Data sources and rule engine among microservices

Another important factor is applying a rules engine and deciding upon data sources in our distributed system. Rules are an essential part of any system as they help us to govern the entire system. Many organizations use a centralized rules engine or workflow processes following the BPMN standards example, Drools. An embedded rule engine can either be placed within the service or can be external to the service based on usage. If there are complex rules, a central authoring repository with an embedded engine would be the best choice. Since it is centrally distributed, there can be technology dependencies, rules running rules within some application server boundaries, and so on.

 Business Process Modeling Notations (BPMN) are standardized notations with the objective of creating visual models of any business or any organizational process. Often in business capabilities, we need a definitive workflow that may change as per requirements. We never hardcode any processes or write our own engine and leverage BPMN tools for it.

Just like the rules engine, deciding on data stores among microservices is also crucial. Transactional boundaries should be set up within our defined business capabilities. For example, in our shopping cart microservices, at the checkout we need to maintain transactions and we can go with RDBMS as a data source to ensure integrity and follow ACID principles. However, product catalog databases don't have any transactions and we can use NoSQL databases for them.

Summary

In this chapter, we began designing our microservices for the shopping cart services. We analyzed our requirements based on technical, functional, and business capabilities, which are the primary drivers in scoping microservices. We designed our schema, analyzed our microservice structure, and ran it on Docker. Finally, we looked at some of the best practices for microservice design and learned how to scope microservices based on our business capabilities.

In the next chapter, we are going to learn how to introduce a gateway to our microservices and understand the problem a gateway solves. We are going to see how API Gateway solves centralized concerns in distributed systems. We will get acquainted with some API Gateway design patterns and design our gateway for the shopping cart microservices.

5
Understanding API Gateway

After designing some microservices, we will talk about microservices gateways here. When compared to monolithic applications, microservices do not communicate via in-memory calls and rather use the network calls. Hence, network design and implementation plays an important role in the stability of the distributed system. We will debunk API Gateway and learn how it handles important concerns in microservices-based architecture.

This chapter will commence with an understanding of API Gateway and why we need to use it. It will then talk about all the centralized concerns that an API Gateway handles, as well as the benefits, and drawbacks of introducing a gateway. We will design our gateway for shopping cart microservices and see all available options for a gateway, and get acquainted with design patterns and aspects involved in API Gateway. This chapter will talk about the following topics:

- Debunking API Gateway
- Concerns API Gateway handles
- API Gateway design patterns
- Circuit breakers and its role
- The need for gateway in our shopping cart microservices
- Available gateways options
- Designing our gateway for shopping cart microservices

Debunking API Gateway

As we go deeper into our microservices development, we see various pitfalls ahead. Now that our microservices are ready and when we think of clients utilizing those microservices, we will encounter the following issues:

- The consumer or the web client runs on a browser. We don't have any discovery client on the frontend, which takes care of identifying where the container/VM service is located or neither take care of load balancing. We need an extra piece of the puzzle which connects the microservices living in different containers in the backend and abstracting that implementation from the client.

- Untill now, we haven't spoken about centralized concerns like authenticating services, versioning services, filtering or transforming any request/response. Upon reflection, we realize that they need a central point of control from which they can be applied throughout the system without re-implementing the same logic everywhere.

- Further more, different clients may have different contract requirements. One client may expect an XML response while other needs JSON response. We need a center component which takes care of routing a request, translating the response as per protocol needs, and composing various responses as per need.

- If we want to scale any of the microservice independently on demand, new instances need to be added on demand whose location should be abstracted from the client. So we need a central client who constantly communicates with all microservices and maintains a registry. Further, if the service is down, it should inform the client of this and break the connection there, thus preventing failure to propagate. Further, it can act as a place for central cache management.

An API Gateway is a type of service which solves all mentioned problems. It is the entry point in our microservices world and it provides a shared layer for clients to communicate with internal services. It can perform tasks like route requests, transform protocols, authenticate, rate limiting to a service, and so on. It is a center point for governance and it helps to achieve various things like the following:

- Monitor the entire distributed moving system and take action accordingly
- Decouple consumers from microservices by abstracting the instance and network location, and routing every request via the API Gateway

- Avoid code duplication by keeping reusable code in a single place
- Achieve scaling on demand, and take action on faulty services from a single place
- Define API standards, for example, Swagger, Thrift IDL, and so on
- Design contracts
- Track the life cycle of APIs with various things like versioning, utilization, monitoring and alerting, throttling, and so on
- Avoid chatty communication between client and microservices

With being a single entry point into a totally moving distributed system, it becomes very easy to enforce any new governance standards (for example, every consumer should have JWT token), have some real-time monitoring, auditing, API consumption policies, and so on.

 The JWT token pattern leverages an encryption algorithm: method of token validation. After any successful authentication, our system generates a unique token which has the userID, and a timestamp value. This token is returned to the client which needs to be sent alongside further requests. On receiving any service requests the server reads and decrypts the token. This token is usually termed as **JSON Web Token** or **JWT**. To prevent attacks like **cross-site request forgery** (**CSRF**) we use this kind of technique.

The gateway provides flexibility to freely manipulate microservice instances as the client is totally abstracted from this logic. It is the best place to handle transformation requirements based on a client device. The gateway acts as a buffer zone against any sorts of attacks. The service is contaminated and it will not compromise the whole system. Gateway handles security by meeting all these standards, confidentiality, integrity, and availability. With increasing benefits, if the gateway is not properly handled there can be loads of drawbacks too. A gateway can introduce an exponential level of complexity with the increased dynamic system. With the added layer of communication, it will increase the response time.

In the following diagram, API Gateway is explained in detail:

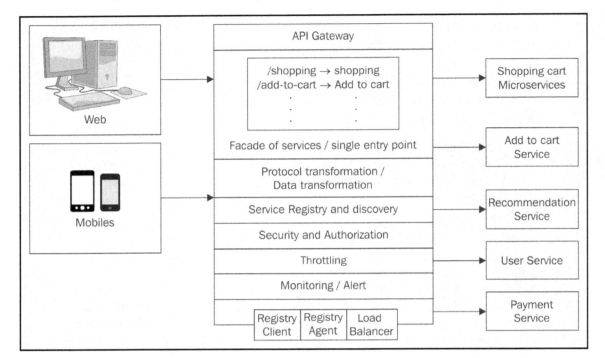

Now that we know what a gateway does, let us now understand the basics of what a gateway does and what things it handles overall.

Concerns API Gateway handles

An API Gateway becomes one of the most important components in microservices architecture as it is the only place where core concerns are handled. Hence, a common implementation seen across all microservices implementation is introducing API Gateway which provides critical functionalities. Furthermore, API Gateway is the part which is connected to service discovery which maintains routes of all newly added services dynamically. In this section, we will look into gateway features and understand the role and impact of the overall architecture of our central operational layer.

Security

With an increase in distribution, there is a considerably high level of freedom. There are lots of moving services which may go up or down at any point in time. Considering from a security point of view, when there are a lot of moving parts, things can go considerably wrong. Hence, certain rules are needed which govern security. Therefore, we need to secure remote service invocations of all public facing API endpoints. We need to handle various things like authentication, threat vulnerabilities, authorizations, message protection, and secure communications. We will add SSL/TLS compliant endpoints to safeguard against various attacks like a man in the middle, bidirectional encryption against tampering. Furthermore, to handle DDoS attacks, API Gateway will handle various factors like limiting the rate of requests, number of connections on demand, and many more. Gateway will close slow connections, blacklist or whitelist IP addresses, limiting connections to other backend microservices, maintaining a number of database connections, and so on. API Gateway will handle things like authentication and authorizations. We can introduce federal identities such as **OpenID**, **SAML**, and **OAuth** here. Also, this layer would generate JWT and authenticate all requests.

 One of the tricky parts of microservices development is identity and access management. In huge enterprises, this is usually handled through common systems like LDAP. Federal identities are kind of authorization servers (they are used across varied applications: for example, you can consider single a Google Account linked to various services such as Google Docs, Google Drive, and so on which authorize the user and then gives ID token and access token). Famous federal identities providers include OAuth and **Security Assertion Markup Language (SAML)**.

Dumb gateways

One of the most fundamental principles of a gateway is *gateways are always dumb*. While designing gateways, an important aspect to take care of is, that gateways should not be overly ambitious; that is it should not contain non-generic logic or any business requirements. Making it overly ambitious defeats the purpose of the gateway and can make it a single point of failure and also make it difficult to test and deploy. Smart gateways cannot be easily version controlled or integrated into the large pipeline. Furthermore, it introduces tight coupling as when you upgrade your gateway, you often have to work on upgrading its dependencies and core logic associated with it.

To briefly summarize, API Gateways should contain anything that we can validate or maintain within itself without the help of other services or shared states. Anything apart from that should be moved out of the API Gateway. The following points briefly summarize the dumbness of API Gateway and its functionalities:

- Validations like JWT token validation (we are not requesting any external service)
- Improving quality of service (things like shrinking responses, HTTP header caching, sending cached data, and so on)
- Request and response manipulation (handling multiple content types and manipulating request and response accordingly)
- Interaction with service discovery (non-blocking interactions with service registry to get service request details)
- Rate limiting and throttling (isolated features)
- Circuit breaker (detect failures and handle failures accordingly)

Transformation and orchestration

We have divided our microservices well into single responsibility principle; however, in order to achieve a business capability, we often require a combination of microservices. For example, a person buying a product is a mixture of payment microservice, inventory microservice, shipping microservice, and checkout microservice. Just like a Linux pipe which combines various commands, we need a similar orchestrator solution. This is essential for the consumers as it is an absolute nightmare to call every fine-grained service individually. Consider an example for our shopping cart microservices. We have the following two microservices:

- **Audience targeting**: These microservices take in user information and return a list of all the recommendations (it returns a list of product IDs)
- **Product detail**: These microservices takes in product IDs and respond by giving product metadata and detailed information

Let's say we are designing a recommendation page for 20 items. If we keep it as it is, then the consumer will have to make a total of 21 HTTP calls (1 call to get a list of product IDs, 20 calls to get product detail information), which is a nightmare. To avoid this, we need orchestrator (something which combines all these 21 calls). Furthermore, microservices have to deal with different clients who have need of varying responses. The API Gateway is a place for transformation where all things such as communication protocol, response formats, protocol transformations can be taken care of. We can put things like JSON to XML conversion in API Gateway, HTTP to gRPC or GraphQL protocols transformations, and so on.

Monitoring, alerting, and high availability

There are a lot of moving parts in microservices architecture. Hence, it becomes vital to have system-wide monitoring and avoid cascading failures. API Gateway provides a one-stop solution to that problem. We can monitor and capture the information about all data flow which can be kept for security purposes. We can monitor health, traffic, and data. API Gateway can monitor various things such as network connectivity, log maintenance, backups and recovery, security, and system status and health. Further, API Gateway can monitor basic things like a number of requests coming for API, maintain remote hosts, browsers, OS, performance statistics, the stack trace of messages, violations for breaching gateway policies, and so on. API Gateway can integrate with alert tools such as consul alerts (`https://github.com/AcalephStorage/consul-alerts`) and appropriate actions can be taken accordingly on it to achieve high availability. We must deploy multiple instances of API Gateway behind the load balancer to effectively load balance the traffic among many instances of API Gateway. We must plan for high volume and load. If deployed in the cloud we can have auto-scaling enabled if not, then we must make sure it has enough data resources to handle future load.

Caching and error handling

In order to have maximum optimization and performance, caches are often introduced in distributed systems. Redis has seen a huge increase as it is lightweight and can serve the purpose of cache very well. Further, in some business capabilities, stale data can be tolerated in the age of offline first. API Gateway can take care of this part, providing a cached response if the microservice is down or to prevent too many database calls. The golden rule while designing a cache mechanism can be those service calls which never actually need to be made should be the fastest calls. For example, consider the Avengers 4 page is updated in IMDB. It's getting more than 20,000 hits per second.

The database is hammered with these hits as it also has to fetch other things (like comments, reviews, and so on). That's where cache be comes useful. Things which will rarely change like actors description, movie description, and so on come from the cache layer. The response returned is super fast and it saves a network hop as well as it does not increase CPU performance. By implementing a caching layer, API Gateway ensures that the user experience is not impacted. In a distributed system, due to being chatty, an error is meant to occur, hence errors should be properly handled through patterns like timeouts and circuit breakers which should give out cached responses.

We can manage to cache at the following two levels:

- **Caching at the API Gateway level:** With this option, we cache the service response at the gateway or central level. It provides us the advantage of saving the service call as we can return the data at the gateway level itself. Also, in case of service unavailability or non-responsiveness, API Gateway could return the data from the cache.
- **Caching at the service level:** With this option, each service manages to cache its own data. API Gateway is not aware of the inner cache or inner anything to be precise. Service can easily invalidate the cache on a need basis. However, while implementing this option we should have a default response ready at central cache level.

 Netflix Hystrix is one such useful library which has powerful options like timing out the calls which exceed a specific threshold, not to wait needlessly, define fall back action such as returning default value or returning value from the cache. It has a Node.js client too (`https://www.npmjs.com/package/hystrixjs`).

Service registry and discovery

One of the key advantages of microservices is ease of scaling. At any point in time new microservices can be added to adapt to incoming traffic, can be scaled, and existing monolithic can be broken down to several microservices. All these service instances have dynamically assigned network locations. An API Gateway can maintain a connection to service registry which can keep a track of all these service instances. API Gateway communicates with service registry which is a database containing network locations of all instances. Each service instance tells its location to the registry on startup and shutdown. Another component which is connected to API Gateway is service discovery. The client consuming various microservices needs to have a simple discovery pattern in order to prevent the application from becoming too chatty.

Consul is one of the most widely used tools for service registry and discovery. It knows how many active containers fail for a specific service, and if that number is zero it marks that service as broken.

There are the following two types of approaches:

- `push`: Microservice itself takes care of making its entry acknowledged to the API gateway
- `pull`: Where API Gateway takes care of checking in all microservices

Circuit breakers

Yet another important concern API Gateway handles is breaking the connection whenever the service is down. Let's say one microservice is down and starts throwing out a high number of errors. Queuing further requests of that microservice is unwise as it will soon have a high resource utilization. An API Gateway introduced here can implement things such as breaking the connection or simply saying when a certain threshold is passed, the gateway will stop sending data to that failing component unless the component is resolved, analyze the logs, implement a fix, push an update, and thus prevent failure cascading in the entire system. Scaling the underlying and popular microservices thus becomes very easy. The gateway can therefore be scaled horizontally as well as vertically. API Gateway helps to achieve zero downtime by deploying configuration in a rolling fashion, that is, while in new deployments, the circuit is tripped, new requests are not served, older requests are honored in a single cluster, and the other cluster meanwhile takes new requests. We will see circuit breaker live example in `Chapter 7`, *Service State and Interservice Communication*.

Versioning and dependency resolution

When microservices are very fine grained and designed based on the single responsibility principle they deal with only specific concerns, and hence they become chatty (too many network calls): that is, to perform a usual set of tasks, many requests need to be sent to different services. Gateways can provide virtual endpoints or facades that can internally be routed to many different microservices. API Gateway can resolve all dependencies and segregate all responses in a single response, thus making it easy to consume for the client. Furthermore, with increasing changing business needs and capabilities we need to maintain versioning, so at any point in time, we can go back in time to old services.

API versioning is managed in two ways—either by sending it in URI (a URI not to be confused with URL is uniform resource identifier with information contained in itself, for example `http://example.com/users/v4/1234/`) or by sending it along the header. API Gateway can handle this problem with the following two approaches:

- **Microservices discovery**: This is the most widely used pattern wherein coupling between microservices and client application is totally removed as microservices are dynamically registered (we will see this in more detail in the next chapter). This component is in direct touch with API Gateway and provides information about service location to it, thereby preventing traditional SOA monolithic approach.
- **Microservices description**: This approach, on the other hand, focuses more on communicating via contracts. It expresses features of microservices in a very well written descriptive contract which can be understood by other client applications. The contract contains metadata information too, such as API version, requirements, and so on.

In this section, we looked at all the concerns which an API Gateway vice handles. Special care should be made for API Gateway for the following aspects:

- It should not be a single point of failure
- It should not be centralized or have synchronous coordination
- It should not depend on any state
- It should be just another microservice
- Business logic should not be encapsulated inside

API Gateway design patterns and aspects

Now that we know what API Gateway handles, lets throughout now look at common design aspects involved in API Gateway. In this section, we will look at all design aspects to be considered while designing API Gateway. We will understand modes of designing API Gateway which will help us to design a scalable system with high availability.

Being a core part which handles centralized concerns and being the starting point in microservices, API Gateway should be designed so that:

- **It embraces concurrency**: Being heavily distributed due to designing based on single responsibility, server-side concurrency is needed which can reduce the network chattiness. Node.js being non-blocking and asynchronous, each request executes in parallel with other requests and thereby a single heavy client request is not much better than many light non-concurrent requests. While business use cases may need blocking calls to backend systems, API Gateway should compose these calls via an efficient way through reactive frameworks, which does not increase resource pool utilization.

- **It should be reactive**: Reactive programming offers varying operators capable of filtering, selecting, transforming, combining, and composing observables thus by enabling efficient execution and composition in API Gateway layer. It promotes the idea of variables which are filled over time. It promotes non-blocking architecture as in the observable pattern, the producer just pushes the values to the consumer whenever the values are available rather than blocking the thread in that time. Values can arrive at any point in time asynchronously or synchronously. It has added advantages like the producer can give an ending signal to the consumer that there is no more data or if an error has occurred.

- **The service layer follows an observable pattern**: When all methods in API Gateway return an `Observable<T>` concurrency is enabled by default. The service layer then adheres to things like returning a cached response based on conditions and if resources are not available or if service is not available, then block the request. This can happen without changing anything on the client end.

- **It handle backend services and dependencies**: A gateway abstracts away all the backend services and dependencies behind the virtual facade layer due to which any inbound request access business capability rather than the entire system. This will allow us to change underlying implementations with limited impact on code that depends on it. Thus service layer ensures that all models and tight couplings stay inbound and are abstracted and are not allowed to leak in the endpoints.

- **They should be stateless**: API Gateways should be stateless by nature, which means not creating any session data. This will enable us to scale the gateway as there won't be any need later to replicate the session in case of disaster. However, API Gateway can maintain cached data, which can either be replicated using a peer-to-peer relationship or introducing a cache library such as Redis rather than going for in-memory calls. The following is a list of some of the general guidelines by seeing most common pitfalls:
    - To achieve the best availability API Gateway should be used in the Active-Active mode. It means that the system should always be fully operational and able to maintain current system state.

- Proper analysis and monitoring tools to prevent message flooding. In that case, that traffic to that service should be limited.
- Using tools to constantly monitor the system either via some available tools or system logs or network management protocols.

 The Active/Active mode is a method to deal with failover, load balancing, and keeping our system highly available. Here two or more servers are used which aggregate the network traffic load and they work together as a team to distribute it to the available network servers. Load balancers also persist information requests and keep this information in cache. If they return looking for the same information the user will be directly locked on to the server which previously served its request. This process reduces network traffic load intensely.

Circuit breakers and its role

In the practical world, errors do occur. Services can timeout, become unreachable, or take longer to complete. Being a distributed system, the entire system should not go down. The circuit breaker is the solution to this problem and it is a very important component in API Gateway.

The pattern essentially works in two states. If the circuit is closed, everything is normal, the request is dispatched to the destination, the response is received. But if there are errors or timeouts the circuit is open which means that route is not available as of now, we need to go a different route or way to achieve the service request. To achieve this functionality, Netflix has open sourced their project—Hystrix. This is, however, the Node.js version of the same: `https://www.npmjs.com/package/hystrixjs` (it's not official from Netflix, but rather an open source project). It even has the Hystrix dashboard for monitoring purposes. According to Hystrix's library, it has the following capabilities:

- Protect system against any failures which occur because of network issues or any third-party clients or libraries
- Stop propagating failures and avoid dispersion of error
- Fail fast, fail often, fail better, fail forward, and recover rapidly with counter-measures
- Degrade failures with fallback mechanisms like returning response from the cache
- Provide dashboard for monitoring purposes

Take a look at the following diagram:

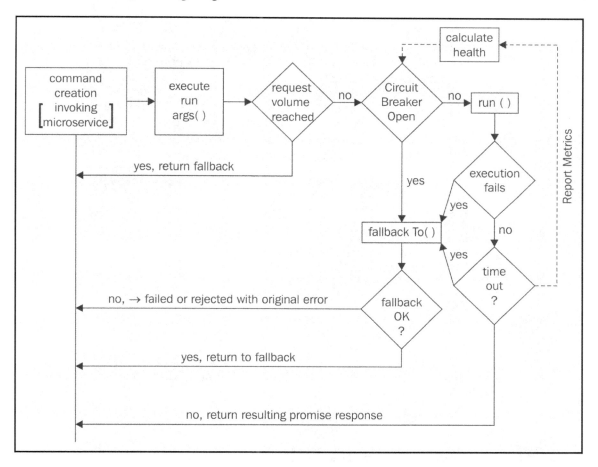

The circuit breaker follows the same set of rules as the original **Hystrix** module. To calculate the health of a command, the following steps are executed:

1. Maintain a watch on volume across the circuit as follows:

   - If the network volume across the circuit doesn't exceed the predefined value, then Hystrix can simply execute the run function without comparing anything at all. Metrics can log all told cases for future references.

- If the network volume across the circuit exceeds the configured brink value, Hystrix can check the health first to take preventive measures.
- When checking the health, if the error percentage exceeds the pre-defined threshold, the transition of circuit happens from closed to open and all subsequent requests would be rejected with the open circuit error preventing further requests.

2. After an organized time Hystrix can enable one request to go through to examine whether the services are recovered. If it passes an expectation test, the circuit once more transitions to a closed state and all the counters are reset. To use it in your application just create service commands and add values:

```
var serviceCommand = CommandsFactory.getOrCreate("Service on port
:"+ service.port +":"+ port)
 .circuitBreakerErrorThresholdPercentage(service.errorThreshold)
 .timeout(service.timeout)
 .run(makeRequest)
 .circuitBreakerRequestVolumeThreshold(service.concurrency)
 .circuitBreakerSleepWindowInMilliseconds(service.timeout)
 .statisticalWindowLength(10000)
 .statisticalWindowNumberOfBuckets(10)
 .errorHandler(isErrorHandler)
 .build();
serviceCommand.service = service;
commands.push(serviceCommand);
```

3. To execute those commands just use the execute method. A complete gist can be found in the source inside `hystrix` folder.

Need for gateway in our shopping cart microservices

After debunking gateways in detail lets come back to our shopping cart microservices system. We will look at the need for a gateway in our system and the things it will handle with our context and then move on to design the gateway. In this section, we will look at various design aspects that we need to consider while designing the gateway.

Handle performance and scalability

Being an entry point in system performance, scalability and high availability of API Gateway is a very crucial factor. As it will handle all the requests, making it on asynchronous non-blocking I/O seems very logical which is what Node.js is. All the requests coming from our shopping cart microservices need to be authenticated, cached, monitored and constantly send out health aware checks. Consider a scenario where our products service has larg traffic. API Gateway should then automatically spawn new instances of the server and maintain addresses of the new instances. The new instances then need to constantly send health checks to gateway so it would know which instances are alive. Consider the same example which we saw earlier where we have product microservice and we need to show the client a detailed listing of 20 items. Now the client is not going to make 21 HTTP requests but instead, we need a core composition component which combines responses from various requests.

Reactive programming to up the odds

In order to make sure that we don't have to frequently change the client code, the API Gateway simply routes the client request to a microservice. It may make other requests by making multiple backend service calls and then aggregate all the results. In order to make sure that there is minimum response time, the API Gateway should make independent calls concurrently which is where a reactive model of programming comes into the picture. API Composition is needed in various cases like fetching the users past orders, where we first need to fetch the user details and then their past orders. Writing compositional logic using traditional asynchronous callbacks will soon lead to the problem of callback hell which will produce coupled, tangled, difficult to understand and error-prone code which is where reactive programming is very helpful.

Invoking services

Microservices do need to communicate with each other synchronously or asynchronously based on the business capability. There must be inter-process communication mechanisms. Our shopping cart microservices can have two modes of communication. One involves a message broker which queues up messages and sends them to services on availability. The other involves brokerless communication and the service directly communicates with an other service and this may have data loss. There are lots of event-driven message brokers such as AMQP, RabbitMQ, and so on, others such as Zeromq are brokerless.

Some business capabilities need asynchronous modes of communication such as during the checkout of a product, we need to call payment services. If there is successful payment, then and only then can the product be purchased. API Gateway needs to support a variety of mechanisms based on business capabilities. We will see a live example in Chapter 7, *Service State and Interservice Communication*, in the *NetFlix Case study* section.

Discovering services

With constantly dynamic and evolving services, our gateway needs to know the location (IP address, service port) of every microservice in the system. Now, this can be hotwired in the system but as they are evolving we need a more dynamic method as services constantly auto-scale and upgrade. For example, in our shopping cart microservices, we may constantly add new services based on use case. Now API Gateway needs to know the location of these services so it can query any of the services any time to return the response to the client. API Gateway must maintain communication with service registry which is just a database of all microservices locations and their instances.

Handling partial service failures

Yet another need to address is handling partial failures. When one service calls another service it may not receive a response at all or it may get delayed response. With the increased number of services, any service may go down at any point in time. API Gateway should be able to handle partial failures by implementing some/all of the following strategies:

- Asynchronous mode of communication by default. Using synchronous mode only when needed.
- A number of retries should be handled with exponential backoffs that is 1, 2, 4, 16, and so on.
- Well defined network timeouts to prevent blocking of resources.
- Circuit breaker pattern to trip the request if service is down or overloaded.
- Fallbacks or returning cached values. For example images of a product will never change frequently, they can be cached.
- Monitoring the number of queued requests. If the number goes beyond a limit, then it doesn't make sense to send further requests.

Design considerations

A good API Gateway should adhere to the following design considerations in order to have a rock solid microservice design:

- **Dependency:** There should not be a dependency on any other microservice. An API Gateway is just another microservice. If any service ID is unavailable for a preconfigured time or does not follow the SLAs then API Gateway should not wait for that service. It should rather fail fast using circuit breaker or another fall back strategy like returning cached responses.

- **Database and business logic:** API Gateway should not have database connectivity. Gateways are dumb that is they do not have any state. If you need a database then we need to create a separate microservice. Likewise business logic should reside in the service itself. Gateway just routes any service requests to an appropriate destination.

- **Orchestration and handling multiple content types:** Service choreography (a pattern where microservices communicate with each other) should be done at API Gateway rather than orchestration. Gateway should be connected to service registry which gives us a location of dynamically moving services.

- **Versioning:** Gateway should have appropriate versioning strategy. Its like we need to move a huge rock up the mountain, but as it is too big we break the rock into smaller pieces and distribute it to every person. Now each person will go at its own pace, but that doesn't imply that he has to meet the other person's expectation too, because, in the end, it is the whole rock that matters and not smaller pieces. Likewise, any particular version of a service should not break contract exposed. New contracts should be updated on a need basis so other clients can then know the new expectations until which backwards compatibility should be there.

- **High Availability:** It should be highly available and scalable. Planning should be done for high volume and high load. If deployed in the cloud we can go with: AWS auto-scaling.

In the next section, we will dive into available gateway options and discuss them in detail. We will look at some cloud provider options too and see pros and cons of each.

Available API Gateways options

Now let us look at some of the practical implementations of API Gateway available. In this section, we will look at options like Express Gateway, Netflix OSS, message brokers, NGINX as a reverse proxy, and tools available for designing gateway.

HTTP proxy and Express Gateway

HTTP proxy is an HTTP programmable library for proxying. This is helpful for applying things such as reverse proxy or load balancing. `http-proxy` available in npm has more than 1 lakh download per day. To achieve request dispatching we can use `http-proxy`. This is a piece of cake and can be achieved like this:

```
const express = require('express')
const httpProxy = require('express-http-proxy')
const app = express();
const productServiceProxy= httpProxy('https://10.0.0.1/')
//10.0.0.1 is product container location
// Authentication
app.use((req, res, next) => {
    // TODO: Central Authentication logic for all
    next()
    })
// Proxy request
app.get('/products/:productId', (req, res, next) => {
    productServiceProxy(req, res, next)
```

One of the gateways built on top of Express.js and Node.js, Express Gateway is the most simple to use with wide options such as language agnostic for a microservices use case and portable as it can be run anywhere in Docker in public or private cloud. It can work with any DevOps tools and it comes with pre-bundled proven and popular modules. We can extend this with any express middleware and this is totally config based and configs are auto-detected and hot reloaded. The following are core components in the express gateway:

Endpoints (API and service)	They are nothing but URLs. Express Gateway maintains them in two forms. API endpoints and service endpoints. API endpoints are exposed and it proxies API requests to microservices asked for in service.
Policies	Set of conditions or actions or contract that is evaluated and acted upon for any request that is passed through the gateway. Middlewares are utilized.
Pipelines	Set of policies linked to microservices to be executed sequentially. For policy execution an API requested is passed through the pipeline where in the end it encounters a proxy policy which guides request to service endpoint.
Consumers	Anyone who consumes microservices. To handle varying consumers Express Gateway comes with a consumer management module. The golden rule for which is an app must belong to a user.

| Credentials | Types of authentication and authorizations. Consumer or user may have one or more than one set of credentials. Credentials are linked to a scope. Express Gateway comes with the credential management module. |
| Scopes | Labels used to assign authorization. Authorization policies protecting the endpoints look up at the credential to make sure the integrity of the system and consumer has that corresponding scope. |

Let's now look at one example of Express Gateway. Following is the sample `gateway.config.yml` file which is generated using Express Gateway (`https://www.express-gateway.io/`.):

```
http:
  port: 8990
  serviceEndpoints:
    example: # will be referenced in proxy policy
    url: 'http://example.com'
  apiEndpoints:
  api:
    path: '/*'
  pipelines:
  example-pipeline:
    apiEndpoints: # process all request matching "api" apiEndpoint
    - api
  policies:
  - jwt:
  - action:
  secretOrPublicKeyFile: '/app/key.pem'
  - proxy:
  - action:
  serviceEndpoint: example # reference to serviceEndpoints Section
```

The preceding configuration is a minimalist example of a JWT at gateway and proxy routes and is self explanatory.

Zuul and Eureka

The next option that we are going to look at is the Zuul proxy server provided by Netflix. Zuul is an edge service with objective of proxying requests to various backing services. Thus it acts as a "unified front door" to consume services. Zuul can be integrated with other open sourced tools by Netflix such as Hystrix for fault tolerance, Eureka for service discovery, routing engine, load balancing, and so on. Zuul is written in Java but can be used for microservices written in any language. Zuul provides ease in doing the following things:

- Validating contract requirements for each resource. If contract is not fulfilled, then rejecting those requests that do not meet them.

- Give us accurate view of production by tracking meaningful data and statistics.
- Connecting to service registries and dynamically routing to different backend clusters as needed.
- In order to gauge performance gradually increasing traffic in a cluster.
- Dropping requests that go over a limit, thus by achieving load shedding by allocating capacity for each type of request.
- Handling static or cached responses, thus by preventing internal container trips.

Zuul 2.1 is under active development with the objective of achieving asynchronous operations at the gateway level. Zuul 2 is however non blocking and thoroughly relies on RxJava and reactive programming. To run Zuul as an API Gateway perform the following steps:

1. Zuul requires a Java environment. Clone the following Spring boot project: `https://github.com/kissaten/heroku-zuul-server-demo`
2. Start the project using `mvn spring-boot:run`.
3. Inside the project's `src/main/resources/application.yml` file we will write our Zuul filters logic.
4. We will add failover logic there. For example consider the following sample configuration:

```
zuul:
  routes:
    httpbin:
      path: /**
      serviceId: httpbin
    httpbin:
    ribbon:
      listOfServers: httpbin.org,eu.httpbin.org
    ribbon:
eureka:
  client:
    serviceUrl:
    defaultZone:
    ${EUREKA_URL:http://user:password@localhost:5000}/eureka/
```

This configuration tells `zuul` to send all requests to the `httpbin` service. If we want to define multiple routes here we can. The `httpbin` service then defines the number of available servers. If the first host goes down, then proxy will fail over to the second host.

The next chapter enables service discovery through another Netflix library: Eureka.

API Gateway versus reverse proxy NGINX

In this section, we are going to look at possible options available at server levels. A reverse proxy (NGINX or Apache httpd) can do tasks like authenticating a request, handling transportation security, and load balancing. NGINX is one of the widely used tools to use a reverse proxy at gateway level in microservices. The following code sample depicts configuration with a reverse proxy, SSL certificates, and load balancing:

```
#user gateway;
 worker_processes 1;
 events {worker_connections 1024;}
 http {
     include mime.types;
     default_type application/json;
     keepalive_timeout 65;
     server {
         listen 443 ssl;
         server_name yourdomain.com;
         ssl_certificate cert.pem;
         ssl_certificate_key cert.key;
         ssl_session_cache shared:SSL:1m;
         ssl_session_timeout 5m;
         ssl_ciphers HIGH:!aNULL:!MD5;
         ssl_prefer_server_ciphers on;
         location public1.yourdomain.com {proxy_pass
         http://localhost:9000;}
         location public2.yourdomain.com {proxy_pass
         http://localhost:9001;}
         location public3.yourdomain.com {proxy_pass
         http://localhost:9002;}
     }
 }
```

The preceding configuration adds SSL certificates at a central level and adds proxies at three domains and load balances all requests among them.

RabbitMQ

One of the most widely deployed message brokers, RabbitMQ operates on AMQP protocol. The `amqplib` client for Node.js is widely adopted and has more than 16,000 downloads per day. In this section, we will look at a sample implementation of `amqp` and understand the options given by it. RabbitMQ follows more of an event based approach where each service listens to RabbitMQ "tasks" queue and on listening for an event, the service completes its task and then sends it to a `completed_tasks` queue. API Gateway listens for the `completed_tasks` queue and when it receives a message, it sends the response back to the client. So let us design our RabbitMQ class by performing the following steps:

1. We will define our constructor as follows:

```
constructor(host, user, password, queues, prefetch) {
    super();
    this._url = `amqp://${user}:${password}@${host}`;
    this._queues = queues || [ 'default' ];
    this._prefetch = prefetch;
}
```

2. Next we will define our connection method as follows:

```
connect() {
    return amqp.connect(this._url)
    .then(connection => (this._connection =
    connection).createChannel())
    .then(channel => {
        this._channel = channel;
        channel.prefetch(this._prefetch);
        var promises = [];
        for (var queue of this._queues) {
            promises.push(
            channel.assertQueue(queue, { durable: true })
            .then(result => channel.consume(result.queue,
            (message) => {
                if (message != null) {
                    this.emit('messageReceived',
                    JSON.parse(message.content),
                    result.queue, message);
                }
            }, { noAck: false }))
            );
        }
        return Promise.all(promises);
    });
}
```

3. Next we will have a `send` method which sends a message to the RabbitMQ channel as follows:

```
send(queue, message) {
    var messageBuff = new Buffer(JSON.stringify(message));
    return this._channel.assertQueue(queue, { durable: true })
    .then(result => this._channel.sendToQueue(result.queue,
    messageBuff, { persistent: true }));
}
```

You can see the full file here, where you will find all available options. Similar to earlier use cases, you can also find types for the `amqp` module at the definitely typed repository https://gist.github.com/insanityrules/4d120b3d9c20053a7c6e280a6d5c5bfb.

4. Next we just have to use the class. For example, take a look at the following code:

```
...
constructor(){ this._conn = new RabbitMqConnection(host, user,
password, queues, 1);}
...
addTask(queue, task) {
    return this._conn.send(queue, task);
}
...
```

 As a prerequisite of for this project RabbitMQ must be installed on the system, which requires the installation of Erlang. Once RabbitMQ is up and running, you can check by typing `rabbitmqctl status` to make sure that RabbitMQ service is running.

Designing our gateway for shopping cart microservices

After seeing various options let's now get our hands dirty and start implementing our microservices gateway for shopping cart microservices. In this section, we will implement gateway from scratch which will have functionalities such as dispatching requests from public endpoints to internal endpoints, aggregate responses from multiple services, and handle transport security and dependency resolution. Let's look at all the concepts that we will use in this module before proceeding with code.

What are we going to use?

In this section, we will look at all the following node modules and concepts in order to efficiently construct our gateway:

- **ES6 proxy**: Generally speaking, a proxy server is one which acts as an intermediary server for requests coming in from clients. One of the most powerful and interesting features in ES6 was proxy. ES6 proxy acts as an intermediary among API consumers and objects in services. We usually create proxies when we want our own desired behavior whenever the properties of the underlying target object are accessed. To configure traps for your proxy which has control of the underlying target object we use handler functions.
- **NPM module dockerode**: Its Node.js reactive module for Remote API for docker. It has some nice features such as streams for reactive programming, support for additional demultiplexing and promises and callback based interfaces for easy programming.
- **Dependency injection**: One of the most important design patterns (initially started in Java, now it is present everywhere) in which one or more dependencies of a service are injected or passed by reference to a dependent object.

 Please check source code of chapter 5 for custom implementation which includes service discovery. You can revisit this exercise after completing chapter 6.

Summary

In this chapter, we debunked API Gateway. We understood the pros and cons of introducing API Gateway and what concerns API Gateway can handle centrally. We looked at design aspects of API Gateway and understood the need for API Gateway in our system. We had a look at the circuit breaker and why it was vital to have. We looked at available gateway options like Zuul, Express Gateway, reverse proxy, and designed our own gateway for shopping cart microservices.

In the next chapter, we will learn about service registry and service discovery. We will see how gateway connects with service discovery to automatically know the location of moving services. We will see ways in which a service can be registered and learn the pros and cons of each approach. We will see some options like consul and implement them in our shopping cart microservices.

Service Registry and Discovery 6

After handling core concerns in our distributed system through a gateway, we will now talk about service registry and discovery in this chapter. The more services we have, the more complicated it becomes to handle them using only predefined ports. In the previous chapter, we saw the gateway interacting with the service registry, which maintains the service location in a database. The client request is dispatched to service based on the information contained in a database. In this chapter, we will see how the service registry is populated, and in what ways services, clients, and gateways interact with it.

This chapter will commence by understanding service discovery, how the service registry is maintained dynamically, different ways of registering services in the registry, and pros and cons of each way. We will understand the end to end process of maintaining a service registry and how a service is discovered based on a registry. We will see the available options for designing a service registry, get acquainted with each of the steps, and then we will design our dynamic service registry using the best practices available. In this chapter, we will look at the following topics:

- Introduction to the service registry
- The what, why, and how of service registry and discovery
- Service discovery patterns
- Service registry patterns
- Service registry and discovery options
- How to choose the service registry and discovery

Introduction to the service registry

In this section, we will see the need for service discovery and the need for the service registry and try to understand the difference between service registry and discovery. We already have some of our shopping cart microservices set ups, but with core dependency on a network location that was static. Our code reads a value from a configuration file and on any change in the location of a service, we update it in our configurations. In the practical world, it is very difficult to maintain this as service instances are dynamically assigned locations. Moreover, service instances change dynamically based on the needs for autoscaling, failure handling, and updating process that is abstracted from a consumer client in the microservice world. Hence, clients need to use a more enhanced service discovery mechanism.

Service discovery can be defined as:

> *A complete end to end process of registering services in a central place (API Gateway or database) and reaching out to targeted service of consuming via looking up in the service registry.*

In the microservices world, different microservices are typically distributed in a **platform as a service** (**PaaS**) environment. The infrastructure is typically immutable as we usually have containers or immutable VM images. Services can usually scale up or down based on traffic and pre-fixed metrics. As everything is constantly dynamic, the exact address of the service may not be known until the service is ready to be used and deployed. This dynamic nature is one of the most important aspects to be handled in the microservice world. A logical and obvious solution is persisting these endpoints somewhere and that itself is the basis of a service registry. In this approach, each microservice registers with a central broker (the component that we saw in `Chapter 5`, *Understanding API Gateway*) and it provides all details about that microservice, such as the endpoint address, the contract details, the communication protocol, and so on. Consuming services usually query the broker to find the available location of a service at that point and then invoke it based on the location retrieved. Some of the commonly available options for this are Zookeeper, Consul, Netflix Eureka, and Kubernetes, which we will look at in much more detail soon.

What, why, and how of service registry and discovery

After looking briefly at service registry, we will understand the what, why, and how of service registry and discovery in this section. From understanding the need for service discovery, we will then understand the process and components involved in that process.

The why of service registry and discovery

Whatever container technology we go for, in production environments we will always have three four hosts and a number of containers inside each. In general, the way we distribute our services across all available hosts is totally dynamic and dependent on business capabilities, and can change at any point in time as hosts are just servers and they are not going to last forever. This is where service discovery and registry comes in. We need an external system that solves the limitations of a common web server, keeps an eye on all the services at all times, and maintains a combination of IP and port so that clients can seamlessly route to those service providers.

To understand the need for service registry and discovery, we will take a classic example. Let's say we have 10 instances of our product catalog microservice running on an arbitrary number of nodes. Now in order to have a resilient system, someone needs to keep track of those 10 nodes because whenever there would be a need to consume a product catalog service, at least one proper IP address or hostname should be available or else the consumer must query a central place where it can find the location of the product-catalog service. This approach very much resembles a DNS, the difference being that this is just for internal services to service communication. Most microservice-based architecture is dynamically moving. Services scale up and down based on development, depreciation, and traffic. Whenever a service endpoint changes, the registry needs to know about the change. The service registry is all about this: maintaining all information about how to reach every service.

There are lots of available tools in the market to solve this problem and as an architect, we need to decide the right tool based on our need. We need to consider factors such as how much automation can be done and how much control we have over the tool. There exist right from low-level tools such as Consul, to high-level tools such as Kubernetes or Docker swarm,which take care of advanced requirements such as load balancing containers and container scheduling capabilities.

How service registry and discovery?

Today, three basic approaches are prevalent for service registry and discovery:

- The first rudimentary and preliminary approach is using existing DNS infrastructure. A well deployed DNS would be highly available and distributed. Examples of this approach include `httpd`, `confd`, `systemd`, and so on. In this approach, standard DNS libraries are used as registrar clients. Each microservice entry receives an entry in a DNS zone file and does a DNS lookup to connect to or locate a microservice. Another approach is using proxies such as NGINX, which periodically poll DNS for service discovery. The advantage of this approach includes being language agnostic: it works with any language with minimal or zero changes. However, it has several flaws, such as DNS does not provide a real-time view, managing new zone files on service registrations and deregistrations, and maintaining the high availability of this component for resiliency.

- The second approach is more dynamic and more suitable to microservices using consistent key-value data stores such as Hashicorp's Consul, Apache Zookeeper, etcd, and so on. These tools are highly distributed systems. With the key-value store and sidecar pattern, it solves all the issues that we had while using DNS. This approach is meant to be completely transparent to any developer writing the code. A developer can write code in any programming language and not think of how microservices interact with other services. It has several limitations, such as sidecar being limited to service discovery of hosts and not more granular routes. It also adds extra latency by introducing an extra hop for every microservice.

- The final approach for service discovery is adopting ready-made frameworks such as Netflix Eureka, specially designed and optimized for service discovery. This model exposes functionality directly to end developers.

Whichever tool we select, each of the microservices needs a central client to communicate for service discovery, whose main function is to allow service registration and resolution. Whenever a service starts, the service discovery uses the registration process to signal its availability to other services. Once available, other services use service resolution to locate the service on the network. The two processes involved around are as follows.

Service registration

On startup and shutdown, the service registers itself, or through third-party registration, a service registration client also sends constant heartbeats so that the client knows that the service is alive. A heartbeat is a message that is sent periodically to other services to say that the service is running and alive. They should be sent asynchronously or implemented as event-based, in order to avoid performance issues. Other approaches include polling the service constantly. The service registration stage is also responsible for setting the contract of the service, that is, service name, protocol, version, and so on.

Service resolution

This is the process of returning the network address of microservices. An ideal service discovery client has several critical features such as caching, failover, and load balancing. In order to avoid network latency when caching services, addresses are critical. The cache layer subscribes to updates from service discovery to ensure that it is always up to date. A typical microservice implementation layer is deployed in various locations for high availability; the service resolution client must know how to return the address of service instances based on load availability and other factors.

The what of service registry and discovery

In this section, we will look at the what of service registry and discovery. We will see all aspects involved in a service registry and have a look at all the possible options involved regarding maintaining it.

Maintaining service registry

In this section, we will see how a consumer ultimately finds a service provider. We will see all available approaches and look at the pros and cons of each option:

- **Updation through sockets**: Regular polling soon becomes a problem as consumers are least concerned with registering themselves with the discovery service, and it also becomes painful for the discovery service to maintain a list of the consumers. A better solution would be for the client to open up a socket connection with the discovery service and continuously get an up-to-date list of all the service changes.

- **Service discovery as a proxy**: This is more of a server-side implementation where logic for routing is present in the discovery service, making it not necessary for the clients to maintain any lists. They simply make outbound requests to the discovery service, which forwards the request to an appropriate service provider and returns the results to the providers.

Timely health checks

There are two approaches for performing timely health checks for discovery. One method states that services should send a message to a centralized discovery service, whereas another method has the discovery service sending requests to the service providers:

- **Service polls registrar**: In this approach, a service provider actively sends messages at a predefined regular interval to the registrar discovery service. The discovery service keeps track of all the last time requests were received and considers a service provider dead if a certain time threshold has not been made.

- **Registrar polls service**: This is the approach where a central discovery service sends requests to the service providers. However, a shortcoming to this approach is that a centralized discovery service may get exhausted with the task of making so many outbound requests. Furthermore, if service providers disappear, then the registrar has to make a lot of failed health lookups, which would be network waste.

Service discovery patterns

Discovery is the counterpart of service registry from the view of clients. Whenever a client wants to access a service, it must find details about the service, where it is located, and other contract information. This is typically done using two approaches, client-side discovery and server-side discovery. Service discovery can be briefly summarized as follows:

- Microservices or consumers don't have any prior knowledge about the physical location of other services. They don't know when a service goes down or another node of the service is going up.
- Services broadcast their existence and disappearance.
- Services are able to other service instances based on other broadcasted metadata.

- Instance failures are detected and any request to that failed node is prevented and is made invalid.
- Service discovery is not a single point of failure.

In this section, we will both look at the patterns of service discovery and understand the pros and cons of each pattern.

Client-side discovery pattern

While using a client-side pattern, it is the client's or the gateway's duty to determine the location of a network of available service instances and also to load balance the requests among them. The client queries a service registry, which is nothing but a set of available service instances, stores its response, and then routes the request according to the location address in that response. The client uses some famous load balancing algorithms to choose one of the service instances and make a request to that instance. The physical network location of that service instance is registered with the registry whenever the service starts and deregistered when the service goes down. The service instance registration is refreshed using a heartbeat mechanism or polling or through sockets for real-time updates.

Advantages:

- The pattern is pretty static except for the service registry, so it is a lot easier to maintain
- As the client is aware of the service instance, the client can make intelligent, application-specific, situation-dependent load balancing decisions such as constantly using a hash

Pain areas:

- The client is tightly coupled to the service registry
- There would be a need to implement client-side service discovery in every programming language and framework that is used by a service client

A famous tool for client-side registration process is Netflix Eureka. It provides a REST API for managing service instance registrations and for querying available instances. A full list of APIs and available options can be found at `https://github.com/Netflix/eureka/wiki/Eureka-REST-operations`, which has all available operations that can be done.

Server-side discovery pattern

The counter approach to this is having a separate component for a registry, which is the server-side discovery pattern. In this approach, a client makes a request to the service through a load balancer in between. The load balancer then queries the service registry and routes each request to an available service instance to provide a service response to the consumer. A classic example of such an approach is an inbuilt AWS load balancer. An Amazon **Elastic Load Balancer** (ELB) is commonly used to handle the huge external traffic from the internet and load balance among the incoming traffic, but the use of an ELB goes way beyond this. An ELB can also be used to load balance traffic internal traffic to the VM. When a client makes a request to an ELB through its DNS, the ELB load balances the traffic among a set of registered EC2 instances or containers.

One of the approaches in maintaining server-side discovery is using a proxy on each host. This proxy plays the role of server-side discovery load balancer. A proxy transparently forwards the request to available service instances running anywhere on that server. Kubernetes runs on a similar approach. Some of the available tools are NGINX and Consul templates. These tools configure reverse proxying and reload NGINX or HAProxy servers.

Advantages of the server-side discovery pattern:

- Simpler code for client-side discovery on the server side as we don't have to write code for discovery in each service and it is totally abstracted from the client
- Functionalities such as load balancing are taken care of through this approach

Disadvantages of the server-side discovery pattern:

- The router is yet another component that needs to be maintained on the server. If the environment is clustered, then it needs to be replicated everywhere.
- Unless the router is a TCP router, the router should have support for protocols such as HTTP, RPC, and so on.
- It needs more network hops compared to client-side discovery.

Let's look at both approaches in this diagram:

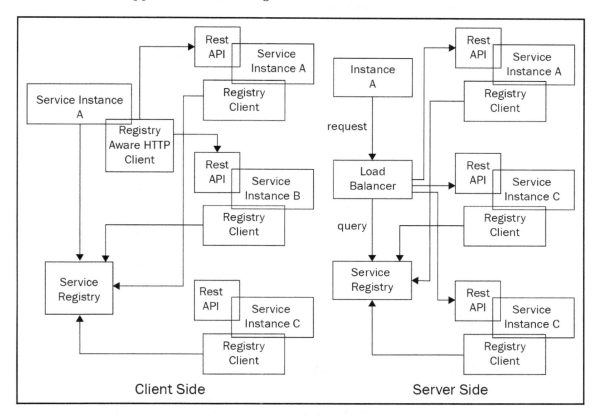

Client-side vs server-side service discovery

Service registry patterns

One of the key aspects of discovering services in a distributed system is service registry. The service registry is just a database that has all the network locations of service instances. As it contains crucial information, it must be highly available and stay up to date on an efficient system. Based on the system clients (in our case, API Gateway), we can even cache network locations obtained from the service registry. However, it must be updated on a daily basis, otherwise clients won't be able to discover service instances and communicate per service. A service registry, in order to be highly available, consists of clusters where a replication protocol is used to maintain consistency. The service registry saves the metadata of microservice instances, which includes things such as actual locations, host ports, communication protocol, and so on. Startup and shutdown processes of microservices are constantly monitored. In this section, we will look at service registry and common service registration options. We will look at the pros and cons of each approach.

All service instances must register and deregister from the central registry in order to have a fault tolerant system. There are various ways to handle this registration and deregistration process. One option is the service registry providing endpoints and the service instance registers itself, that is, self-registration. Another option is using some other system components to manage the registration of service instances. Let's dive deep into both of these patterns to understand them in detail.

Self-registration pattern

While using the self-registration process, a service instance itself is responsible for registering and deregistering within the service registry. Also, the service instance must constantly send heartbeat requests in order to let the registry know the status of the service. If the registry doesn't receive heartbeats, the registry can assume that the service no longer exists and can deregister or stop listening for that service. The self-registration pattern forces microservices to communicate with the service registry by themselves. Whenever a service goes up or down, it has to communicate with the registry to inform it of its status. Microservices deal with single concerns, so introducing yet another concern everywhere might be an extra burden and may seem an anti-pattern; however, it has the added advantage that a service maintains its own state model, knowing the current state, that is, **STARTING, AVAILABLE, SHUTDOWN**, without being dependent on any other third-party services.

A well-known example of a self-registration process is the Netflix OSS Eureka client. The Eureka client handles all aspects of client registration and deregistration. We will see a detailed implementation of Eureka in a later section.

Disadvantages of the self-registration pattern:

- The service is coupled to the service registry. It must constantly communicate with the server to tell it about the service's state.
- Service registry logic is not centralized and must be implemented in every language we have in the ecosystem.

Third-party registration pattern

When using a third-party registration process and service instances, microservices stick to the principle of single responsibility and are no longer responsible for registering themselves with the service registry. Instead, we introduce a new component in the system, *service registrar*, which handles the responsibility of maintaining service registry. The service registrar, in order to maintain the registry, keeps track of instances either by polling the environment or by subscribing to startup and shutdown events. Whenever it notices a newly available service, it registers the instance with the registry. Likewise, if it fails to receive health checks, then it deregisters that service from the registry. Unlike the self-registration pattern, the microservice code is far less complex as it is not responsible for registering itself, but it has drawbacks too. If the registrar is not selected carefully, it becomes yet another component that has to be installed, configured, maintained, and highly available since it is a critical component of the system. Third-party registration is normally the preferred choice in industry as it automatically manages the registry. Additional data required for the registry can be provided in the form of policies or contracts, which can be updated in the database. Tools such as Apache Zookeeper or Netflix Eureka, in combination with others, are widely used.

Third-party registration has various advantages. Say a service goes down, a third-party registrar can take appropriate action such as providing safe fallbacks, triggering a self-repair mechanism, and so on. If there is heavy traffic on a service, the registry process can automatically add a new endpoint by requesting a new instantiation of that microservice. These health checks performed on services can help in auto-deregistering to stop the failure cascading to the entire system. A well-known example is Registrator, which we are going to see later in this chapter.

Some of the famous available examples of third-party registration patterns include:

- **Netflix Prana:** Outsourced by Netflix, Netflix OSS Prana is especially for non-JVM languages. It is an implementation of the sidecar pattern, which runs side by side with service instances and exposes them over HTTP. Prana registers and deregisters service instances over HTTP with Netflix Eureka.

- **Built-in components such as the ELB:** Most deployment environments have inbuilt components. EC2 instances created automatically through scaling are automatically registered to the ELB. Similarly, Kubernetes services are automatically registered and made available for discovery (we will look at this in more detail in the scaling section of `Chapter 10`, *Hardening Your Application*).

Advantages of the third-party registration pattern are as follows:

- The code is less complex as each service doesn't have to write code for registering and deregistering itself
- The central registrar also contains code for performing health checks and this doesn't need to be replicated everywhere

Disadvantages of third-party registration pattern are as follows:

- Unless it is provided by a service discovery tool, it is yet another component that needs to be maintained and made highly available

Service registry and discovery options

In this section, we will look at some of the commonly available options in the market for service discovery and registry. Options range right from low-level solutions providing a high degree of control to the architect (etcd from CoreOS and Consul from HashiCorp) to high-end solutions providing container scheduling solutions (Kubernetes from Google, Docker swarm, and so on). In this section, we will understand various options and look at the pros and cons of each.

Eureka

Eureka is a service registry and discovery framework outsourced by Netflix with a need for primary usage of locating services for the purpose of load balancing and failover for any middle-tier servers. In this section, we will look at service discovery and registry using Eureka.

The overall Eureka architecture consists of two components: the Eureka server and client. The Eureka server is a standalone server application that is responsible for:

- Managing a registry of service instances
- Providing the means to register any service, deregister any microservice, and query instances as part of service discovery
- Registry propagation of instances to other Eureka servers and clients provides a mechanism similar to heartbeats to constantly monitor services

The Eureka client is a part of an ecosystem and has the following responsibilities:

- Register and unregister bound microservices with the Eureka server on processes such as startup, shutdown, and so on
- Keep the connection alive with the Eureka server by constantly sending heartbeats
- Retrieve other service instance information, cache it, and update it on a daily basis

We will be using the following terminology in Eureka frequently:

Eureka server	It is the discovery server. It has a registry of all services with their current state by means of registering and deregistering any service, and APIs for discovering any service.
Eureka service	Anything that is found in Eureka service registry and anything that is registered for others and is meant to be discovered. Each service has a logical identifier that can refer to the instance ID of that application and it is called the VIP or service ID.
Eureka instance	Any application that registers with the Eureka server so that it can be discovered by other services.
Eureka client	Any microservice application that can register and discover any microservice.

In this section, we will set up the Eureka server register a sample microservice with the Eureka server, and find the location of that microservice in our other microservice. So, let's get started.

Setting up the Eureka server

The Eureka server is a Netflix OSS product and a service discovery pattern implementation where every microservice is registered and a client looks up on the server to get dependent microservices. A Eureka server runs on the JVM platform, so we will directly use an available template.

 To run a Eureka server, you will need Java 8 and Maven set up.

Let's take a look at the steps to set up Eureka server:

1. Go to the eureka folder inside the extracted source code for this chapter. You will find a ready-to-use Java project for Eureka server named euraka-server.

2. Inside the root directory, open up the Terminal and run the following command:

   mvn clean install

3. You should see dependencies getting installed and at the end, you will get a message confirming a successful build and that your target folder is generated.

4. Open the target folder, inside which you will be able to see Eureka server .jar file (demo-service-discovery-0.0.1-SNAPSHOT.jar).

5. Open up a Terminal and hit the following command. You should see your server startup:

   java -jar demo-service-discovery-0.0.1-SNAPSHOT.jar

The output for the preceding command is shown in the following screenshot:

```
C:\Windows\System32\cmd.exe - java -jar demo-service-discovery-0.0.1-SNAPSHOT.jar                                    —   □   ×
Microsoft Windows [Version 10.0.16299.371]
(c) 2017 Microsoft Corporation. All rights reserved.

C:\Users\parth.ghiya.KADC\Desktop\tsms chapter2\typescript microservices\chapter 6\eureka\eureka-server\target
>java -jar demo-service-discovery-0.0.1-SNAPSHOT.jar
2018-05-08 22:50:39.071  INFO 14932 --- [           main] s.c.a.AnnotationConfigApplicationContext : Refreshing org.springframework.context.annotatio
n.AnnotationConfigApplicationContext@6ae40994: startup date [Tue May 08 22:50:39 IST 2018]; root of context hierarchy
2018-05-08 22:50:40.436  INFO 14932 --- [           main] f.a.AutowiredAnnotationBeanPostProcessor : JSR-330 'javax.inject.Inject' annotation found a
nd supported for autowiring
2018-05-08 22:50:40.598  INFO 14932 --- [           main] trationDelegate$BeanPostProcessorChecker : Bean 'configurationPropertiesRebinderAutoConfigu
ration' of type [org.springframework.cloud.autoconfigure.ConfigurationPropertiesRebinderAutoConfiguration$$EnhancerBySpringCGLIB$$7adf301] is not eli
gible for getting processed by all BeanPostProcessors (for example: not eligible for auto-proxying)

  /\\ / ___'_ __ _ _(_)_ __  __ _ \ \ \ \
 ( ( )\___ | '_ | '_| | '_ \/ _` | \ \ \ \
  \\/  ___)| |_)| | | | | || (_| |  ) ) ) )
   '  |____| .__|_| |_|_| |_\__, | / / / /
  =========|_|==============|___/=/_/_/_/
  :: Spring Boot ::        (v1.5.10.RELEASE)

2018-05-08 22:50:42.381  INFO 14932 --- [           main] c.c.c.ConfigServicePropertySourceLocator : Fetching config from server at: http://localhost
:8888
2018-05-08 22:50:43.788  WARN 14932 --- [           main] c.c.c.ConfigServicePropertySourceLocator : Could not locate PropertySource: I/O error on GE
T request for "http://localhost:8888/EmployeeEurekaServer/default": Connection refused: connect; nested exception is java.net.ConnectException: Conne
ction refused: connect
2018-05-08 22:50:43.791  INFO 14932 --- [           main] .m.d.d.DemoServiceDiscoveryApplication : No active profile set, falling back to default p
rofiles: default
2018-05-08 22:50:43.858  INFO 14932 --- [           main] ationConfigEmbeddedWebApplicationContext : Refreshing org.springframework.boot.context.embe
dded.AnnotationConfigEmbeddedWebApplicationContext@610694f1: startup date [Tue May 08 22:50:43 IST 2018]; parent: org.springframework.context.annotat
ion.AnnotationConfigApplicationContext@6ae40994
2018-05-08 22:50:46.517  INFO 14932 --- [           main] o.s.cloud.context.scope.GenericScope     : BeanFactory id=a48b8ffc-2350-3262-b16c-201e15747
48c
2018-05-08 22:50:46.550  INFO 14932 --- [           main] f.a.AutowiredAnnotationBeanPostProcessor : JSR-330 'javax.inject.Inject' annotation found a
nd supported for autowiring
```

Starting up Spring Eureka server

6. Hit `http://localhost:9091/` and you should be able to see Eureka server started. You should see something like this:

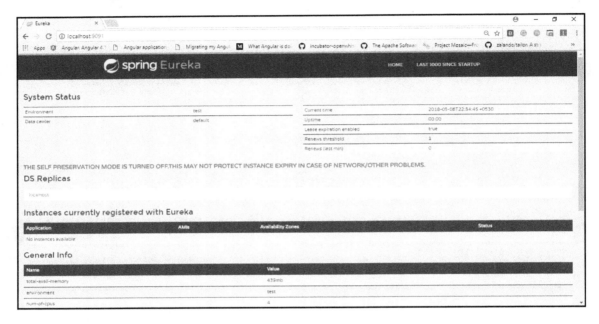

Spring Eureka server

Now that we have started Eureka server, we will register our services with it. We will be able to see our service under **Instances currently registered with Eureka** after registering with Eureka server.

Registering with Eureka server

Now that our Eureka server is up and running and ready to accept the registration of microservices, we will register a demo microservice and see it on the Eureka dashboard. You can follow along with the source code attached to the source files (`first-microservice-register`). Let's get started:

1. Pull up our first microservice code from `Chapter 2`, *Gearing up for the Journey*. We will be using the `eureka-js-client` (`https://www.npmjs.com/package/eureka-js-client`) module in the project, which is a JavaScript implementation of Netflix OSS Eureka.

2. Open up a Terminal and install eureka-js-client:

```
npm i eureka-js-client --save
```

3. Next, we will install the types of eureka-js-client to be used in our TypeScript project. At the time of writing, the types available in the DefinitelyTyped repository were not up to date. So, we will now write our custom types.

4. Create a folder, custom_types, and inside it add eureka-js-client.d.ts. Copy the contents either from attached source code or from my gist at https://gist.github.com/insanityrules/7461385aa561db5835c5c35279eb12bf

5. Next, we will register our Express app with Eureka. Open Application.ts and inside it write the following code:

```
let client = new Eureka(
  {
    instance: {
      app: 'hello-world-chapter-6',
      hostName: 'localhost',
      ipAddr: '127.0.0.1',
      statusPageUrl: `http://localhost:${port}`,
      healthCheckUrl: `http://localhost:${port}/health`,
      port: {
        '$': port,
        '@enabled': true
      },
      vipAddress: 'myvip',
      dataCenterInfo: {
        '@class':
'com.netflix.appinfo.InstanceInfo$DefaultDataCenterInfo',
        'name': 'MyOwn',
      },
    }, eureka: {
      host: 'localhost',
      port: 9091,
      servicePath: '/eureka/apps/'
    }
  })
```

What did we just do? Have a look at the following points for a better understanding:

- We registered our app instance named `hello-world-chapter-6` with a key, `myvip`, and data center, `myOwn`, with Eureka
- We provided `statusPageURL` and `IpAddress`
- We added Eureka information with host, port, and service paths
- The full list of configurations can be found here (`https://www.npmjs.com/package/eureka-js-client`)

6. Next, we will start with the client; just add the following:

```
client.start()
```

7. Our register is all ready; we can now start our service with `npm start`. Now, navigate to `localhost:9091` to check the server instances:

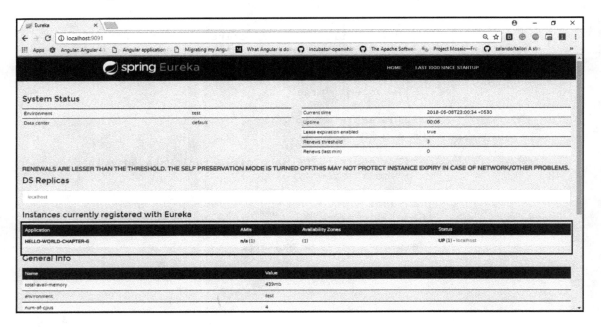

Service registered in Eureka server

8. Our service will constantly fetch service registries and send heartbeats to tell that service is running. Let's stop and deregister the service when our microservice is killed. Just add the following code to `Application.ts`:

```
process.on('SIGINT', function() {client.stop(); });
```

Now that our service is synced with Eureka, in the next section we will see how to discover a service.

Discovering with Eureka server

In this section, we will discover our register service in another microservice. We will be getting a response from that service without knowing the service address or hardcoding the location anywhere. Copy the structure of `first-microservice` from Chapter 2, *Gearing up for the Journey*. As we will need Eureka client everywhere, we will create `EurekaService.ts`. You can find the full source code in the `eureka/eureka-service-discovery/src` folder of the project.

Let's take a look at the steps to discover our registered service:

1. Create a file called `EurekaService.ts`, and create static methods for initializing clients:

```
static getClient(): Eureka{
  if (!this._client) {
    this._client = new Eureka({
      instance: {}, //set instance specific parameters,
      Eureka: {} //set Eureka parameters
    })
  }
}
```

2. In `Application.ts`, start your client and add stop processes as follows:

```
EurekaService.getClient().start();
...
process.on('SIGINT', () => {
  /*stop client*/
  EurekaService.getClient().stop();
  this.server.close()
});
```

3. In our `HelloWorld.ts` we will call the service from `first-microservice-register` and fetch its response. We won't hardcode locations. Add the following LOCs in `HelloWorld.ts`:

```
let instances: any =
  EurekaService.getClient().getInstancesByAppId("HELLO-WORLD-
CHAPTER-6");
let instance = null;
let msg = "404 Not Available";
if (instances != null && instances.length > 0) {
  instance = instances[0];
  let protocol = instances[0].securePort["@enabled"] == "true"
? "https" : "http";
  let url = protocol + "://" + instance.ipAddr + ":" +
                         instances[0].port.$ + "/";
  const { res, payload } = await Wreck.get(url);
  msg = payload.toString();
}
```

As you can see, we selected the protocol, port, and IP address from our service registry.

4. Run your application and you will be able to see the response from `first-microservice-register`.

Key points for Eureka

After this exercise on Eureka service registry and discovery, let's take a look at some salient points on Eureka:

- Eureka consists of a server component and a client-side component. The server component is the one that all microservices communicate with. They register their availability by constantly sending out heartbeats. The consuming services also use server components for discovering services.

- When a microservice is bootstrapped using our Eureka service, it reaches out to the Eureka server and broadcasts its existence with contract details. After registration, the service endpoint sends heartbeat requests every 30 seconds to renew its lease period. If a service endpoint fails to do so a certain number of times, it gets taken out of service registry.

- You can enable debug logs by setting either of the following options:
  - `NODE_DEBUG=request`
  - `client.logger.level('debug');`

- The client constantly fetches the registry at every predefined point and caches it. Hence, when it wants to discover another service, the extra network hop is prevented.
- Eureka client provides a list of available services with options to provide them by hostname or instance name.
- Eureka server is zone aware. Zone information can be supplied when registering a service in the same zone. To further introduce a load balancer, we can use a resilient client (`https://www.npmjs.com/package/resilient`) which is equivalent to Netflix Ribbon.
- It has options for a health check, status page, registering, deregistering, maximum number of retries, and so on.
- Eureka is a classic example of a server-side client registry and self-registration option.

Consul

Another option we have for service registry and discovery is HashiCorp Consul (`https://www.consul.io/`). Consul is an open source implementation of a distributed key-value store and other service discovery and registry features. It can run either as the master or as an agent. The master orchestrates the whole network and maintains the registry. A Consul agent acts as a proxy to the master and forwards all requests to the master. In this section, we will understand service discovery and registry using Consul.

In this exercise, we will do service registry and discovery using Consul. We will look at ways of self-registering/deregistering using Consul. Let's get started; we'll be using Linux OS in this exercise.

Setting up the Consul server

Let's take a look at the steps to set up Consul sever:

1. Setting up Consul server is pretty straightforward. Just download the executable from `https://www.consul.io/downloads.html` and unzip it to the location of your choice. After unzipping, hit the following command to make it available to the binary executions:

```
cp consul /usr/local/bin/
```

2. Test your Consul installation by opening up a Terminal and typing `consul -v`; you should be able to see version 1.0.7.

3. Now, we will open Consul UI terminal. Consul comes by default with a UI dashboard; to start the Consul terminal with a UI dashboard, hit the following command:

```
consul agent -server -bootstrap-expect=1 -data-dir=consul-data
-ui -bind=<Your_IPV4_Address>
```

4. Open up `localhost:8500`; you should be able to see something like this:

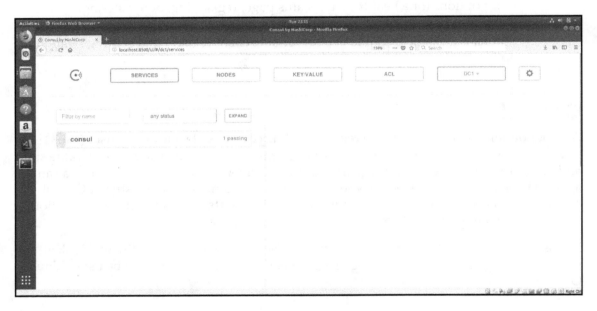

Consul server

We have successfully started Consul server; next we will register some services inside Consul.

Talking with Consul server

Like Eureka, Consul has also exposed some REST endpoints that can be used to interact with the Consul server. In this section, we will see how to:

- Register a service instance
- Send heartbeats and do a health check

- Deregister a service instance
- Subscribe to updates

Registering a service instance

Let's start by taking clones of the first microservice from `Chapter 2`, *Gearing up for the Journey*. You can find the entire source code in the `chapter-6/consul/consul-producer` folder:

1. Open up the Terminal and hit the following command:

```
npm install consul  @types/consul --save
```

2. Now in `Application.ts`, we will initialize our Consul client. Write this code:

```
import * as Consul from 'consul';
import { ConsulOptions } from 'consul';
...
let consulOptions: ConsulOptions =
  { host: '127.0.0.1', port: '8500', secure: false, promisify:
false }
....
let details =
  {
    name: 'typescript-microservices-consul-producer',
    address: HOST,
    check: { ttl: '10s', deregister_critical_service_after:
'1m' },
    port: appPort, id: CONSUL_ID
  };
let consul = new Consul(consulOptions);
```

3. Next, we will register our service with Consul:

```
consul.agent.service.register(
  details, err => {
    if (err) {
      throw new Error(err.toString());
    }
    console.log('registered with Consul');
  }
```

4. Run the program and you should be able to see successful logs. You will be able to see output similar to the following:

Service registry with Consul and Consul dashboard

Sending heartbeats and doing a health check

Now, we will add one scheduler that constantly sends heartbeats to tell our Consul server that it is active. In the same code as the previous exercise, just add the following lines of code:

```
setInterval(() => {
  consul.agent.check.pass({id:`service:${CONSUL_ID}`},
  (err:any) => {
      if (err) throw new Error(err);
      console.log('Send out heartbeat to consul');
      });
}, 5 * 1000);
```

What did we do?

- Every five seconds, we send out heartbeats to Consul, to ensure that our service with the CONSUL_ID that we generated is active.

- Periodic heartbeats are sent out to make sure that Consul knows that our service is active and it doesn't disconnect our service. Earlier, we kept TTL values in our settings as 10 seconds, which means that if Consul server doesn't receive heartbeats after 10 seconds, it will assume that the service is down.

- A higher TTL value means that Consul will know very late when the application is dead or unable to serve requests. A short TTL value, on the other hand, means that we are sending too much data over the network, which can flood Consul, so this value should be selected carefully.

- You always need to pass a unique ID, so in this exercise, we generated UUID and mixed host and port with it.

- The health check API is available over HTTP. All we have to do is hit the following:

```
GET /agent/check/pass/service:<service_id>
```

Deregistering an application

In this section, we will deregister our application whenever the server terminates or someone kills the server. This ensures that Consul doesn't have to wait until the TTL period to actually know that the service is down. Simply add the following lines of code in `Application.ts`:

```
process.on('SIGINT', () => {
console.log('Process Terminating. De-Registering...');
let details = { id: CONSUL_ID };
consul.agent.service.deregister(details,
  (err) => {
    console.log('de-registered.', err);
    process.exit();
  });
```

Now, when you check Consul server when you gracefully kill the application, you won't be able to see our Consul producer registered.

Subscribing to updates

Just like Eureka, we will constantly get the Consul registry, so whenever we need to communicate to another registry we won't need to make another registry call, as the registry is already cached at our end. Consul takes care of this by providing a feature called `watch`. Responses to a service will have an index number, which can be used for future requests to compare. They are nothing but a cursor to keep track of where we have left off. Let's add watchers to our application:

1. Create a new watcher by adding the following code. Here, we have created a watcher on the service named `data` in Consul:

   ```
   let watcher = consul.watch({
     method: consul.health.service,
     options: {
       service: 'data',
       passing: true
     }
   });
   ```

2. Next, we will add a change event on our watcher, so whenever it receives new updates we will just cache the registry for our service data. Create one array and persist the entries that it receives while watching:

   ```
   let known_data_instances: string[];
   ..
   watcher.on('change', (data, res) => {
     console.log('received discovery update:', data.length);
     known_data_instances = [];
     data.forEach((entry: any) => {
       known_data_instances.push(`http://${entry.Service.Address}:
       ${entry.Service.Port}/`);
     });
     console.log(known_data_instances);
   });
   ```

3. Add an error handler:

   ```
   watcher.on('error', err => {
     console.error('watch error', err);
   });
   ```

4. That's it. Now, run the program using `npm start` and register another service with the name `data` (the steps are the same as registering a new service). Then, you should be able to see output like the following:

```
received discovery update: 1
[ 'http://parth-VirtualBox:8081/' ]
```

That's it. We just did service registry and interacted with Eureka server. Whenever the data service goes down, this value will also be dynamically updated. Now that we have the dynamic address and port, we can use it anytime to discover the location of services.

Key points for Consul

After completing the exercise on Consul, let's now summarize the key points for Consul:

1. Consul works on the gossip protocol (tell everyone who is alive and has been in constant touch with others) to form dynamic clusters.
2. It has an inbuilt key-value store that not only stores data, but is also used to register watches, which can be used for a number of tasks, such as notifying others about data changes, running different health checks, and some custom commands depending on use cases.
3. Service discovery is embedded, so we do not need any third-party tools. It has inbuilt features such as health checks, watches, and so on.

It has out-of-the-box support for multiple data centers, and the gossip protocol works across all data centers as well. It can also be used to discover information about other deployed services and nodes on which they reside. It has inbuilt health checks, TTLs, and custom command support where we can add our own middleware functions.

Registrator

While Consul seems a great alternative for service discovery and registration, there is quite a big drawback where each service needs to maintain their startup and shutdown codes, which seems like quite a lot of duplicated code everywhere. We need a tool that auto-registers a service to the Consul server based on listening to their startup and shutdown events. Registrator is just the right tool for that. It is a service registry bridge for Docker with options to plug adapters as per the need. Registrator automatically registers and deregisters services when they come online or go dead. It has pluggable options for service registries, meaning it can be used with various other service registry clients such as Consul, etcd, and more.

Let's get started with using Registrator. In this exercise, we will use service registry for Consul, plug it into Registrator, and then start a service and let Registrator autoregister it in Consul server:

1. First of all, start the Consul server using the following command:

   ```
   consul agent -server -bootstrap-expect=1 -data-dir=consul-data
   -ui -bind=<Your_IPV4_Address>
   ```

2. Now, we will pull the Docker image of Registrator and specify to plug it into Consul registry, so that when Registrator finds any services they will be automatically added to Consul server. Open up the Terminal and hit the following command:

   ```
   sudo docker run -d
       --name=registrator
       --net=host
         --volume=/var/run/docker.sock:/tmp/docker.sock
         gliderlabs/registrator:latest
         consul://localhost:8500
   ```

   We run the container in detached mode and name it. We run in host network mode to make sure that Registrator has the hostname and IP address of the actual host. The last line is our registry URI. Registrator needs to be run on every host; for our exercise, we went ahead with a single host. To start Registrator, the essential configuration that we need to provide is how to connect to a registry, in this case Consul.

3. To ensure that Registrator has successfully started, hit the following command and you should be able to see logs streaming and the message `Listening for Docker events ...`:

   ```
   sudo  docker logs registrator
   ```

4. Now, we will just start any service using Docker and our service will be automatically registered with Consul. Open up Terminal and just start our service from `Chapter 2`, *Gearing up for the Journey* in Docker using the following:

   ```
   sudo docker run -p 8080:3000 -d firsttypescriptms:latest
   ```

   Or you can just start any service, let's say `redis`, by simply typing the following:

   ```
   sudo docker run -d -P --name=redis redis
   ```

5. Open up Consul user interface and you will be able to see our service registered there.

Here, we efficiently implemented auto discovery using Registrator and Consul. It works as auto discovery.

Key points for Registrator

Let's discuss the key points for Registrator:

1. Registrator acts as an auto-discovery agent, where it listens for Docker startup and shutdown events.

2. Registrator has the following inbuilt options taken from their GitHub `Readme` file:

```
Usage of /bin/registrator:
  /bin/registrator [options] <registry URI>
  -cleanup=false: Remove dangling services
  -deregister="always": Deregister exited services "always" or
"on-
    success"
  -internal=false: Use internal ports instead of published
ones
  -ip="": IP for ports mapped to the host
  -resync=0: Frequency with which services are resynchronized
  -retry-attempts=0: Max retry attempts to establish a
connection
    with the backend. Use -1 for infinite retries
  -retry-interval=2000: Interval (in millisecond) between
retry-
    attempts.
  -tags="": Append tags for all registered services
  -ttl=0: TTL for services (default is no expiry)
  -ttl-refresh=0: Frequency with which service TTLs are
refreshed
```

3. Using Registrator with Consul gives a very viable solution for our service discovery and registry without duplicating code everywhere.

These are some of the widely used solutions available right now. Besides these, there are other solutions too such as ELB, Kubernetes, and so on.

In this section, we saw service registry and discovery using Eureka, Consul, and Registrator and saw some other options based on our service discovery and registry patterns. In the next section, we will understand how to choose the correct service registry and discovery solution.

How to choose service registry and discovery

Previously, we saw various service registry and discovery options based on service registry and discovery patterns. So, the next question that arises is pretty obvious, which solution to go for? That question is pretty wide and it actually depends on the requirements. Your requirements are most likely to be different than most other companies, so rather than going with the most common solutions, a better approach would be to evaluate your requirements and devise your own strategy based on that. To devise a strategy, the following questions should be properly evaluated:

- Is the system going to be coded in only one language or is there a polyglot environment? Writing the same code in different languages is pretty cumbersome. In this case, Registrator is pretty helpful.
- Is there a legacy system involved? Are both the systems going to run for some time? In this case, self registering solutions can be pretty helpful.
- How simplified is service discovery process? Is there going to be a gateway? Is there going to be a load balancer in between?
- Is there a requirement for an API for the service discovery? Do individual microservices need to communicate with other microservices? In this case, HTTP or DNS-based solutions are pretty helpful.
- Are service discovery solutions embedded in each microservice or is there a need to embed the logic centrally?
- Do we need separate application configurations or can we store these in key-value stores such as Redis or MongoDB?
- What is the deployment strategy? Is there a need for deployment strategies such as the blue-green strategy? Based on appropriate service discovery, solutions should be selected.

 Blue-green is a deployment strategy where the downtime is reduced by running two identical production environments named blue and green.

- How is the system going to run? Are there going to be multiple data centers? If that's the case, then running Eureka is most appropriate.

- How do you maintain your acknowledgments? How is the access control list maintained? If that's the case, then Consul has inbuilt solutions.
- How much support is there? Is it open sourced and does it have widespread support? Are there too many issues?
- How are auto-scaling solutions decided?

Based on these questions, and after properly evaluating them, we can decide on appropriate solutions. After carefully evaluating these, we can select any solution. Given here is a list of careful points that need to be taken care of while selecting any solution.

Take care of these points while selecting either Consul or Eureka.

If you select Consul

While Consul has lots of benefits, the following points need to be taken care of while selecting Consul:

- Clients need to write their own load-balancing, timeout, and retry logic. To avoid writing complete logic, we can utilize the following `node` module at `https://www.npmjs.com/package/resilient`.
- The client needs to implement fetch logic, and cache, and Consul failure handling individually unless we utilized Registrator. These needs to be written separately for each language in the ecosystem.
- Priorities cannot be set for servers; custom logic needs to be written.

If you select Eureka

While Eureka has many added advantages, the following points need to be taken care of while selecting Eureka:

- Clients have to add their own load-balancing, timeout, and retry logic, so we need to integrate it with external tools such as Netflix Ribbon.
- Documentation is very poor. If you have a non-JVM environment, you won't be able to use Eureka. Eureka server needs to be run on JVM platforms. Documentation is very vague for non-JVM clients.
- Web UI is extremely dull and noninformative.

In this section, we learned about major takeaways while selecting Eureka or Consul. We summarized major points to actually help us decide a service registry and discovery solution.

Summary

In this chapter, we learned about service registry and discovery. We went through the when, what, and why of service discovery and understood the service registry and discovery patterns. We saw the pros and cons of each pattern and the available options for each of them. Then, we implemented service discovery and registry using Eureka, Consul, and service registrator. In the end, we saw how to choose a service discovery and registry solution and the key takeaways while selecting Eureka or Consul.

In the next chapter, we will see service state and how microservices communicate with each other. We will learn more design patterns such as event-based communication and the publisher-subscriber pattern, see a service bus in action, share database dependencies, and so on. We will learn about stateful and stateless services with some live examples.

7
Service State and Interservice Communication

Now that we have developed some microservices, seen API Gateway, and understood service registry and discovery, it's time to dive deeper into microservices and understand the system from an individual microservice point of view. To gain the most benefits out of microservices architecture, every component in the system has to collaborate in just the right way—a way that ensures that there is most likely no coupling between microservices, which will enable us to be Agile.

In this chapter, we will understand various communication styles between microservices and see how services exchange data among themselves. Then we will move on to the service bus, an enterprise way of how system components communicate with each other. Many services would need to persist some state in one form or another. We will see how to make our service stateless. We will see the current database landscape and understand service state. We will understand pub-sub pattern and look at tools such as Kafka, and RabbitMQ, to understand event-driven architecture. This chapter covers the following topics:

- Core concepts—state, communication, and dependencies
- Communication styles
- Synchronous versus asynchronous way of data sharing
- Microservice versioning and failure handling
- Service bus
- Data sharing between microservices
- Cache via Redis
- Publish-subscribe pattern

Core concepts – state, communication, and dependencies

Each microservice implements a single capability such as shipping, and deducting from the inventory. However, to deliver an end user, a service request such as business capability, user need, or user-specific requests; it may or may not be a set of business capabilities. For example, a person who wants to buy the product is a single service request from the user's point of view. However, multiple requests are involved here, such as add to cart microservice, payment microservice, shipping microservice. Hence, to deliver, microservices need to collaborate among each other. In this section, we will look at core concepts of microservice collaboration such as service state, communication styles, and more. Choosing the correct communication style helps us to design a loosely coupled architecture that ensures that each microservice has clear boundaries and it stays inside its bounded context. In this section, we will look at some core concepts that will affect our microservice design and architecture. So, let's get started.

Microservice state

While we should indeed thrive on making services as stateless as possible, there are some instances where we do need stateful services. A state is simply any condition or quality at any specific point in time. A stateful service is one that is dependent on the state of the system. Being stateful means to rely on these moments in time, whereas statelessness means to be independent of any sort of state.

Stateful service is essential in instances where we have a workflow that calls some REST services, we need to support retries on failures, we need to track progress, store intermediate results, and so on. We need to keep state somewhere outside of our service instances boundaries. This is where databases come into the picture.

Databases are an important and interesting part to think on. Introducing database in a microservice should be done in such a way that no other team can directly talk to our database. They, in fact, shouldn't even know the type of our database. The current database landscape has various options available to us, both in the SQL and NoSQL category. There are even graph databases, in-memory databases, and databases with either high read and write capabilities.

Our microservices can have both stateless and stateful microservices. If a service relies on the state it should be separated out in a dedicated container that is easily accessible and not shared with anyone. Microservices have the ability to scale better when stateless. We scale the container rather than scaling the VM. Hence each state store should be in a container that can be scaled at any point in time. We use Docker to scale the database store, which creates a separate persistence layer that is host-independent. The new cloud data stores such as Redis, Cassandra, and DynamoDB maximize availability with a minimum delay in consistency. Designing a stateful microservice with asynchronous and scalable nature needs some thinking on the problem—to find some means of communication state between any sequential messages and to ensure that messages don't mix up with any context where they don't belong. We will see various synchronous patterns such as CQRS and Saga for achieving this in this chapter.

Maintaining state is not something that can be done on the service level only. Actually, there are three places wherein state can be maintained in the network:

- **HTTP**: This is actually the application layer from where the state is maintained mostly session-based or persisting in the database. Generally speaking by maintaining a communication layer between a client and an application or a service.
- **TCP**: This is actually the transportation layer. The objective of maintaining state here is to ensure a reliable delivery channel between the client and an application or a service.
- **SSL**: This is the layer without any home between the TCP and HTTP layer. It provides confidentiality and privacy in data. State here is maintained, as encryption and decryption rely solely on information that is unique to the connection between client and application or a service.

So even if our services are stateless, the TCP and SSL layer do need to maintain state. So you are never pure stateless. Anyway, we will just stick to the application layer for the scope of the book.

Interservice communication

Being finely grained and closely bound to a scope, microservices need to collaborate in some way or another to deliver functionality to end users. They either need to share state or dependencies or talk to other services. Let's take a look at a practical example. Consider the frequent buyers rewards program microservice. This microservice is responsible for rewards for frequent buyers business capability. The program is simple—whenever customers purchase something, some points are accumulated in their account. Now, when a customer buys something, he can use those rewards points for a discount on the selling price. The rewards microservice depends on the customer purchase microservice and other business capabilities. Other business capabilities depend on the rewards program. As shown in the following diagram, microservices need to collaborate with other microservices:

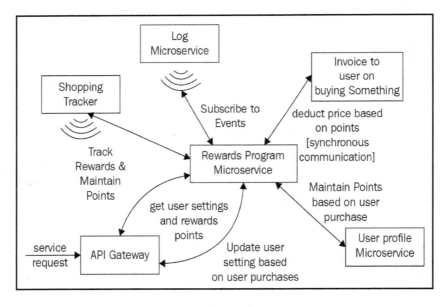

Need of microservices

As seen in the preceding diagram, microservices are finely divided into business capabilities. However, end user functionality needs several business capabilities for which microservices must need to collaborate with each other to deliver use cases to end users. When any microservices collaborate, the collaboration style follows in majorly three categories—**commands**, **queries**, and **events**. Let's understand all the three categories with some examples.

Commands

Commands are used whenever any microservice wants another microservice to perform an action. They are synchronous in nature and are generally implemented using HTTP POST or PUT requests. For example, in the preceding figure, the rewards program microservice sends a command to user profile microservice or invoice microservice regarding promotional offers based on rewards. When sending a command fails, the sender won't know if the receiver processed the command or not. This can result in errors or some degraded functionalities if a set of rules is not followed by the sender as well as receiver side.

Queries

Similar to commands, queries are used when one microservice needs some information from another microservice. For example, during invoice in our shopping cart microservice, we need information on the total number of reward points so as to give a promotional discount, so the invoice microservice queries the rewards points microservice. This is a synchronous mode of communication and is generally implemented using HTTP GET requests. Whenever a query fails, the caller does not get the data it needs. If the caller handles exceptions well enough then there is a minimal impact with some degraded functionality. If it does not handle errors well enough, the error propagates throughout the system.

Events

While deviating from the standard approaches, the third approach is more of a reactive approach. Events are generally preferred whenever a microservice needs to react to something that has occurred in another microservice. The custom logging microservice listens to all other services for log entries so that it can push logs to Elasticsearch. Similarly, the rewards microservices listens to shopping tracker microservices in order to update user rewards accordingly based on user shopping. When a subscriber polls any event feed and if the call fails the impact is very limited. The subscriber can still poll the event feed later until the event feed is up and start receiving events at any time. Some of the events will be delayed, but this should not be a problem as everything is done asynchronously.

Exchanging data formats

The essence or fundamental of interservice communication is the exchange of messages in any formats. Messages usually contain data and so a very important design aspect is the format of data. This can greatly impact the efficiency of communication, the usability and changes, and evolving the service in time. It is very necessary to select cross-message format. There are two types of message formats—**text** and **binary**. In this section, we will look at both.

Text-based message formats

Commonly used message formats such as JSON and XML are human-readable and self-describing. These formats enable a user to pick out the values that the consumer is interested in and discard the rest. Any changes to the schema format can easily be backward-compatible. The downsides to using text-based formats include being too verbose in nature and overhead of parsing the entire text. For stronger efficiency, binary formats are recommended to be used.

Binary message formats

These formats provide a typed identity language for defining a structure for the messages. A compiler then generates the code that serializes and deserializes the messages for us (we will be seeing Apache Thrift later in the chapter). If the client has a statically typed language then the compiler checks if the API is used correctly or not. Avro, Thrift, and Google's protobuf are prominent binary message formats.

Now that we have a clear idea about communication essentials, we can move on to the next section on dependencies. Let's summarize the points before moving on.

You can opt for using commands and queries if the following use cases are met:

- In order to process the service request, the service client needs a response to move further along its process. For example, for the payment microservice, we need customer information.
- The situation demands asynchronous operation. For example, inventory should only be deducted if payment has been made and product processed for customer delivery.
- Request to other services is a simple query or command, that is, something that can be processed via HTTP GET, PUT, POST, and DELETE methods.

You can opt for using events if the following use cases are met:

- When you need to scale the application as pure commands and queries do not scale over a larger problem set.
- Producer or sender does not care how much extra processing is done on the receiver or consumer's end and it has no such effect on the producers end.
- When multiple clients read a single message. For example, an order has been invoiced, then multiple processes need to be done such as getting it ready to be dispatched, updating inventory, sending client notifications, and so on.

Dependencies

Now that we are aware of communication styles in microservices, we will learn about the next obvious thing in development—dependencies and avoiding dependency hell. With developing more and more microservices, you will spot code duplication across multiple microservices. To resolve these, we need to understand dependencies and how to separate supporting code. Node.js has the package manager NPM that grabs application dependencies (as well as dependencies of your dependencies). NPM has support for private repositories, directly downloaded from GitHub, setting up your own repository (such as JFrog, Artifactory), which not only helps to avoid code but also in deployment processes.

However, we must not forget **Microservices 101**. We make microservices to ensure that each service can release and deploy independently, for which we must avoid dependency hell. To understand dependency hell, let's consider the following example, shopping cart microservice has API listing products that have now upgraded to API listing products with specific brands. Now all dependencies on the shopping cart microservice may send a message to listing products with specific brands, which are originally meant for listing products. If backward-compatibility is not handled, then this evolves into dependency hell. To avoid dependency hell, strategies that can be used are—APIs must be forward and backward-compatible, they must have accurate documentation, contract testing must be done (we will see this in Chapter 8, *Testing, Debugging, and Documenting*, under *PACT*), and using an appropriate tooling library that has a clear objective to throw out errors if there is an unknown field encountered. To make sure that we want to avoid dependency hell we must simply follow these rules:

- A microservice cannot call another microservice nor access its data source directly
- A microservice can only call another microservice only through either event-based mechanism or some microservice script (a script can be anything such as API Gateway, UI, service registry, and so on)

In the next section, we will look at microservice communication styles and see how they collaborate with each other. We will look at the widely used patterns based on different classification factors and understand the scenarios for using which pattern at what moment.

Communication styles

A microservice ecosystem is essentially a distributed system that is running on multiple machines. Each service instance is just another process. We saw in the earlier diagram different process communications. In this section, we will learn about communication styles in much more detail.

A service consumer and service responder may communicate through many different types of communication styles, each one targeting some scenario and outcome in mind. The communication types can be categorized into two different aspects.

The first aspect deals with the type of protocol, whether it is synchronous or asynchronous:

- Communication invoked via commands and queries such as HTTP are synchronous in nature. The client sends a request to wait for a response from the service. This waiting is language-dependent, that is, it can be synchronous (languages such as Java) and it can be asynchronous (response can be processed via callbacks, promises, and so on, in our case, Node.js). The important point is that a service request can only be served once the client receives a proper HTTP server response.
- Other protocols such as AMQP, sockets, and so on are asynchronous in nature (the log and shopping tracker microservice). The client code or message sender does not wait for a response, it simply sends the message to any queue or message broker and simply.

The second aspect deals with the number of receivers, whether there is just a single receiver or there are multiple receivers:

- For a single receiver, each request has to be processed by only one receiver or service. Command and query pattern are examples of this kind of communication. One-to-one interaction includes models such as request/response, one-way requests such as notifications, and request/async responses.
- For multiple receivers, each request can be processed by zero or multiple services or receivers. This is an asynchronous mode of communication with an example of the publisher-subscriber mechanism promoting event-driven architecture. Data updates between multiple microservices are propagated through events that are implemented through some service bus (Azure service bus) or any message brokers (AMQP, Kafka, RabbitMQ, and so on).

NextGen communication styles

While we saw some common communication styles, the world is constantly changing. With evolution everywhere, even the fundamental HTTP protocol has evolved and we now have the HTTP 2.X protocol with some added advantages. In this section, we are going to look at next-gen communication styles and see the advantages they have to offer.

HTTP/2

HTTP/2 gives significant enhancements and focuses more on improving the usage of TCP connections. The following are some major enhancements as compared to HTTP/1.1:

- **Compression and binary framing**: HTTP/2 has header compression inbuilt in order to reduce the footprint of HTTP headers that can grow in kilobytes (say, for example, cookies). It also controls headers that are repeated across multiple requests and responses. Also, the client and the server maintain a list of frequently visible fields along with their compressed values, so when these fields are repeated, the individual simply includes the reference to the compressed value. Besides this, HTTP/2 uses binary encoding for frames.
- **Multiplexing**: As compared to a single request and response flow (client has to wait for a response before issuing next request), HTTP/2 introduces fully asynchronous multiplexing of a request by implementing streams (behold reactive programming!). Clients and servers can both start multiple requests on a single TCP connection. For example, when a client requests a web page, the server can start a separate stream to transfer images and videos that are needed for that web page.
- **Flow Control**: With multiplexing introduced, there is a need for a flow control in place to avoid destructive behavior across any of the streams. HTTP/2 provides building blocks for client and server to have proper flow controls suitable for any specific situations. Flow control can allow the browser to get only a part of the particular resource, put that operation on hold by reducing window down to zero, and resuming at any point in time. Also, priorities can be set.

In this section, we are going to look at how to implement HTTP/2 in our microservice system. You can check example http2 under chapter 7, source code to follow the implementation:

1. HTTP/2 is supported on Node.js 10.XX, but there are other ways to achieve support without upgrading to the latest version, which was introduced just two weeks ago (Node.js 10.XX was introduced just two weeks ago at the time of writing). We will use node module spdy, which provides HTTP/2 support to our Express application. Copy our first-microservice skeleton from Chapter 2, *Gearing up for the Journey*, and install spdy as a node module by using the following command:

```
npm install spdy --save
```

2. For HTTP/2 to work, the SSL/TLS has to be enabled. For our development environment to work properly we will self-generate the CSR and certificates that can easily be replaced by procuring certificates in production environments. To generate the certificates, follow along with these commands:

```
// this command generates server pass key.
openssl genrsa -des3 -passout pass:x -out server.pass.key 2048
//we write our RSA key and let it generate a password
openssl rsa -passin pass:x -in server.pass.key -out server.key
rm server.pass.key //this command removes the pass key, as we
are just on dev env
//following commands generates the csr file
openssl req -new -key server.key -out server.csr
//following command generates server.crt file
openssl x509 -req -sha256 -days 365 -in server.csr -signkey
server.key -out server.crt
```

The outcome of all these steps will result in three files: `server.crt`, `server.csr`, and `server.key`.

3. Next, we need to change the way we start our express server. Instead of using default methods, we need to use one provided by `spdy`. Make the following changes in `Application.ts`. Replace `this.express.app.listen` with the following code:

```
import * as spdy from 'spdy';
 const certsPath = path.resolve('certs');
 const options={
    key:fs.readFileSync(certsPath+"/server.key"),
    cert:fs.readFileSync(certsPath+"/server.crt")
 }...
this.server=spdy.createServer(options,this.express.app)
              .listen(port,(error:any)=>{
              if(error){
                  logger.error("failed to start
                  server with ssl",error);
                  return process.exit(1);}else{
                  logger.info(`Server Started! Express:
                  http://localhost:${port}`); }})
```

4. We are ready to start dishing out HTTP/2 requests. Start the server and open up `https://localhost:3000/hello-world`. Open up the **Developer** console and you should be able to see HTTP/2 just like in the following screenshot:

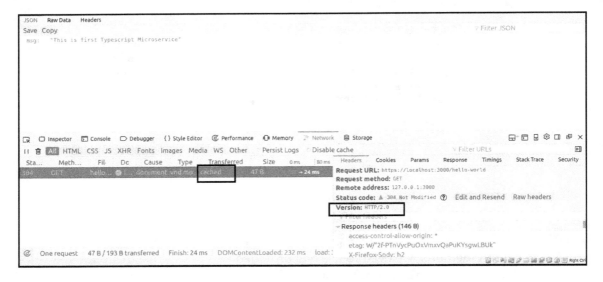

HTTP support

These are HTTP calls. In the next section, we will look at the RPC mechanism, which is another way to do collaboration among microservices.

gRPC with Apache Thrift

gRPC is a framework designed for writing cross-language RPC (remote procedure calls) clients and servers. It works on binary formats and focuses on an API First approach for designing any services. It provides fixed IDL (interactive data language fixed formats) to later generate client-side stubs and server-side skeletons adhering to that fixed IDL format. The compiler can generate code for most of the languages and they exchange data using HTTP/2, which is beneficial in the long run. Apache Thrift is a great alternative for writing cross-language RPC clients and servers. It has a C-style IDL Definition language. The compiler generates code for a variety of languages, which includes C++, Java, and even TypeScript. A Thrift definition is very analogous to the TypeScript interface. Thrift methods can give out any value or they can be just one-way communication. Methods that have a return type implement the request/response model, whereas methods that do not have a return type are defined to implement the notification model. Thrift has support for JSON as well as binary. Let's get started with an example. You can follow along with the `thrift-rpc` folder in `Chapter 7`, *Service State and Interservice Communication*, in the extracted source code.

The overall process that we are going to do is as follows:

- Write ourselves a `.thrift` file that will describe our product microservice and popularity microservice
- Generate source code for TypeScript, the language in which we are going to write our service communication
- Import the generated code and start writing our service
- Include the generated source of popularity in product and write our service
- Create API Gateway as a single entry point

 Though Thrift provides Node.js and TypeScript libraries, we are going to use npm modules of **CreditKarma** (`https://github.com/creditkarma`), as original modules lack in generating strict types. So let's get started.

Now, let's perform the following steps:

1. Initialize a Node.js project. Instead of downloading Thrift, I am going to use `npm` modules. Hence, install the following modules as dependencies:

```
npm install @creditkarma/dynamic-config @creditkarma/thrift-
client @creditkarma/thrift-server-core @creditkarma/thrift-
server-express @creditkarma/thrift-typescript --save
```

2. Create one folder called `thrift` and inside it create two Thrift files—`PopularityService.thrift` (`thrift/popularity/PopularityService.thrift`) and `ProductService.thrift` (`thrift/product/ProductService.thrift`). A Thrift file is like a TypeScript interface:

```
namespace js com.popularity
struct Popularity {
    1: required i32 id
    2: required i32 totalStars
    3: required string review
    4: required i32 productId}
exception PopularityServiceException {
    1: required string message}
service PopularityService {
    Popularity getPopularityByProduct(4: i32 productId)
    throws (1: PopularityServiceException exp)}
```

Since we need popularity inside the product, we will import that in `ProductService.thrift`, and you can check other default syntax here `https:/ /thrift.apache.org/docs/idl`.

3. Now we will generate our code using IDL files defined in the preceding step. Open up `package.json` and add the following scripts inside the `scripts` tag:

```
"precodegen": "rimraf src/codegen",
"codegen": "npm run precodegen && thrift-typescript --target
thrift-server --sourceDir thrift --outDir src/codegen"
```

This script will generate the code for us, as we simply will have to type `npm run codegen`.

4. The next part involves writing `findByProductId` and `findPopularityOfProduct` methods. Check out `src/popularity/data.ts` and `src/product/data.ts` for dummy data and dummy find methods in the extracted source code.

5. We will now write code for starting `PopluarityThriftService` and `ProductThriftService`. **Create one** `serviceHandler` **inside** `src/popularity/server.ts` as follows:

```
const serviceHandler:
PopularityService.IHandler<express.Request> = {
    getPopularityByProduct(id: number, context?:
    express.Request): Popularity {
        //find method which uses generated models and types.
},
```

6. Start this `server.ts` **as** `express` **by adding** `ThriftServerExpress` **as middleware:**

```
app.use(serverConfig.path,bodyParser.raw(),
ThriftServerExpress({
    serviceName: 'popularity-service',
    handler: new PopularityService.Processor(serviceHandler),
}), )
app.listen(serverConfig.port, () => {//server startup code)})
```

7. Now, inside `src/product/server.ts`, add the following code that will make an RPC call to the `PopularityService` to get popularity by `productId`:

```
const popularityClientV1: PopularityService.Client =
createHttpClient(PopularityService.Client, clientConfig)
const serviceHandler: ProductService.IHandler<express.Request>
= {
    getProduct(id: number, context?: express.Request):
    Promise<Product> {
        console.log(`ContentService: getProduct[${id}]`)
        const product: IMockProduct | undefined =
findProduct(id)
        if (product !== undefined) {
            return
popularityClientV1.getPopularityByProduct(product.id)
            .then((popularity: Popularity) => {
            return new Product({
            id: product.id,
            feedback:popularity,
            productInfo: product.productInfo,
            productType: product.productType,
        })
})} else {
throw new ProductServiceException({
    message: `Unable to find product for id[${id}]`,
})}},}
```

8. Similarly, `create gateway/server.ts`. Define a route for `/product/:productId` and it will make an RPC call to `ProductMicroservice` to fetch the data of `productId` passed.

9. Run the program and make a request to `localhost:9000/product/1` and you will be able to see combined communicated response via RPC calls.

In this section, we had hands-on experience with some microservice communication styles along with some practicals. In the next section, we are going to see how to version microservices and make our microservices have a fail-safe mechanism.

Versioning microservices and failure handling

Evolution is necessary and we can't prevent it. Whenever we allow one of the services to evolve, one of the most considerable aspects of maintaining is service versioning. In this section, we are going to see various aspects related to handling changes in the system and overcoming failures if any are introduced in the system.

Versioning 101

Service versioning should be thought of firstly and not be taken up as an after-development exercise. An API is a published contract between a server and consumer. Maintaining versions helps us to release new services without breaking anything for existing customers (not everyone accepts change in the first attempt). Both the old version and the new version should coexist side by side.

Prevalent styles of versioning are using the semantic versions. Any semantic version will have three major components—**major** (whenever there is a groundbreaking change), **minor** (whenever there is a backward-compatible behavior), and **patch** (backward-compatible with any bug fix). Versioning is extremely problematic whenever there is more than a single service inside a microservice. A recommended way is to version any services at the service level rather than doing it at the operations level. If there is a single change in any of the operations the service is upgraded and deployed to **Version2 (V2)**, which is applicable to all operations in the service. There are three ways in which we can version any service:

- **URI versioning**: The version number of the service is included in the URL itself. We just need to worry about major versions of this approach, as that would change the URL route. If there is a minor version or any patch available the consumer does not need to worry about the change. Keeping an alias for the latest version to non-versioned URI is one of the good practices that needs to be followed. For example, the URL `/api/v5/product/1234` should be aliased to `/api/product/1234`—aliased to v5. Moreover, passing version number can also be done as follows:

  `/api/product/1234?v=1.5`

- **Media type versioning**: The media type versioning follows a slightly different approach. Here the version is set by the client on the HTTP Accept header. Its structure is something similar to, `Accept: application/vnd.api+json`. The Accept header gives us a way to specify generic and less generic content types as well as giving fallbacks. A command such as `Accept: application/vnd.api.v5+json` specifically asks for v5 of the API. If the Accept header is omitted, the consumer interacts with the latest version, which may not be production-grade. GitHub uses such kinds of versioning.
- **Custom header**: The last approach is to maintain our own custom header. Consumers would still use an Accept header and add a new one on top of that. It would be something like this: `X-my-api-version:1`.

When comparing the preceding three approaches, it is simple for clients to consume services in a URI approach, but also managing nested URI resources can be complex in a URI approach. Migrating clients is complex when it comes to a URI-based approach as compared to media type versioning, as we need to maintain caching of multiple versions. However, most of the big players, such as Google, Salesforce, and so on, go with the URI approach.

When a developer's nightmare comes true

All systems will experience failures. Microservices being distributed, the probability increases very high. How we handle failures and respond to failures is what defines a developer. While making the overall product ecosystem resilient is spectacular (activities involve clustering servers, setting up application load balancers, distributing infrastructure between multiple locations, and setting up disaster recovery), our work does not stop there. This part only addresses the complete loss of a system. However, whenever a service is running slow or there is memory leak, it is extremely difficult to detect the problem for the following reasons:

- A service degradation starts slow, but rapidly gains momentum and spreads just like an infection. The application container exhausts its thread pool resources completely and the system goes down.
- Too many synchronous calls where a caller has to wait endlessly for the service to return a response.
- Applications don't deal with partial degradations. As long as any service is completely down, the application continues to make calls to that service that soon exists in resource exhaustion.

The worst thing about such situations is that such failures cascade up and adversely affect the system just like a contagion. A single poorly performing system can soon take out multiple dependent systems. It becomes necessary to protect a service's resources from getting exhausted because of some other poorly performing service. In the next section, we will look at some of these patterns to avoid failure cascading in the system and causing the ripple effect.

Client resiliency patterns

Client resiliency patterns allow the client to fail fast and not block database connections or thread pools. These patterns are implemented in the client layer, which calls any remote resource. There are the following four common client resiliency patterns:

- Bulkhead and retry
- Client-side load balancing or queue-based load leveling
- Circuit breaker
- Fallback and compensating transaction

The four patterns can be seen in the diagram as follows:

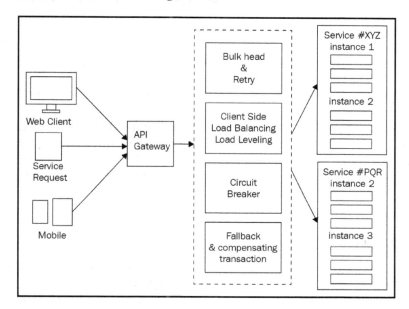

Client resiliency patterns

Bulkhead and retry pattern

The bulkhead pattern is similar to the pattern of building a ship, where a ship is divided into completely isolated and watertight compartments called bulkheads. Even if the ship's hull is punctured, the ship is not affected as it is divided into watertight compartments. The bulkheads keep the water confined to the specific region of the ship where the puncture occurred and prevent the ship from sinking.

A similar concept is applied in the bulkhead pattern for a service interacting with many remote resources. By using this pattern we break the calls to remote resources into their own bulkheads (their own thread pools) and reduce the risk and prevent the application from going down because of a slow remote resource. If one service is slow, then the thread pool for that type of service will become saturated to stop processing further requests. Service calls to another service won't be hampered as each one has its own thread pool. The retry pattern helps an application to handle any anticipated, temporary failure whenever it tries to connect to a service or any network resource by transparently retrying an operation that has previously failed due to some criteria. Instead of waiting, it rather does a fixed number of retries.

Client-side load balancing or queue-based load leveling pattern

We saw client-side load balancing in `Chapter 6`, *Service Registry and Discovery*. It involves having the client look up all of a service's individual instances from any service discovery agent (Eureka/Consul) and then caching the location of available service instances. Whenever any further request comes, the client-side load balancer will return a location from the pool of service locations it is maintained at the client-side. Locations are periodically refreshed based on some interval. If the client-side load balancer detects a problem in any service location, it removes it from the pool and prevents any further requests from hitting that service. For example, Netflix Ribbon. Another resiliency approach includes adding a queue that acts as a buffer between any task and/or service that it invokes so as to smoothly handle any intermittent loads and prevent loss of data.

Circuit breaker pattern

We already saw this pattern in `Chapter 1`, *Debunking Microservices*. Let's quickly recall that. Whenever we have a circuit breaker installed and a remote service is being called, the circuit breaker monitors the call. If calls are taking too long, the circuit breaker will kill the call and make the circuit open, making it impossible to allow any further calls. This is the concept of fail fast, recover fast.

The fallback and compensating transaction pattern

In this pattern, whenever a remote service call fails, rather than generating an exception, the consumer will try to carry out an alternative way to do that action. Ways to achieve this usually include looking for data from an alternate data source (let's say cache) or queuing user's input for future processing. Users will be notified that their requests will be addressed later on and if all routes fail the system tries to compensate whatever actions that have been processed. Some common approaches to fallback that we use are (as highlighted by Netflix):

- **Cache**: Get data from local or remote cache if the real-time dependency is missing, periodically refresh cache data to avoid stale data
- **Eventual Consistency**: Persist data in queues to be processed further when service is available

- **Stubbed Data**: Keep default values and use those when personalized or service responses are not available
- **Empty Response**: Return null or empty list

Now, let's look at some practical case studies to handle failures and prevent them from cascading or causing a ripple effect.

Case Study – The NetFlix Stack

In this case study we are going to embrace the Netflix stack and adopt it in our microservices. Since the beginning in time we heard : polyglot development environment. We are going to do the same here. In this section we will set up API Gateway using ZUUL, add auto discovery using Java and Typescript. The user will not know which request actually hit, as he is only going to access the Gateway. The first part of the case study deals with Introducing Zuul, Eureka and registering some services in it and how communication occurs via central Gateway. The next part will deal with more significant things such as how to deal with load balancing, security, etc. So let's get started. You can follow along with the example in `Chapter 7/netflix` cloud folder. We don't reinvent the wheel until and unless it is very much necessary. Lets leverage things the most we can. The following case study supports and encourages polyglot architecture. So let's get moving.

Part A – Zuul and Polyglot Environment

Let's have a look at the following steps:

1. First off we need is a gateway (`Chapter 5`, *Understanding API Gateway*) and service registry and discovery (`Chapter 6`, *Service Registry and Discovery*) solution. We will leverage Zuul and Eureka from the Netflix OSS.

2. First off we need a Eureka server, copy the source from `Chapter-6/eureka/eureka-server` to a new folder or follow the steps from `Chapter 6`, *Service Registry and Discovery*, in the Eureka section to create a new server which would run on JVM.

3. Doing nothing fancy, just add annotations `@EnableEurekaServer` and `@SpringBootApplication` at relevant places—`DemoServiceDiscoveryApplication.java`.

4. Configure properties like port number, health check in the `application.properties` file by adding the following:

```
eureka:
  instance:
    leaseRenewalIntervalInSeconds: 1
    leaseExpirationDurationInSeconds: 2
  client:
    serviceUrl:
      defaultZone: http://127.0.0.1:8761/eureka/
    registerWithEureka: false
    fetchRegistry: true
  healthcheck:
    enabled: true
  server:
    port: 8761
```

5. Run the Eureka server by the following command:

```
mvn clean install && java -jar target\demo-service-
discovery-0.0.1-SNAPSHOT.jar
```

You should be able to see Eureka server up and running in port 8761.

6. Next up is Zuul or our API Gateway. Zuul will act as routing point for any service requests as well as it will be in constant touch with Eureka Server. We will enable auto registration of service with Zuul, that is, if any service registers or deregisters we won't have to restart Zuul. Having our Gateway in JVM rather than Node.js will also give a significant durable boost.

7. Open `https://start.spring.io/` and generate project by adding Zuul and Eureka discovery as dependency. (You can find `zuuul-server` under `Chapter 7/netflix cloud`).

8. Open `NetflixOsssApplication` and add the following annotations on top of it.

```
@SpringBootApplication
@EnableDiscoveryClient
@EnableZuulProxy
public class NetflixOsssApplication { ...}
```

9. Next up we will configure our Zuul server with application level properties:

```
server.port=8762
spring.application.name=zuul-server
eureka.instance.preferIpAddress=true
eureka.client.registerWithEureka=true
eureka.client.fetchRegistry=true
eureka.serviceurl.defaultzone=http://localhost:9091/eureka/
```

10. Run the application by `mvn clean install && java -jar target\netflix-osss-0.0.1-SNAPSHOT.jar`

11. You should be able to see your Zuul server registered in Eureka dashboard meaning that Zuul has run up and successfully.

12. Next up is we create a service in Node.js and Java and register it in Eureka, as Zuul has Auto registration enabled, our services will be directly routed without any other configurations. Wow!

13. So first let's create a Node.js microservice. Register your microservice with Eureka by adding following code in `Application.ts` (place where Express is initialized):

```
let client=new Eureka({
    instance: {
        instanceId:'hello-world-chapter-6',
        app: 'hello-world-chapter-6',
        //other attributes
    }, vipAddress: 'hello-world-chapter-6',
    eureka: {
        host: 'localhost',
        port: 8761,
        servicePath: '/eureka/apps/',
    }
});
```

 We did nothing new, this is same code we had in `Chapter 6`, *Service Registry and Discovery*. Just remember that `instanceId`, `vipAddress` should be same.

14. Now run the service by `npm start`. It will open in port `3001`, but our Zuul server is listening at port `8762`. So hit the URL `http://localhost:8762/hello-world-chapter-6` where `hello-world-chapter-6` is the `vipAddress` or the application name. You will be able to see the same output. This confirms our working of Zuul server.

15. To further understand microservices, I have added a microservice (`http://localhost:8080/product`) in Java (nothing fancy, just a GET call, check folder `java-microservice`). After registering microservice which runs at port `8080`, when i check via my gateway (`http://localhost:8762/java-microservice-producer/product`) it works like a charm.

 Another feasible option for us includes using Netflix Sidecar. 14. Let's take a break and pat yourself. We have achieved auto registration/deregistration which can handle service in any language. We have created a polyglot environment.

Part B – Zuul, Load balancing and failure resiliency

Whoa!! *Part A* was awesome. We will go on the same track. The next part which comes in our plate is, what will happen when there is heavy traffic. In this part we will see how to leverage Zuul which has in built Netflix Ribbon support to load balance the requests without much huss or fuss. Whenever a request come to Zuul, it pick up one of the available locations it finds and forwards the service request to the actual service instance present there. The whole process of caching the location of instances and periodically refreshing it and
forwarding the request to actual location is given out of the box without any configurations needed. Behind the scenes Zuul uses Eureka to administer the routing. Furthermore we will be seeing circuit breaker in this example and configure it in Hystrix dashboard to see real time analytics. In this section we will configure circuit breaker and send those streams to Hystrix. So let us get started. You can follow along the example at `Chapter 7/ hystrix`:

1. In extracted source grab the `standalone-hystrix-dashboard-all.jar` and hit the `java -jar standalone-hystrix-dashboard-all.jar` command. This will open up Hystrix dashboard in port `7979`. Verify URL `http://localhost:7979/hystrix-dashboard` to check:

2. Time to write a simple program which will trip open a circuit at some time. We will be leveraging opossum module (https://www.npmjs.com/package/opossum) to trip open a circuit. Install the opossum module by the npm install opossum --save command and write down its custom types as they are not available yet.

3. We would write a simple logic. We will initialize a number, if it reaches threshold, then the circuit would be broken—open state and our fallback function will hit. Let's do the needful.

4. Let's define our variables:

```
private baseline:number;
private delay:number;
private circuitBreakerOptions = {
    maxFailures: 5,
    timeout: 5000,
    resetTimeout: 10000, //there should be 5 failures
    name: 'customName',
    group: 'customGroupName'
};
```

5. We start with count 20 and use two variables to compare in time:

```
this.baseline=20;
 this.delay = this.baseline;
```

6. We define `circuitBreaker` and instruct our express app to use it:

```
import * as circuitBreaker from 'opossum';
    const circuit = circuitBreaker(this.flakeFunction,
    this.circuitBreakerOptions);
    circuit.fallback(this.fallback);
    this.app.use('/hystrix.stream',
    hystrixStream(circuitBreaker));
    this.app.use('/', (request:any, response:any) => {
        circuit.fire().then((result:any) => {
            response.send(result);
        }).catch((err:any) => {
            response.send(err);
        });
    });
});
```

7. We define a function which increases over time, until it trips open. And we define a fall back function like Oops! Service down:

```
flakeFunction= () => {
    return new Promise((resolve, reject) => {
        if (this.delay > 1000) {
            return reject(new Error('Flakey Service is
Flakey'));
        }
        setTimeout(() => {
            console.log('replying with flakey response
            after delay of ', this.delay);
            resolve(`Sending flakey service. Current Delay at
              ${this.delay}`);
            this.delay *= 2;
        }, this.delay);
    });
}
callingSetTimeOut(){
    setInterval(() => {
        if (this.delay !== this.baseline) {
            this.delay = this.baseline;
            console.log('resetting flakey service delay',
            this.delay);
        }
    }, 20000);
}
fallback () => { return 'Service Fallback'; }
```

8. That's it! Open up Hystrix, enter URL `http://localhost:3000/hystrix.stream` in Hystrix streams, and you will be able to see live monitoring of the circuit:

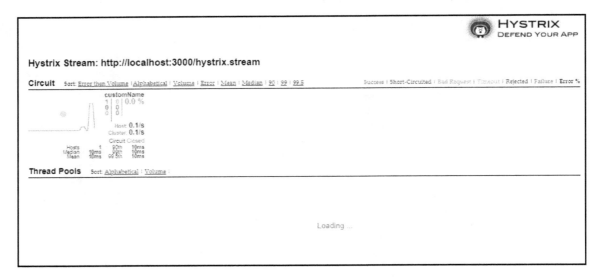

Once it reaches the peak stage, it will trip open:

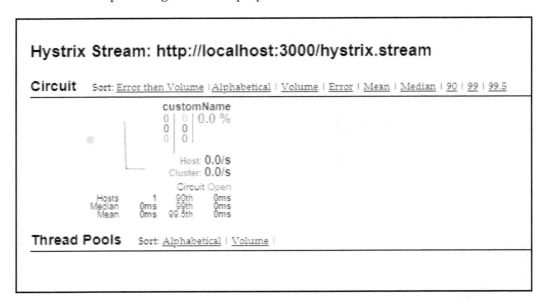

After preconfigured time, it will again be closed state and ready to serve requests. A full detailed API can be found here `https://www.npmjs.com/package/opossum`.

Message queues and brokers

A message queue is an answer for problem of application to application communication. This communication occurs regardless of where my application or my data is, whether I am on same server, separate server, server with different OS or anything similar. Message queuing is build for scenarios such as a task list or work queue. A message queue solves the problem by passing and sending data via queues. Application then make use of information in the messages to interact further. The platform provided is secured and reliable. Whereas a Message broker is build to extend the functionality of message queue and it is able to understand the content of each message which moves through out the broker. A set of operations defined on each message are processed. Message processing nodes which are packaged along with message broker are able to understand messages from various sources such as JMS, HTTP, and files. In this section we will explore message bus and message brokers in detail. Popular message brokers include Kakfa, RabbitMQ, Redis, and NSQ. We will see Apache Kakfa in much detail in the next section which is a advanced version of messaging queues.

Introduction to pub/sub pattern

Just as message queuing, pub-sub (publish-subscribe) pattern moves information from producer to a consumer. However the major difference here is this pattern allows multiple consumers to receive each message in a topic. It ensures that the consumer receives messages in a topic in exact same order in which it was received in the messaging system. This pattern can be better understood by taking a real life scenario. Consider a stock market. It is used by large number of people and applications, all of whom should be send messages real time and just the exact sequence of prices. There is a huge difference between a stock going up to down and stock going down to up. Lets see an example Apache Kafka is one of the shining solution when it comes to pub sub pattern. As per docs of Apache Kafka—Kafka is a distributed, partitioned, replicated commit log service. It provides the functionality of a messaging system, but with a unique design.

Kafka is a streaming platform that allows applications to get and take messages. It is used for making real time data pipeline streaming apps. Let's get acquainted with Kafka terminology:

- Producers are someone who send data to Kafka.
- Consumers are someone who read data from Kafka.
- Data is send in the form of record. Each record is associated with a topic. A topic has a category and it consists of a key, a value and a timestamp.
- Consumers usually subscribe to given topics and get a stream of records and they are alerted whenever a new record comes.
- If a consumer goes down, they can restart streaming by tracking the last offset. Order of messages is guaranteed.

We will commence this case study with three phases:

1. Install Kakfa Locally:
    1. To setup Kakfa locally, download the bundle and extract it to a location of choice. Once extracted we need to setup Zookeeper. To do so start `zookeeper` by the following command—`bin\windows\zookeeper-server-start.bat config\zookeeper.properties`. Java 8 is essential for this case study. Since I am working on windows for this example, my commands has `Windows` folder in it. Be sure to be aware about the `.sh` and the `.bat` difference.

       2. Next we will start the Kakfa server. Hit the the following command—`bin\windows\kafka-server-start.bat config\server.properties`.

       3. We will create a topic named offers with a single partition and only one replica—`bin\windows\kafka-topics.bat --create --zookeeper localhost:2181 --replication-factor 1 --partitions 1 --topic offers`. You will get a prompt **Created topic offers**. To see the topic we can hit `bin\windows\kafka-topics.bat --list --zookeeper localhost:2181`.

       4. Kakfa is up and running on `localhost:2181`. We can even create topics via our broker or Node.js client.

2. Creating a Kafka producer
    1. We will leverage `kakfa-node` module (https://www.npmjs.com/ package/kafka-node). As per need we can either setup a separate service or integrate in existing application service.
    2. Right now we will just write two seperate files in two different projects to test out our application.
    3. You can check `Chapter-8/kakfka/node-producer` to check the source:

```
const client = new
kafka.Client("http://localhost:2181", "kakfka-client",
{
    sessionTimeout: 300,
    spinDelay: 100,
    retries: 2
});
const producer = new kafka.HighLevelProducer(client);
producer.on("ready", function() {
    console.log("Kafka Producer is ready.");
});
// For this demo we just log producer errors
producer.on("error", function(error:any) {
    console.error(error);
});
const KafkaService = {
    sendRecord: ({ type, userId, sessionId, data
}:any,
        callback = () => {}) => {
        if (!userId) {
            return callback(new Error(`A userId
                has to be provided.`));
        }
        const event = {
            id: uuid.v4(),
            timestamp: Date.now(),
            userId: userId,
            sessionId: sessionId,
            type: type,
            data: data
        };
        const buffer:any = new
          Buffer.from(JSON.stringify(event));
        // Create a new payload
        const record = [
        {
            topic: "offers",
```

```
                    messages: buffer,
                    attributes: 1
                }
                ];
                //Send record to Kafka and log result/error
                producer.send(record, callback);
            }
        };
```

3. You can bind the on message event like this. Through the same module we can create client who is going to listen on message of offers and process event accordingly:

```
const consumer = new kafka.HighLevelConsumer(client, topics,
options);
consumer.on("message", function(message:any) {
    // Read string into a buffer.
    var buf = new Buffer(message.value, "binary");
    var decodedMessage = JSON.parse(buf.toString());
    //Events is a Sequelize Model Object.
    return Events.create({
        id: decodedMessage.id,
        type: decodedMessage.type,
        userId: decodedMessage.userId,
        sessionId: decodedMessage.sessionId,
        data: JSON.stringify(decodedMessage.data),
        createdAt: new Date()
    });
});
```

Kafka is a powerful player which can be used in variety of things where we actually need real time data processing. The pub/sub pattern is a great way to achieve event driven communication.

Sharing dependencies

Microservices are great when it comes to building scalable code bases with independent deployments, separating concerns, better resilience, polyglot technologies and better modularity, reusability, and development life cycle. However, modularity and reusability come at a cost. More modularity and reusability may often result in high coupling or code duplications. Having many different services attached to the same shared library will soon lead us back to square one and we will end up with monolithic hell.

In this section, we are going to see how to overcome this hell. We will see some options with practical implementations and understand the sharing code and common code process. So let's get started.

The problem and solution

Sharing code between microservices is always tricky. We need to make sure that a common dependency does not break our microservices freedom. The major goals that we want to achieve while sharing code are:

- Share common code among our microservices, while making sure that our code is **Don't Repeat Yourself (DRY)**—it is a coding principle with the main aim to reduce any repetition of code
- Avoid tight coupling through any common shared library, as it eliminates the freedom of microservices
- Enable simple changes in order to sync the code we can share between our microservices

Microservices are something that introduce code duplications. Creating an npm package with a new code base for any such business use case is highly impractical as it will generate a lot of overhead to make it harder to maintain any code changes.

We are going to use **bit** (https://bitsrc.io/) to solve our dependency problem and to achieve our goals. Bit operates on the philosophy that components are the building blocks, you are the architect. Using bit, we don't have to create a new repository or add packages to share code instead of duplicating it. You just need to define reusable parts of any existing microservices and share them to other microservices as any package or tracked source code. This way, we can easily make parts of any service reusable without modifying any single line of code and not introduce tight coupling among services. The major advantage of bit is that it gives us the flexibility to make the changes to code that are shared with any other service, thus allowing us to develop and modify the code from anywhere in our microservice ecosystem.

Getting started with bit

Coupling microservices via common libraries is very bad. Bit promotes building components. We simply isolate and sync any reusable code and let bit handle how to isolate and track source code among the projects. This can still be installed with NPM and make changes from any end. Let's say you are making some great system with top-notch functionalities that are common everywhere. You want to share code among these services. You can follow along with the code inside the `bit-code-sharing` folder in Chapter 7, *Service State and Interservice Communication*:

1. Bit would be installed as a global module. Install `bit` by typing the following:

   ```
   npm install bit-bin -g
   ```

2. For this example, check out `demo-microservice`, which has common utilities such as fetching from the cache, common logging utility, and so on. We want these functionalities everywhere. That's where we are going to use `bit` to make our file `common/logging.ts` available everywhere.

3. Time to initialize `bit` and tell `bit` to add `logging.ts` in the tracking list. Open up `demo-microservice` in the Terminal and type the `bit init` command. This will create a `bit.json` file.

4. Next, we will tell `bit` to start tracking the `common` folder. Hit the following command in Terminal:

   ```
   bit add src/common/*
   ```

   Here we used * as a global pattern so we can track multiple components on the same path. It will track all the components inside the `common` folder and you should be able to see a message tracking two new components.

5. Bit components are added to our bit tracking list. We can simply hit `bit status` to check the current status of bit in our microservices. It will show two components under the **New Components** section.

6. Next, we will add build and test environments so we don't introduce any abnormalities in our ecosystem before sharing the component. First off is our build environment. The build environment is essentially a build task that is used by bit to run and compile the component, since our file is written in TypeScript. To import dependencies you need to create an account at `https://bitsrc.io` and sign up for the public tier.

7. Import the TypeScript compiler by adding the following line:

```
bit import bit.envs/compilers/typescript -c
```

You will need to enter the user credentials for the account you just made. Once installed, we will go with a public scope as of now.

8. Hit the command `bit build` to see the `distribution` folder with our generated files. You can write tests similarly to check whether unit test cases pass or not. Bit has support in-built for mocha and jest. We will just create a `hello-world` test right now. We need to specify to bit for what component, which would be the `test` file explicitly. So let's untrack previously added files, as we need to pass on our spec files:

```
bit untrack --all
```

9. Create a `test` folder inside `src` and install testing libraries by hitting the following command:

```
npm install mocha chai @types/mocha @types/chai --save
```

10. Create `logging.spec.ts` inside the `tests` folder and add the following code. Similarly, create `cacheReader.spec.ts`:

```
import {expect} from 'chai';
describe("hello world mocha test service", function(){
    it("should create the user with the correct name", ()=>{
        let helloDef=()=>'hello world';
        let helloRes=helloDef();
        expect(helloRes).to.equal('hello world');
    });});
```

 We will see detailed testing concepts in `Chapter 8`, *Testing, Debugging, and Documenting*.

11. To tell `bit` about our testing strategy, hit the following commands:

```
bit import bit.envs/testers/mocha --tester
bit add src/common/cacheReader.ts  --tests
'src/tests/cacheReader.spec.ts'
bit add src/common/logging.ts --tests
'src/tests/logging.spec.ts'
```

12. Hit the command `bit test` and it will print the test results against each component added.

13. We are all done. Time to share our brand new component with the world. First, we will lock a version and isolate it from other components from this project. Hit the following command:

    bit tag --all 1.0.0

    You should be able to see an output stating added components `common/logging@1.0.0` and `common@cache-reader@1.0.0`. When you do a `bit status` you will be able to see that these components have moved from new components to staged components.

14. To share it with other services we export it using `bit export`. We will push it to the remote scope so it can be accessed from anywhere. Go to `http://bitsrc.io/`, log in, and then create a new scope there. Now we will push our code to that scope:

    bit export <username>.<scopename>

    You can log in to your account and then check code in pushed repositories.

15. To import in other workspaces, you can follow these steps:
    1. We need to tell the node that bit is one of our registries from where to download modules. So add the `bit` repository as one of the registries with alias `@bit` in `npm config`:

       npm config set '@bit:registry' https://node.bitsrc.io

    2. To download from any other project, use the following:

       npm i @bit/parthghiya.tsms.common.logging

The command is similar to `npm i <alias we created>/<username>.<scopename>.<username>`. Once installed, you can use it just like any other node module. Check out `chapter 9/bit-code-sharing/consumer` for this.

You can also use `bit import` and other utilities such as making changes, syncing code, and so on.

Sharing code is a must for development and maintenance offers. However, tightly coupling services through shared libraries ruins the point of having microservices. Creating new repositories in NPM for any new common use case is impractical as we have to make many changes. Tools such as bit have the best of both worlds. We can easily share code and also make and sync changes from any end.

The problem of shared data

Having common shared data among microservices is a huge pitfall. Firstly, all the microservice's requirements may not be satisfied with a single database. Also, it increases development time coupling. For example, `InventoryService` will need to coordinate the schema changes with the developers of other services that use the same tables. It also increases runtime coupling. If, for instance, a long-running `ProductCheckOut` service holds a lock on the `ORDER` table, then any other service using that same table will be blocked. Each service must have its own databases and data must not be directly accessible by any other service.

However, there is a huge situation that we need to take care of. The problem of transactions and how to handle them. Even though keeping transaction-related entities in the same database and leveraging database transactions seems the only option, we cannot go with that. Let's see what should we do:

- **Option 1**: If any update happens only in one microservice, then we can leverage an asynchronous messaging/service bus to handle that for us. Service bus will maintain two-way communication so as to ensure business capability is achieved.
- **Option 2**: This is where we want transactional data to be handled. For example, checkout should only occur if payment is done. If not, then it should not proceed further with anything. Either we need to merge the services or we can use transactions (something like Google Spanner for Distributed transactions). We are stuck with two options, either settle via transactions or handle situations accordingly. Let's look at how to handle these scenarios in various ways.

To manage data consistency, one of the most widely used patterns is the saga pattern. Let's understand a practical use case that we have. We have a customers rewards point service that maintains the total allowed points to buy. The application must ensure that new orders must not exceed customers allowed rewards points. Since orders and customers rewards points are in different databases, we must maintain data consistency.

As per the saga pattern, we must implement each business transaction that spans across multiple services. It would be a sequence of local transactions. Each individual transaction updates the database and publishes a message or an event that will trigger the next local transaction in the saga. If the local transaction fails, then saga executes a series of compensating transactions that actually undo changes that were made by the previous transaction. Here are the steps that we will execute in our case. This is one case for maintaining consistency for consistency via events:

- Rewards service creates an order in pending state and publishes a points processed event.
- Customer service receives the event and attempts to block rewards for that order. It publishes a rewards blocked event or a rewards blocked failed event.
- The order service receives the event and changes the state accordingly.

The most predominant patterns used are as follows:

- **State store**: A service records all the state changes in a state store. When any failure occurs, we can query the state store to find and recover any incomplete transactions.
- **Process manager**: A process manager that listens to events generated by any operations and decides on whether to complete the transaction or not.

- **Routing slip**: Another dominant approach is making all operations asynchronous. A service makes a message with two request commands (a debit and shipping instruction) in a slip called a routing slip. This message is passed to the debit service from the routing slip. The debit service executes the first command and fills the routing slip before passing the message to a shipping service that completes the shipping operation. If there is a failure, the message is sent back to error queue, where the service can watch the state and error status to compensate if needs arise. The following diagram describes the same process:

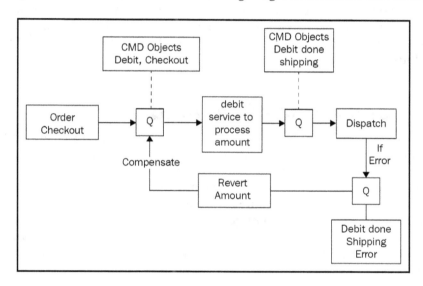

Routing slip

Data sharing in microservices always remains a pain if not handled properly. There are various solutions to distributed transactions across microservices. We saw widely used solutions such as saga and went through various ways to handle data eventual consistency.

Cache

Now we are pretty much in the driver's seat of our microservice development. We have developed microservices, connected them via a gateway, and set up a communication layer between them. Since we have distributed our code into various services, one of the problems that may arise is accessing the much-needed data at the right time. Using in-memory has its own set of challenges that we never want to introduce (for example, you need to introduce load balancers, session replicators, and so on). We need some way to access temporary data across services. This would be our caching mechanism: one service creates and stores data in cache, while others may use it on need and situation basis or fail basis. This is where we will introduce Redis as our cache database. Prominent caching solutions include Redis and Hazelcast.

Blessing and curse of caching

Whenever we are told to optimize the performance aspects of our application, the first thing that comes to mind is caching. Caching can be defined as a process of temporarily holding retrieved or computed data in either data store (server's RAM, a key-value store like Redis) in the hope that future access to this information will be faster. Updating of this information can be triggered or this value can be invalidated after some fixed interval of time. The advantages of caching seem huge at first. Calculating resources once and then fetching from cache (read-efficient resources) avoids frequent network calls and hence it can result in shorter load times, more responsive websites, and a more revenue-generating end user experience.

However, caching is not a one-stop solution. Caching is indeed an effective strategy for static content and for APIs that can tolerate stale data up to some point, but it is not applicable elsewhere in situations as data is very huge and dynamic. For example, consider the inventory of a given product in our shopping cart microservices. This count will change very rapidly for popular products, while it might change for some other products. So determining the right age for the cache is quite a conundrum here. Adding caching introduces other components needed to be managed (such as Redis, Hazelcast, Memcached, and so on). It adds costs, the process of procuring, configuring, integrating, and maintaining. Caching can introduce other dangers too. Sometimes reading from the cache can be slow (cache layer not properly maintained, the cache is within network boundaries, and so on). Maintaining cache with updated deployments is also a huge nightmare.

The following are some of the practices that need to be maintained in order to use cache effectively, that is, to make our service work less:

- Using HTTP standards (standards such as If-modified-Since and Last-Modified response headers).
- Other options include ETag and If-none-match. A unique **Entity tag (ETag)** is generated and sent to service request after the first call, which the client sends in *if-none-match-header*. When the server finds that ETag has not been changed it sends an empty body with a `304 Not Modified` response.
- The HTTP Cache-Control header can be used to help the service to control all caching entities. It has various attributes such as **private** (not allowed to cache the content if this header is included), **no-cache** (force server to resubmit to make a fresh call), **public** (mark any response as cacheable), and **max-age** (maximum time to be cached).

Look at the following diagram to understand some caching scenarios:

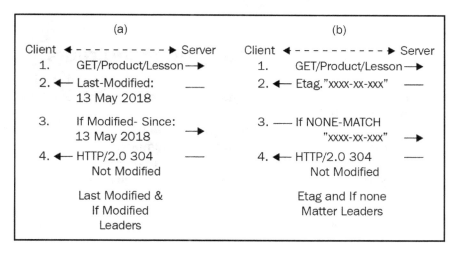

Cache scenarios

Introduction to Redis

Redis is a simple NoSQL database which focuses on simple data structure (key-value pair) with high availability and read efficiency. Redis is open source, in memory data structure store which can be used as database as well as cache or message broker. It has option for built in data structure like strings, hashes, lists, sets, range queries, geospatial indexes,and so on. It has out of the box built in replication, transactions, different levels of disk persistence, and options of high availability and automatic partitioning. We can also add persistent storage as well rather than going for in-memory storage.

Redis when combined with Node.js is like a match made in heaven as Node.js is highly efficient in network I/O. NPM repository has a lot of Redis packages to smoothen our development. The forerunners are `redis` (https://www.npmjs.com/package/redis), `ioredis` (https://www.npmjs.com/package/ioredis) and `hiredis` (https://www.npmjs.com/package/hiredis). The `hiredis` package has lots of performance benefits. To get started with our development we first need to install `redis`. In the next section, we will setup our distributed caching in our project.

Setting up our distributed caching using redis

To understand the caching mechanism let's take a practical example and implement distributed caching. We will evolve around the shopping cart example. As dividing business capabilities in to different services is a good thing, we are dividing our inventory service and checkout service into two different services. So whenever a user adds anything to cart, we will never persist the data, but rather store it temporarily as this ain't permanent or functionality changing data. We would persist such kind of ephemeral data into Redis as its read efficiency is super awesome. Our solution for this problem would be divided in to following steps:

1. First we focus on setting up our `redis` client. Like everything pull out a docker image by `docker pull redis`.
2. Once the image is in our local just hit `docker run --name tsms -d redis`. There are also options for persistence storage volume. You just have to append a parameter `docker run --name tsms -d redis redis-server --appendonly yes`.

3. Verify redis running by command just hit `redis-cli`, you should be able see output pong.

4. Time to pull strings at Node.js. Install the module by adding `npm install redis --save` and `npm install @types/redis --save`.

5. Create a client by `import * as redis from 'redis'; let client=redis.createClient('127.0.0.1', 6379);`.

6. Use Redis just like any other datastore:

```
redis.get(req.userSessionToken + '_cart', (err, cart) => { if
(err)
{
    return next(err);
}
//cart will be array, return the response from cache }
```

7. Similarly you can play with redis as and where required. It can be even used as command library. For detailed documentation please check this link (`https://www.npmjs.com/package/redis`).

We had to replicate the code in each of the three service for Redis. To avoid that in the later section we would be using Bit: a code sharing tool.

In the next section, we are going to see How to version microservices and make our microservices to have fail safe mechanism.

Summary

In this chapter, we looked at collaboration among microservices. There are three kinds of microservice collaborations. Command-based collaboration (where one microservice uses an HTTP POST or PUT to make another microservice to perform any action), query-based collaboration (one microservice leverages an HTTP GET to query state of another service), and event-based collaboration (one microservice exposes an event feed to another microservice that can subscribe by polling the feed constantly for any new events). We saw various collaboration techniques, which included the pub-sub pattern and NextGen communication techniques such as gRPC, Thrift, and so on. We saw communication via service bus and saw how to share code among microservices.

In the next chapter, we are going to look into aspects of testing, monitoring, and documentation. We will look into different kinds of tests that we can do and how to write test cases and execute them before releasing them to production. Next we will look into contract testing using PACT. Then we will move on to debugging and looking into how to leverage debugging and profiling tools to effectively monitor the bottlenecks in our collaboration portal. Finally, we will generate documentation for our microservices using Swagger, which can be read by anyone.

8
Testing, Debugging, and Documenting

So far, we've written some microservice implementations (Chapter 4, *Beginning Your Microservice Journey*); set up a single point of contact, API Gateway (Chapter 5, *Understanding API Gateway*); added a registry where each service can log their status (Chapter 6, *Service Registry and Discovery*); set up collaboration between microservices (Chapter 7, *Service State and Interservice Communication*); and written some implementations of them. The implementations seem fine from a developer's point of view, but these days nothing is accepted without testing. This is the age of behavior-driven development and test-driven development. As we write more and more microservices, developing systems without automated test cases and documentation becomes unmanageable and painful.

This chapter will start with understanding the testing pyramid, with an in-depth description of all the different kinds of tests involved in microservices. We will understand the testing frameworks and understand basic unit testing terminology. We will then learn the art of debugging microservices and then, finally, learn how to document our microservices using Swagger.

This chapter covers the following topics:

- Writing good automated test cases
- Understanding the testing pyramid and applying it to microservices
- Testing microservices from the outside
- The art of debugging microservices
- Documenting microservices using tools such as Swagger

Testing

Testing is a fundamental aspect of any software development. No matter how good the development team is, there is always scope for improvement or something has been left out of their training. Testing is usually a time-consuming activity that does not get the required attention at all. This has led to the prevalence of behavior-driven development, where developers write unit test cases, then write code, and then run a coverage report to know the status of the test cases.

What and how to test

As microservices are totally distributed, the main question that comes to mind is what to test and how to test. First, let's have a quick look at the major characteristics that define microservices and need to be tested:

- **Independent deployment**: Whenever any
  - small or a safe change has been deployed to a microservice, the microservice is ready to be deployed to production. But how do we know whether the change is safe or not? This is where automation test cases and code coverage come into the picture. There are several activities, such as code reviews, code analysis, and backward compatibility design, that can come into play, but testing is the activity that gives full confidence in adapting to change.
  - **Replaceable at will**: A good set of tests always helps to understand whether the new implementation is equivalent to the old implementation or not. Any new implementation should be tested against an equivalent implementation with a normal workflow.
  - **Ownership by a small team**: Microservices are small and focused on an individual team to meet a single business requirement. We can write tests that cover all aspects of microservices.

The process of testing has to be fast and repeatable, and should be automated. The next questions are how to test and what to focus on when testing. Typically, all tests are divided into the following four segments:

- **Understanding users**: The primary mode of testing is where the goal is to discover what users need and what problems they are having.

- **Functionality check**: The goal of this mode of testing is to ensure that the functionality is correct and matches the specifications. It involves activities such as user testing, automated tests, and so on.
- **Preventing undesired changes**: The goal of this test is to prevent undesired changes in the system. Whenever a new change is deployed, several automated tests are run, a code coverage report is generated, and a code coverage level can be decided on.
- **Protection against runtime behavior**: The goal of this test is to check what operational problems the system has. Here, we protect the system by doing stress testing, load testing, and monitoring.

In the next section, we will talk about the testing pyramid in microservices.

The testing pyramid – what to test?

The testing pyramid is a tool to guide us through what kinds of tests can be written and at what levels. Tests at the top of the pyramid indicate fewer tests are needed, whereas more testing is required at the bottom of the pyramid. It illustrates what we should aim for and is shown in the following diagram:

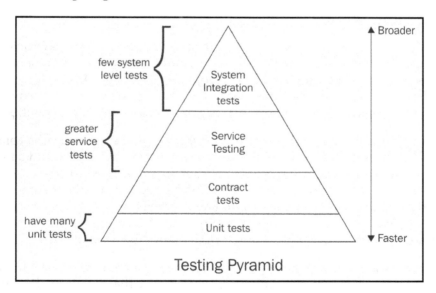

Testing pyramid

The testing pyramid consists of four levels, as explained here:

- **System tests (top level)**: These tests span across the complete distributed microservice system and are usually implemented through the GUI.
- **Service tests (middle level)**: These tests checks the complete execution of the business capability of the system. They check whether a particular business requirement has been fulfilled or not. They are not concerned with how many services behind the scenes are needed to fulfill the requirement.
- **Contract tests (lower level)**: These tests are carried out on the boundary of an external service to verify if meets the contract that is expected by a consuming service.
- **Unit tests (bottom level)**: These are tests that carry out a very small piece of functionality in a microservice. Several lower-level unit tests combine to form a microservice. Unit tests involve only a small aspect inside the microservice, or we can say that they operate at the macroscopic level. For example, our product catalog service has many services. Writing a unit test for it would involve passing a product ID and ensuring that I get the right product.

We will look at all these levels in greater detail in the following sections.

System tests

Sitting at the top of the pyramid are the system tests or E2E tests. They have a very broad scope, or we can say they have a 50,000-foot scope, and they try to cover a lot of things in very few tests. They don't go down the macroscopic level. Whenever a system test fails, it is difficult to identify where the problem is because of its large scope. The test covers the entire distributed system, so the problem can be anywhere, in any component.

An example of a system test in our shopping cart microservices would be the complete checkout process. It uses the web UI of the add to cart system, where we add a number of items, generate an invoice, apply a discount code, and pay using a test credit card. If the test passes, we can assert that the discount code can be applied and payments can be received. If the assertion fails, anything could have caused the failure, such as a wrong price for an item, maybe an extra charge was added, or maybe a payment service failed. To resolve this issue, we need to test all microservices to find the exact culprit.

Covering a huge number of services and a broader area, system tests usually tend to be slow and imprecise (as we can't determine the exact service that is failing). Real service requests are made rather than a mocking system, things are written to real data stores, and even real event feeds are polled to monitor the system.

An important question that comes to mind is regarding the number of system tests that need to be run. System tests, when successful, give a great deal of confidence, but they are also slow and imprecise; we can write system-level tests for only the most important use cases. This can give us coverage of the success paths of all important business capabilities in the system. For complete E2E tests, we can do one of the following:

- Test our API using JSON requests
- Test the UI using Selenium, which emulates clicks on the DOM
- Use behavior-driven development, where use cases are mapped into actions in our application and are later executed on the application that we have built

My recommendation is writing only business facing an important business capabilities system testing, as this exercises much of the fully deployed system and involves utilizing all the components in the ecosystem, such as the load balancer, API Gateway, and so on.

Service tests

These tests are in the middle level of the test pyramid and they focus on interacting with one microservice in its entirety, and in isolation. The collaboration of this microservice with the outside world is replaced by mock JSON. Service-level tests test scenarios, rather than making a single request. They make a sequence of requests that together form a complete picture. These are real HTTP requests and responses, rather than mocked responses.

For example, a service-level test for a credits program can do the following:

1. Send a command to trigger a user in the credits category (the command here follows the CQRS pattern seen in `Chapter 1`, *Debunking Microservices*. CQRS follows a synchronous pattern of communication, so, its testing code would be the same). We send a command to trigger the other service to fulfill our service test criteria.
2. Decide the best loyalty offer based on the user's monthly spending. This can be hardcoded, as it is a different microservice.
3. Record the offer sent to the user, and send back a response to check the functionality of the service.

When all these aspects pass, we can assert that the credits program microservice works successfully and if any one of the functionalities fails, we know for sure that the issue is in the credits program microservice.

Service-level tests are much more precise than system-level tests as they cover only a single microservice. If such a test fails, we can with certainty assert that the problem lies within the microservice, assuming that the API Gateway is not buggy and it delivers the exact same response as written in the mocks. On the other hand, service-level tests are still slow, as they need to interact with the microservice being tested over HTTP and with a real database.

My recommendation is that these tests should be written for the most important viable failure scenarios, keeping in mind that writing service-level tests is expensive as they use all the endpoints in the microservice and involve an event-based subscription.

Contract tests

There is a lot of collaboration going on between microservices in a distributed system. Collaborations need to be implemented as requests from one microservice to another. Any change in an endpoint can break all the microservices calling that particular endpoint. This is where contract tests come into the picture.

When any microservices communicate, the one that makes a request to another has some expectations about how the other microservice will act. This is how the collaboration would work out: the calling microservice expects the called microservice to implement a certain fixed contract. A contract test is a test for the purpose of checking whether the called microservice implements the contract as per the calling microservice's expectation.

Although contract tests are part of the code base of the caller microservice, they also test things in other microservices. As they run against the complete system, it is beneficial to run them against a QA or staging environment and to configure to run contract tests automatically on each deployment. When a contract fails, it implies that we need to update our test doubles or change our code to take in the new changes the contract has made. These tests should be run based on the number of changes in external service. Any failure in a contract test won't break the build in the same way a normal test failure would do if it failed. It's an indicator that the consumer needs to keep up with changes. We need to update the tests and code to bring everything into sync. It will trigger a conversation will the producer service about how that change is affecting others.

My conclusion is that contract tests are very similar to service tests, but the difference is contract tests focus on fulfilling the prerequisites for communicating with a service. Contract tests do not set up mock collaborators and actually make real HTTP requests to the microservice being tested. Therefore, they should be written against each microservice if possible.

Unit tests

These are the tests at the bottom of the test pyramid. These tests also deal with a single microservice, but unlike service tests, they don't focus on the entire microservice, nor do they work over HTTP. Unit tests interact with the parts/units of the microservice being tested directly or through in-memory calls. Testing in unit testing looks exactly like you are making real HTTP requests, except that you are dealing with mocks and playing with assertions. There are usually two kinds of unit testing involved: one that involves making database calls and another that involves playing directly with in-memory calls. A test can be termed a unit test if its scope is a very small piece of functionality, and if the test code and the production code in the microservice run in the same process.

Unit tests have a very narrow scope, making them very precise when identifying the problem. This helps in handling failures and errors effectively. Sometimes, you can have an even narrower scope of microservices by directly instantiating objects and then testing them.

For our credit program, we need several unit tests to test the endpoints and business capabilities. We need to test the user setup with both valid and invalid data. We need tests to read both existing and non-existing users to check our loyalty and monthly benefits.

My recommendation is that we should decide how narrow the narrowest unit test can be. Start with what the test should cover and then gradually add finer details. In general, there are two styles of unit testing that we can use: classic (state-based behavior testing) or mocking (interaction testing supported by mocking actual behavior).

In the following diagram, we can see all the kinds of test applied to a microservice:

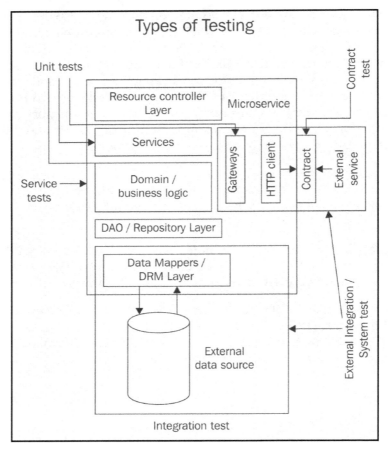

Types of testing

Now that we know about all the kinds of tests needed at the microservice level, it is time to look at our microservice testing frameworks. In the next section, we will look at hands-on implementations of different kinds of testing and carry out the code coverage level of a microservice. Let's get started.

Hands-on testing

It's now time to get our hands dirty with microservice testing frameworks. In this section, we will look at testing basics and then carry on to write some unit tests, contract tests, and service-level tests. Writing tests has great advantages. We are forced to think through breaking the code into sub-functions and writing code based on the principle of single responsibility. Comprehensive test coverage with good tests makes us understand how the application works. In this section, we will be using some famous toolsets: Mocha, Chai, Sinon, and Ava. Ava will be our test runner, Chai will be our assertion library, and Sinon will be our mocking library.

Our libraries and test tool types

Test tools can be divided into various functionalities. In order to get the best out of them, we always use a combination of them. Let's look at the best tools available based on their functionalities:

- Provide a testing base: Mocha, Jasmine, Jest, Cucumber
- Give assertion functions: Chai, Jasmine, Jest, Unexpected
- Generate, display and observe test results: Mocha, Jasmine, Jest, Karma
- Generate and compare snapshots of component and data structures: Jest, Ava
- Provide mocks, spies, and stubs: Sinon, Jasmine, Enzyme, Jest, test double
- Generate code coverage reports: Istanbul, Jest, Blanket
- E2E tests: Casper, Nightwatch

In this section, we will quickly go through Ava, Chai, Mocha, and Sinon, and get to know what they have to offer to us.

 Even though Mocha is a standard library, I have selected Ava because it is very fast compared to Mocha and it runs each test as a separate Node.js process, thereby saving CPU usage and memory.

Chai

This is a fundamental assertion library following TDD/BDD that can be used in conjunction with any other libraries in order to have superior-quality tests. An assertion i

s any statement that has to be fulfilled, or else an error should be thrown and the test should be stopped. This is a very powerful tool to write easy-to-understand test cases.

It provides the following three interfaces to make test cases more readable and powerful:

- `should`
- `expect`
- `assert`

Along with these three interfaces, we can use various natural language words. The full list can be found at `http://www.chaijs.com/api/bdd/`.

> You must be wondering what the difference is between `should` and `expect`. Well, it is a natural question. Although `should` and `expect` do the same thing, the fundamental difference is that the `assert` and `expect` interfaces do not modify `Object.prototype`, while `should` does.

Mocha

One of the most famous and widely used libraries, Mocha follows behavior-driven development testing. Here, the test describes the use case of any service, and it uses assertions from another library to verify the outcome of the executed code. Mocha is a test runner. It is used t

o organize and run tests through `describe` and its operators. Mocha provides various features, such as:

- `beforeEach()`: It is called once before each spec in describe in the test file from which the test runs
- `afterEach()`: It is called once after each spec in describe in the test file
- `before ()`: This runs code prior to any tests
- `after()`: This runs code after all tests have run

Ava

Ava, like Mocha, is a test runner. Ava takes advantage of the parallel and asynchronous nature of Node.js and runs test files in parallel processing through a separate process. As per the stats, switching from Mocha to Ava in `pageres` (a plugin that captures screenshots), brought test time down from 31 seconds to 11 seconds (`https://github.com/avajs/ava/blob/master/readme.md`). It has various options, such as fail fast, live watch (tests are rerun in watch mode when files are changed), storing snapshots, and so on.

Ava is designed for the future and is completely written in ES6. Test run concurrently here with option of going synchronous or asynchronous with the tests. Tests are considered synchronous by default unless they return a promise or an observable. They heavily use async function:

```
import test from 'ava';
const fn = async () => Promise.resolve('typescript-microservices');
test(
  async (t) => {
    t.is(await fn(), 'typescript-microservices');
  });
```

It has a wide range of options such as:

- Reports (beautiful reports showing test coverage)
- Failing fast (stops after the first failed test case)
- Skipping tests
- Futuristic tests

Sinon

Quite often, microservices need to call other microservices, but we don't want to call the actual microservice; we just want to focus on whether the method was called

or not. For this, we have Sinon, a framework that gives us the options of mocks and spies, which fulfill our purpose by providing mock responses or creating a spy service. It provides the following:

- **Stub**: A stub is a dummy object with a prerecorded and specific response.
- **Spy**: A spy is a kind of hybrid between the real object and the mock. Some methods are shadowed by the spy object.
- **Mock**: A mock is a dummy object replacing the actual object.

Istanbul

This is a code coverage tool that covers tracking statements, branches, and functional coverage. The module loader hooks to instrument code on the fly without the need for configuration. It offers multiple report formats, such as HTML, LCOV, and so on. It can also be used on command lines. It can be used as a server-side code coverage tool for Node.js by embedding it as custom middleware.

Contract tests using Pact.js

Each microservice has its own independent implementation; let's say our categories service(product-catalog service). It has an endpoint for fetching a list of categories, getting the list of products associated with those categories, adding any new categories, and so on. Now our shopping cart microservices (consumer) utilizes this service, but at any point in time, the categories microservice (provider) may change.

At any point in time:

- The provider might change the endpoint `/categories/list` to `/categories`
- The provider might change several things in the payload
- The provider might add new mandatory parameters or may introduce a new authentication mechanism
- The provider might remove endpoints that are needed by the consumer

Any of these conditions may lead to a potential catastrophe! These kinds of test would not be handled by unit tests and the traditional approach is to use integration tests. But, however, we can see potential drawbacks of integration tests, such as the following:

- Integration tests are slow. They require setting up integration environments where dependencies for both providers and consumers are fulfilled.
- They are brittle and can fail due to other reasons, such as infrastructure. A failed integration test doesn't necessarily mean a problem with the code. Due to the high scope of integration tests, it becomes very painful to find out the actual problem.

Hence, we need to go for contract tests.

What is consumer-driven contract testing?

Contract testing means that we check our API against a set of expectations (what we define as contracts) which are meant to be fulfilled. This means that we want to check whether, upon receiving any API request call, our API server will return the data we specified in the documentation or not. We often miss out precise information regarding the needs of our API customers. To overcome this problem, consumers can define their set of expectations as mocks, which they use in unit tests, thus creating contracts that they expect us to fulfill. We collect these mocks and check that our provider returns the same or any similar data or not when they get called the same way as mocks are set up, thereby testing the service boundary. This complete approach is called consumer-driven contract testing.

The idea of consumer-driven contracts is just to formalize any or all of the interactions between a consumer and a provider. The consumer creates a contract, which is just an agreement between the consumer and provider on the amount of interaction that will take place between them or simply stating what the consumer expects from the provider. Once the provider has agreed to the contract, both the consumer and provider can take a copy of the contract and use tests to verify that contract violation doesn't occur on any end of the system. The major advantage of these kinds of tests is they can be run independently and locally and they are super fast and can be run without any hassle. Similarly, if a provider has several consumers, we will need to verify several contracts: one for each consumer. This will help us to ensure that changes to the provider do not break any consumer services.

Pact is one of the famous open source frameworks that enable consumer-driven contract testing. There are various implementations for Pact for various platforms, such as Ruby, JVM, and NET. We will be using the JavaScript version Pact JS. So Let's get started. Let's start our journey with Pact.

Introduction to Pact.js

We will be utilizing the `pact` module (`https://www.npmjs.com/package/pact`) available in NPM. The overall process would be as follows, where we would n

need to do operations at both the consumer and the provider levels.

We will be dividing our implementation into two parts. We will set up a provider as well as a client to test whether the services are communicating with one another:

- **On the consumer side:**

   1. We will create a mock web server that will act as a service provider rather than making an actual call. Pact.js provides this functionality out of the box.
   2. For any request that we want to check, we will define the expected response that the mock service needs to return to check whether there are any sudden changes. In Pact language, we call these interactions; that is, for a given request what does the consumer want the provider to return?
   3. We next create unit tests where we will run our service client against the mock provider to check whether the client returns these expected values.
   4. Finally, we will create a pact file containing the consumer expectations as a contract.

- **On the provider side:**

   1. The provider side gets the pact file from the consumer.
   2. It needs to verify that it doesn't violate the expected interactions of the consumer. Pact.js will read the pact file, execute the request for each interaction, and confirm whether the service returns the payload expected by the consumer.
   3. By checking that the provider does not violate any of its consumer's contracts, we can be sure that the latest changes to the provider's code don't break any consumer code.
   4. This way, we can avoid integration testing and still be confident of our system.

After understanding the process, let's now implement it. We will follow the preceding steps regarding the consumer and provider, one at a time. The complete example can be found in `chapter-8/pact-typescript`. Our example project is the categories microservice and we will be playing around with it. So, let's get started:

1. We first create a provider. We will create a service that returns some animals and a specific animal service that gives me an animal on passing an ID.

2. Follow the code from the provider by adding `provider.ts`, `providerService.ts`, `repository.ts` from `packt-typescript/src/provider` and `data.json` from `pact-typescript/data`.

3. Add the following dependencies:

   npm install @pact-foundation/pact --save

4. Now we will create a consumer. The consumer consumes files from providers. We will create a Pact server:

   ```
   const provider = new Pact({
     consumer: "ProfileService",
     provider: "AnimalService",
     port: 8989,
     log: path.resolve(process.cwd(), "logs", "pact.log"),
     dir: path.resolve(process.cwd(), "pacts"),
     logLevel: "INFO",
     spec: 2
   });
   ```

5. We define our expectations next, where we will say:

   ```
   const EXPECTED_BODY = [{..//JSON response here ...//.....}]
   ```

6. Next, we write our usual tests, but before adding the tests, we add these interactions in Pact:

   ```
   describe('and there is a valid listing', () => {
       before((done) => {
         // (2) Start the mock server
         provider.setup()
           // (3) add interactions to the Mock Server,
           //       as many as required
           .then(() => {
               return provider.addInteraction({//define
   interactions here })
                       .then(() => done())
   ```

7. Next, w write the usual tests:

```
// write your test(s)
    it('should give a list for all animals', () => {
  // validate the interactions you've registered
    and expected occurrance
            // this will throw an error if it fails telling you
              what went wrong
});
```

8. Shut down the mock server:

```
after(() => {provider.finalize()})
```

9. Now that we are done on the provider side, we need to verify our provider. Start the `provider` service and in its test file, add the following code:

```
const { Verifier } = require('pact');
let opts = { //pact verifier options};
new Verifier().verifyProvider(opts)
            .then(function () {
                // verification complete.
});
```

Bonus (containerizing pact broker)

In dynamic environments, we need to share Pacts across applications rather than working in a single application. To do so, we will leverage the functionality of the Pact broker. You can simply download it from `https://hub.docker.com/r/dius/pact-broker/`. You can download it through Docker using `docker pull dius/pact-broker`. Once started, you can access the broker with `curl -v http://localhost/9292 #`, which you can visit in your browser too! You can configure it with a database and run a combined `docker-compose.yml` file too. A demo configuration for pact-broker configured with Postgres can be found at `https://github.com/DiUS/pact_broker-docker/blob/master/docker-compose.yml`. Once configured by executing the `docker-compose up` command, the `pact` broker can be accessed on port 80 or port 443 depending on whether SSL is enabled or not.

Revisiting testing key points

Let's recall our key points on testing before moving on to the next section in the book:

- The testing pyramid indicates the number of tests required for each kind of test. Tests at the top of the pyramid should be fewer in number than the level below them.
- Due to their broader scope, system-level tests are meant to be slow and imprecise.
- System-level tests should only be used to provide some test coverage for important business capabilities.
- Service-level tests are faster and more precise then system-level tests, as they have to deal with a reduced scope.
- A practice should be followed to write service-level tests for success and important failure scenarios.
- Contract tests are important, as they verify the assumption one microservice makes about the API and behavior of another microservice.
- Unit tests are meant to be fast and should be kept fast by only including a single unit or using the principle of single responsibility.
- To have wider test coverage, always write service tests first and write unit tests later when it becomes unmanageable to write service tests.
- We use Sinon, Ava, Chai, and Istanbul for testing our microservices.
- To write service level tests:
    - Write mocked endpoints of the microservice under test
    - Write scenarios that interact with the microservice
    - Make assertions both on a response from the microservice and the requests it makes to collaborators
- By using Pact, you can write contract-level tests, thus avoiding integration tests.
- Contract tests are very helpful as they make sure that a microservice adheres to its prefixed contracts and any sudden change in a service does not break any business capabilities.

- **Advanced:** Sometimes you may need to try out snippets of code in a real-time environment, either to reproduce a problem or to try the code in a realistic environment. Telepresence (http://telepresence.io/) is a tool that allows you to swap out running code in Kubernetes.

- **Advanced:** Ambassador (`https://www.getambassador.io/`) is an API Gateway allowing microservices to easily register their public endpoints. It has a variety of options, such as statistics about traffic, monitoring, and so on.
- **Advanced:** Hoverfly (`https://hoverfly.io/`) is a way to achieve microservices virtualization. We can simulate latency and failures in APIs through it.

After going through the testing process, it is now time to solve problems on the fly with debugging. We will learn about debugging and profiling microservices.

Debugging

Debugging is one of the most important aspects in the development of any system. Debugging, or the art of solving problems, is crucial in software development as it helps us to identify issues, profile the system, and identify the culprits responsible for taking down the system. There are some classic definitions of debugging:

> *"Debugging is like solving a murder mystery in which you are the murderer. If debugging is the process of removing bugs, then software development is the process of putting these bugs in it"*

> *– Edsgar Dijkstra.*

Debugging a TypeScript microservice is very similar to debugging any web application. Going for open source free alternatives, we will go for node-inspector, as it also provides very useful profiling tools.

 We already saw debugging through VS Code in `Chapter 2`, *Gearing up for the Journey.*

In the next section, we will learn how to profile and debug our application using node-inspector. We will look at various aspects of remote debugging and how to build a proxy in between a service to debug our microservices. So, let's get started.

Building a proxy in between to debug our microservices

Microservices are distributed based on business capabilities. From the end-user they may seem a single functionality say for instance: buying a product, but behind the scenes, there are many microservices involved, such as the payment service, add to cart service, shipping service, inventory service, and so on. Now, all of these services should not reside inside a single server. They are spread and distributed as per design and infrastructure. Scenarios occur where two servers collaborate with each other and bad behavior may occur at any level if these services are not monitored. It is a very common problem in microservices, which we are going to solve using `http-proxy` and tunneling. We are going to create a very simple example that will log the raw headers of any request. This information can give us valuable information about what is actually going on in the network. This concept is very similar to what we used in the API Gateway. Normally, the API Gateway is a proxy for all requests; it queries the service registry to dynamically fetch the location of a microservice. This proxy layer, our gateway, has various advantages, which we saw in Chapter 5, *Understanding API Gateway*. We will be using the node module `http-proxy` (https://www.npmjs.com/package/http-proxy) and log the request headers there. Initialize one Node.js project, add the `src`, `dist`, and `tsconfig.json` folders, and add the `http-proxy` module and its typings. Then, enter the following code in index.ts to create a proxy server. The full code can be found under the extracted source at `Chapter 8/ts-http-proxy`:

```
export class ProxyServer {
  private proxy: any;
  constructor() {
    this.registerProxyServer();
    this.proxy = httpProxy.createProxyServer({});
    //we are passing zero server options, but we can pass lots of options
such as buffer, target, agent, forward, ssl, etc.
  }
  registerProxyServer(): void {
    http.createServer((req: IncomingMessage, res: ServerResponse) => {
      console.log("===req.rawHeaders====", req.rawHeaders);
      this.proxy.web(req, res, {
        target: 'http://127.0.0.1:3000/
          hello-world'})
      }).listen(4000)
  }}
//after initializing make an object of this class
new ProxyServer();
```

Next, when you hit `localhost:4000`, it will print all the raw headers, which you can check in the source code and see the response of the service.

In the next section, we will have a look at the Chrome debugging extension and profiling tools.

Profiling process

Profiling is a key process these days when it comes to analyzing a service for performance. There are native tools available for Node.js that can profile any running V8 process. These are just snapshots with effective summaries that include statistics on how V8 treats the process when compiling, and the actions and decisions it makes while optimizing the hot code it ran against the V8 engine.

> We can have a v8 log generated in any process simply by passing the `--prof` flag. `prof` stands for a profile. An example is `node --prof index.js`. That won't be much of a readable format. To create a more readable format, run the `node --prof-process <v8.logfilename>.log >` command's profile.

In this section, we will look at how to profile using profile logs, take heap snapshots, and utilize Chrome's CPU profiling for microservices. So, let's get started. You can process the logs of any file using `node --prof <file_name>.js`.

Dumping heap

A heap is a huge memory allocation. When we talk about our case, it is the memory allocated to the V8 process (time to recall how Node.js works—the Event Loop and the memory allocation). By checking the memory usage, you can track down things such as memory leaks or just check which part of the service has the most consumption, based on which you can adjust the code accordingly. We have a very fine npm module (https://github.com/bnoordhuis/node-heapdump), which take a dump that can be used later for inspection. Let's get familiar with reading the dump process and when to take a dump, though the following steps:

1. We install Heap Dump and create a dump ready to be used. Open up any project, and install the heapdump module with:

   ```
   npm install heapdump --save and npm install @types/heapdump --
   save-dev
   ```

2. Next, copy the following lines of code in any process where you want to create the snapshot. I have kept them in Application.ts just as an example. You can follow the code in chapter8/heapdump_demo:

   ```
   import * as heapdump from 'heapdump';
   import * as path from 'path';
   heapdump.writeSnapshot(path.join(__dirname,
   `${Date.now()}.heapsnapshot`),
     (err, filename) => {
       if (err) {
         console.log("failed to create heap snapshot");
       } else {
         console.log("dump written to", filename);
       }
     }
   );
   ```

3. Now, when you run the program, you can find the snapshot in the directory from which we ran the preceding lines of code. You will find output like dump written to /home/parth/chapter 8/heapdump_demo/../<timestamp>.heapsnapshot.

4. We must have something like `<current_date_in_millis>`.heapsnapshot. It will be in a non-readable format, but that's where we will be utilizing Chrome's DevTools. Open Chrome DevTools and go to the **Memory | Select profiling type | Load** option. Open the snapshot file and you will be able to see the following screenshot:

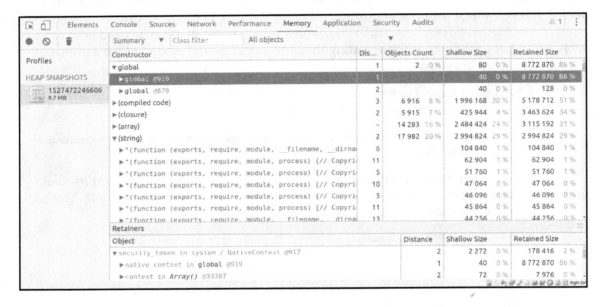

4. Click on **Statistics** and you will be able to see this:

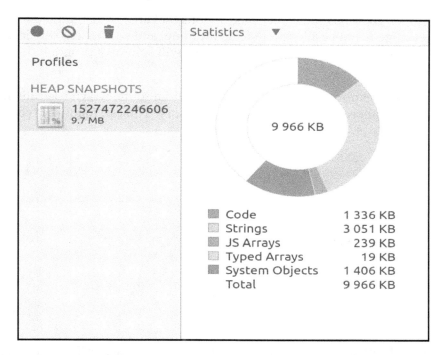

You can go through the following links to get in-depth knowledge about profiling:

- https://developers.google.com/web/tools/chrome-devtools/memory-problems/memory-101h

- ttps://addyosmani.com/blog/taming-the-unicorn-easing-javascript-memory-profiling-in-devtools/

We can periodically take dumps or take dumps in the event of errors, which would be very helpful in order to find the issue in a microservice. Next, we will see how to do CPU profiling.

CPU profiling

Chrome Developer Tools has some very nice options that are not just limited to debugging. We can also leverage memory allocation, CPU profiling, and so on. Let's dig deep into CPU profiling. For the sake of understanding the tool, we will spin up a program that consumes heavy CPU usage:

1. Create any express app and create one random route, which basically iterates 100 times and allocates a buffer 10^8 in the memory. You can follow the code in chapter 8/cpu-profiling-demo:

```
private $alloc(){
  Buffer.alloc(1e8, 'Z');
}

router.get('/check-mem',
  (req, res, next) => {
    let check = 100;
    while (check--) {
      this.$alloc()
    }
    res.status(200).send('I am Done');
  }
)
```

2. The next step is to run the Node.js process in Chrome DevTools. To do so, just add the `--inspect` flag in `node --inspect ./dist/bin/www.js`.

 The Chrome debugging protocol is included in the Node.js core module and we do not need to include it in every project.

3. Open `chrome://inspect` and we will be able to see our process under it. Click on **inspect** and we are ready to debug the Node.js application just like a standard web application.

4. Click on **Profiler**, which is where we will debug the CPU behavior. Click on **Start**, open any tab, and hit `localhost:3000/check-mem`. Come back to our tab. Click on **Stop** when you are able to see **I am done**. You should be able to see something like this like in the figure profiling and profiling detail:

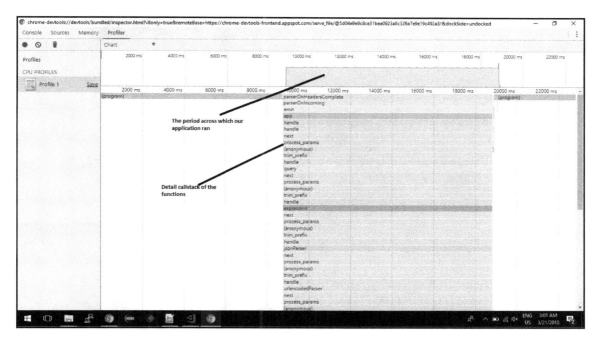

Profiling

5. Now, hover over a single row and you will be able to see a detailed view like this:

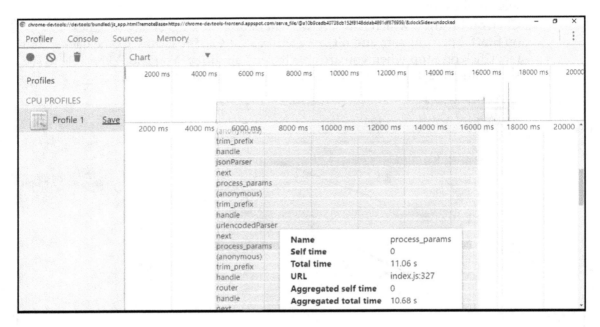

Profiling detail

Live Debugging/Remote Debugging

The penultimate and important feature is to debug a problem live. With the introduction of the inspector protocol inside Node.js, this becomes a piece of cake as all we have to do is create an `--inspect` version of running the process. This will print the URL of the process on which debug is open, something like this:

```
Debugger listening on ws://127.0.0.1:9229/1309f374-
d358-4d41-9878-8448b721ac5c
```

You can install the Chrome extension **Node.js V8 --inspector Manager (NiM)**, from `https://chrome.google.com/webstore/detail/nim-node-inspector-manage/gnhhdgbaldcilmgcpfddgdbkhjohddkj` for debugging remote applications or you can even spawn a process for debugging and specify a port with:

```
node inspect --port=xxxx <file>.js
```

You can find other options here: `https://nodejs.org/en/docs/guides/debugging-getting-started/#command-line-options`. When any process is started with the `--inspect` switch, Node.js listens to it via sockets for diagnostics commands uniquely identified by the host and the port. Each process is assigned a unique UUID for tracking. Node-Inspector also provides an HTTP endpoint to serve metadata about debugger, including its WebSocket URL, UUID, and Chrome DevTools URL. We can get this information by hitting `<host:port>/json/list`.

Debugging is great, but we should make sure that it does not come with a side effect. Debugging means opening up a port, which will have security implications. The following points should be taken care of with utmost precautions:

- Exposing the debug port publicly is not safe
- Local applications running inside have full access to the application inspector
- The same origin policy should be maintained

This concludes our debugging and profiling session. In the next section, we will revisit key points before moving on to documenting.

Key points for debugging

In this section, we saw debugging and core aspects involved in profiling. We learned how to diagnose a leak or observe heap dump memory to analyze a service request. We saw how a proxy can often help, even if it increases a network hop:

- To avoid overloading, we have a module providing as in, code `503` middleware. Refer to `https://github.com/davidmarkclements/overload-protection` for implementation details.
- Chrome Inspector is a very useful tool for debugging Node.js microservices, as it not only provides a debugging interface, but also heap snapshots and CPU profiling.
- VS Code is also a very user-friendly tool.
- Node.js embraced node-inspector and included it in the core module, thus making remote debugging very easy.

Now that we know the fundamental aspects of debugging, let's move on to the final part of making a developer's life easy. Yes, you guessed it correct: proper documentation, which always saves the day not just for the technical team but also non-technical persons.

Documenting

Documenting is a contract between the backend and the frontend that takes care of dependency management between the two sides. If the API changes, the document needs to adapt to it quickly. One of the easiest fails in development can be the lack of visibility or lack of awareness about other people's work. Often, the traditional approach is to write service specification documents or use some static service registries that maintain different things. No matter how hard we try, documentation always goes out of date.

Need of Documentation

Documentation of development and organizational understanding of the system increases developers, skill and speed while dealing with two of the most common challenges that come with microservice adoption—technical and organizational change. The importance of thorough, updated documentation cannot be underestimated. Whenever we ask someone about problems they face while doing anything new, the answer is the same. We all face the same issue: we don't know how this thing works, it's a new black box and the documentation given is worthless.

Poor documentation of dependencies or internal tools makes developer's lives a nightmare and slows down their ability and the production readiness of a service. It wastes countless hours because the only way that remains is re-engineering the system until we have the resolution. Edison did indeed say, *I have found 2000 ways of how not to make the light bulb,* but I would like to spend my time rather on 2000 ways to get more out of me. Poor documentation of a service also hurts the productivity of the developers who are contributing to it.

The goal of production-ready documentation is to make and organize a centralized repository of knowledge about the service. Sharing this piece of information has two aspects: the fundamental parts of the service and where the service contributes to achieving what piece of functionality. Solving these two problems requires standardizing a documentation approach to sharing microservice understanding. We can summarize the following documentation points:

- Any service should have comprehensive and detailed documentation (should include what the service is and to what it is contributing)
- Documentation should be updated regularly (all the new methods and maintained version)
- It should be understood by all and not just the technical team
- Its architecture is reviewed and audited every fixed interval of time

When approaching microservices, the pain increases exponentially as we divide each business capability into a different service. We need a more generic approach to documenting microservices. Swagger is currently the forerunner in documentation.

With Swagger, you will get the following:

- No inconsistent API descriptions anymore. These will be updated with complete contract details and parameter information.
- You won't need to write any more documentation; it will be auto-generated.
- And, of course, there will be no more arguments regarding poor documentation.

This section will explore how to use Swagger, understand its core tools, its advantages, and working implementations. So, let's get started.

Swagger 101

Swagger is a powerful representation of your microservices or, in fact, any RESTful API. Thousands of developers are supporting Swagger in almost every programming language and environment. With a Swagger-enabled environment, we get interactive documentation, client SDK generation, discoverability, and testing.

Swagger is a part of the Open API Initiative (a committee standardizing how REST APIs should be described). It provides a set of tools to describe and document a RESTful API. Swagger, which began as an API documentation tool, can now also generate boilerplate code via **Swagger Codegen** (`https://github.com/wcandillon/swagger-js-codegen`). Swagger has a large ecosystem of tools, but primarily we will be using the following set of tools. We will understand how to integrate Swagger with an existing application or write an API specific to Swagger standards, through which our documentation will be auto-generated. The overall process involved can be understood from the following diagram:

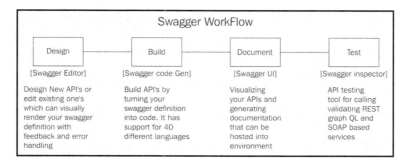

Swagger_workflow

Let us now look at the overall tools involved in the process to get a thorough understanding of all the aspects involved in it.

Swagger Editor and Descriptor

Swagger Descriptor takes a page from design-driven development. Here, we design our endpoints' behavior by describing them in a YML/YAML file or a JSON file. (Of course, as a developer I am too lazy to even write this file and I would prefer this to be autogenerated, which we will look at in a further section.) This is the most important section as it is the contextual information about the service.

Check out `Chapter 8/hello_world_swagger.yaml` to get an idea of the descriptor file.

Key points for Swagger and Descriptor

- Your URL route, parameter, and description is defined inside the `.yaml` file.
- Whether a parameter is required or not, you can pass using the required true, which will validate that parameter while testing it out
- It can also return response codes and their descriptions
- Swagger reads this `.yaml` file to generate its Swagger UI and test services using the Swagger inspector

Swagger Editor

Swagger Editor is an online tool that helps y

ou to edit Swagger API specifications in your browser by previewing the documentation in real time as per Swagger API specifications. This way, we can see how the documentation will look after applying the most recent changes on the fly. The editor has a clean interface and is easy to use with lots of features to design and document various microservices. It is available online at `https://editor2.swagger.io/#!/`. By just writing or importing a `swagger.yaml` file, we can view the Swagger UI in real time.

Let's get our hands dirty with Swagger Editor and Swagger Descriptor:

1. Open up `https://editor2.swagger.io` and enter our previous descriptor (`hello_world_swagger.yaml`).
2. You will be able to see live documentation on the right side:

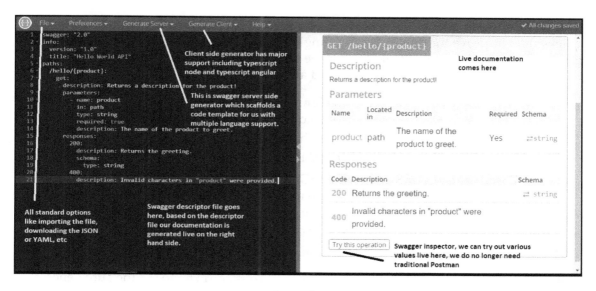

Swagger Editor

3. Try inserting more code in the descriptor file and check out the interactive documentation. Also, try running **Try this operation**. It will give a description of the HTTP request along with all the headers and responses.

Swagger Codegen

Swagger Codegen is a scaffolding engine that gives us the option to generate interactive documentation, API clients, and server stubs from Swagger definitions. The previous options that we saw in Swagger Editor (generating a server and generating a client) resemble the implementation of Swagger Codegen. It has support for a lot of languages.

Client-side scaffolding tool that includes support for languages such as TypeScript Angular, TypeScript Node, JavaScript, Python, HTML, Java, and C#. Server-side scaffolding tool supports languages such as Haskell, Node.js, Go language, and Spring.

Swagger CodeGen (`https://swagger.io/swagger-codegen/`) helps us to build APIs quicker and improve the quality by adhering to OpenAPI-defined specifications. It generates server stubs and client SDKs so we can rather focus on API implementation and business logic rather than code creation and adopt standards:

- **Advantages of Swagger CodeGen**:
  - It generates server code, client code, and documentation
  - It allows for faster changes of API
  - The code generated is open source
- **Disadvantages of Swagger CodeGen**:
  - There is an increase in project complexity by adding extra tools and libraries and the added complexity of managing those
  - It can generate a lot of code that the user might not be able to digest

You can check `Chapter 8/typescript-node-client/api.ts` to see the auto generated code based on our initial Swagger descriptor definition.

Swagger UI

The Swagger UI allows us to visualize a RESTful API. Visualizations are automatically generated from Swagger specifications. The Swagger UI takes in a Swagger descriptor file and creates documentation with the Swagger inspector in the UI. The Swagger UI is what we saw in the preceding screenshot on the right-hand side. Furthermore, this can be given access based on privileges. The Swagger UI is a collection of HTML, JavaScript, andCSS assets that dynamically generate beautiful documentation from a Swagger-compliant API. We will generate documentation for our product catalog microservice and use Swagger UI components in it.

Swagger Inspector

This is a pain-free way to generate documentation based on the OpenAPI specification. Once you have checked **SWAGGER inspector** with its working, then you can create documentation and share it with the world. We can easily autogenerate documentation by selecting the previously tested endpoints from the history and then issuing the command for **CREATE API DEFINITION**. It is much like Postman on the web. You can download Swagger inspector as a Chrome extension. It has these options:

Swagger inspector

Now that we got ourself acquainted with Swagger, let's look at how to use Swagger in our microservices to generate beautiful documentation for us. The next section talks about possible approaches in which we can integrate swagger.

Possible strategies to use Swagger

Swagger is mostly used for documenting services and testing services out. There are two fundamental approaches in implementing Swagger. They are as follows:

- **Top-down or design-first approach:** Here, Swagger Editor is used to create Swagger definitions and then Swagger Code-gen is used to generate code for the client as well as the server. Swagger will be used to design the API and source before any of the code has been written.
- **Bottom-up approach:** Here, for any of the existing APIs, Swagger is used to generate documentation.

We will look at both of the approaches along with the best practices available for us.

Top-down or design-first Approach

Often, generating a valid Swagger file and documentation via just adding a few lines of code seems like a good idea. We have written all the code and then we remember: *Oh my goodness, how will I explain this to others? Will I need to document each and every API?* On the fly generation of documentation at such time simply by adding an annotation seems to be a dream come true in such situations. TSOA (`https://www.npmjs.com/package/tsoa`) is designed on such a principle. Based on TSOA README file, it generates a valid Swagger spec from a written controller and models that include the following. This essentially is a bottom-up approach where we already have an existing REST API and we leverage Swagger to document the existing API.

TSOA generates a valid Swagger `spec` file from controllers and models that include:

- Paths to various REST URLs (example: `Get users :- server_host/users/get_users`)
- Definitions based on TypeScript interfaces (these are the model files or attribute descriptors)
- Parameters types; that is, model properties are marked as required or optionally based on TypeScript syntax (for example, `productDescription?: string` is marked as optional in the Swagger specs)
- jsDoc support for object descriptions (most other metadata can be inferred from TypeScript types)

Like routing-controllers, routes are generated for any middleware of our choice. Options include Express, Hapi, and Koa. Similar to routing-controllers, TSOA has a class validator inbuilt. TSOA minimizes boilerplate code as much as possible and it has plenty of annotations available. You can check the documentation in `npm` for a detailed understanding of the various options available. We will be mainly concerned with the `@Route` annotation, which will generate the Swagger doc for us. In the example, we will use TSOA and generate the documentation.

 Please see extracted source for top-down approach, the example is pretty straight forward strictly adhering to the documentation.

Bottom-up approach

Wow! After going through a top-down approach, it seems like the perfect plan. But what about when we have already developed the project and now we want to generate our documentation. We are left in a conundrum. What should we do? Luckily, we have just the solution. We will leverage `swagger-ui-express` (https://www.npmjs.com/package/swagger-ui-express) to generate the documentation. It has more than 45,000 downloads a week. It is a community-driven package that enables a middleware for your express application, which serves the Swagger UI based on the Swagger documentation file. We will need to add one route, which will host the Swagger UI. Documentation is good and everything is there—whatever we need. So, let's get started. You can follow along with the source code in the `Chapter 8/bottom-up-swagger` folder.

1. Install the module from `npm` as a dependency:

    ```
    npm install swagger-ui-express --save
    ```

2. Next, we will need to add a route, which will host the Swagger UI. We need to generate the Swagger definition and update it on each deployment.

3. We have two options to generate the Swagger documentation. Either we add comments in each of our route handlers or we use the Swagger inspector to test all the REST APIs, club those, and generate a definition file.

4. Whatever route we go for, our objective remains the same: to generate the `swagger.json` file. Going with the first approach, we will use `swagger-jsdoc` (https://www.npmjs.com/package/swagger-jsdoc). Download the module as a dependency with:

    ```
    npm install swagger-jsdoc --save
    ```

5. Let's get started with our configuration. First of all, we need to initialize Swagger JS Doc on Express startup. Create one class, `SwaggerSpec`, and inside it add the following code:

    ```
    export class SwaggerSpec {
      private static swaggerJSON: any;
      constructor() { }
      static setUpSwaggerJSDoc() {
        let swaggerDefinition = {
          info: {
            title: 'Bottom up approach Product Catalog',
            version: '1.0.0',
            description: 'Demonstrating TypeScript microservice
    bottom up approach'
          },
    ```

```
      host: 'localhost:8081',
      basePath: '/'
    };
    let options = {
      swaggerDefinition: swaggerDefinition,
      apis: ['./../service-layer/controllers/*.js']
    }
    this.swaggerJSON = swaggerJSDoc(options);
  }

  static getSwaggerJSON() {
    return this.swaggerJSON;
  }
}
```

Here, we initialized the JSDoc and stored the `swagger.json` inside variable private static `swaggerJSON:any` so it can be used when we want to serve the JSON. We kept the usual configurations inside the `JSDoc` object.

6. Next, on express startup, we need to initialize the `setUpSwaggerJSDoc` method, so we can fill up the JSON at the start of the server.

7. Create a new `Controller`, which gives us `swagger.json` as an HTTP endpoint.

```
@JsonController('/swagger')
export class SwaggerController {
  constructor() { }
  @Get('/swagger.json')
  async swaggerDoc( @Req() req, @Res() res) {
    return SwaggerSpec.getSwaggerJSON();
  }
}
```

8. Hit `http://localhost:8081/swagger/swagger.json` to see the initial Swagger JSON.

9. Now, we need to add JSDoc-style comments to each route to generate the Swagger spec and add comments in YAML to route handlers. Adding appropriate comments like this will populate our `swagger.json`:

```
/**
 * @swagger
 * definitions:
 * Product:
 * properties:
 * name:
 * type:string
 * /products/products-listing:
```

```
 * get:
 * tags:
 * - Products
 * description: Gets all the products
 * produces:
 * - application/json
 * responses:
 * 200:
 * description: An array of products
 * schema:
 * $ref: '#/definitions/Product'
 */
getProductsList() {
 //
}
```

10. Another option is to generate the documentation using Swagger inspector. Now that we are done with Swagger generation, we need to generate the Swagger UI. Add these in `Express.ts` this:

```
app.use('/api-docs', swaggerUi.serve,
swaggerUi.setup(swaggerDocument));
app.use('/api/v1', router);
```

Swagger is a great documentation tool and fulfills all our purposes. Whether we use it from the start or after development, it is a good fit to fulfill our documentation needs. The `./api/v1` file will give you generated Swagger documentation.

Generating a project from a Swagger definition

Until now we were generating swagger definition from our source code. The other way round also holds true. We can easily generate a project from a Swagger definition and type of language (we saw something similar in `Chapter 7`, *Service State and Interservice Communication*. Rings a bell? That is correct. rPC and code generation). Let's download swagger-code-generate and create our project out of it:

1. Check out the updated `hello_world_swagger.yml` in the extracted src `chapter 8/swagger-code-gen`. It has one more added route/endpoint of the API to update the product information.
2. Next step is to download swagger-code-gen from at `https://github.com/swagger-api/swagger-codegen`, so we can even configure it in automation or use it as required, rather than going to the online Swagger editor every time. You can also find swagger-code-gen in the extracted source of this book.

3. Since its a project that runs on JVM, we build the project so we can run it. Hit the command `mvn package` to build the JAR.

4. Next, we will generate the source code:

```
java -jar modules/swagger-codegen-cli/target/swagger-codegen-
cli.jar generate -i ..\hello_world_swagger.yaml -l typescript-
node -o ../typescript-nodejs
```

5. You can explore `typescript-nodejs` inside `chapter-8/swagger-code-gen` to understand the generated structure and play around with it. Similarly, you can go for any other language. Further documentation can be found here `https://github.com/swagger-api/swagger-codegen/blob/master/README.md`.

Swagger is a wonderful utility to generate documentation on-demand. The documentation generated is comprehensible even for product managers or partners, human-readable, and easily adjustable. It makes our lives not only easy, but it makes the API more consumable and manageable, as it adheres to OpenAPI specs. Swagger is widely used by leading companies such as Netflix, Yelp, Twitter, and GitHub. In this section, we saw its varied uses along with its cycle and various approaches.

Summary

In this chapter, we looked at testing, debugging, and documenting. We looked at some fundamental aspects of testing. We looked at the testing pyramid and at how to do unit testing, integration testing, and E2E tests. We looked at contract testing using Pact. Then, we had a look at the debugging and profiling process, which is very helpful in solving critical issues. We saw how to perform debugging in the event of critical failures. Finally, we looked at the documention tool Swagger, which helps to keep central documentation, and we examined strategies to introduce Swagger our microservices.

In the next chapter, we will look at deployment. We will see how to deploy our microservices, get introduced to Docker, and learn about the fundamentals of Docker. We will then see some monitoring tools and logging options. We will integrate ELK stacks for logs.

Deployment, Logging, and Monitoring

9

"Tactics without strategy is the noise before defeat."

- Sun Tzu

We need a very strong deployment strategy before going live to production and starting to earn revenue. Lack of planning always results in an unforeseen emergency, which leads to drastic failures. That's what we are going to do in this chapter. Now that we are done with our development stuff and have added double checks by testing and providing documentation, we are now going to target our *Go Live Phase*. We will see all aspects involved in deployment including current trending terms—continuous integration, continuous delivery, and the new serverless architecture. We will then see the need for logs and how to create a custom centralized logging solution. Moving further, we will look at **Zipkin**—an emerging tool for logging in distributed systems. In the end, we are going to look at monitoring challenges. We will look at two famous tools—**Keymetrics** and **Prometheus**.

This chapter covers the following topics:

- Deployment 101
- Build pipeline
- Introduction to Docker
- Serverless architecture
- Logging 101
- Customized logging using ELK
- Distributed tracing using Zipkin
- Monitoring 101
- Monitoring with tools such as Keymetrics, Prometheus, and Grafana

Deployment

Releasing an application in a production environment with sufficient confidence that it is not going to crash or lose organization money is a developers dream. Even a manual error, such as not loading proper configuration files, can cause huge problems. In this section, we will see how to automate most things and become aware of continuous integration and continuous delivery (CI and CD). Let's get started with understanding the overall build pipeline.

Deciding release plan

While it is good to have confidence, it is bad to have overconfidence. We should always be ready for rolling back the new changes in case of major critical issues while deploying to production. An overall build pipeline is needed as it helps us to plan for the overall process. We will adopt this technique while doing a production build:

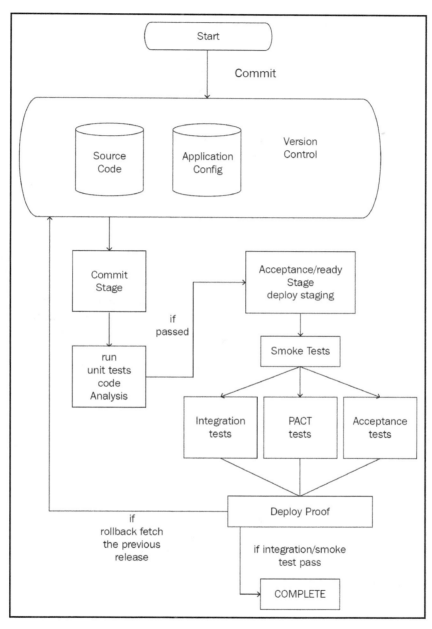

Build pipeline

The overall build process begins by the **Start** block. Whenever any commit occurs, WebHooks (provided by both Bitbucket and GitHub) trigger the build pipeline. Bitbucket has build pipeline tools, too (`https://bitbucket.org/product/features/pipelines`). This build pipeline can be triggered whenever there is a merge in the master branch. Once it comes to the build stage, we first run some code coverage analysis and unit tests. If the test results do not meet required SLAs, we abort the process. If it meets the overall SLAs, we then create an image out of it and build it on the staging server (if we do not have a staging server, we can directly move to the production server). Once you have a docker image ready, you set the environment depending on where you are deploying. Afterwards, some sanity checks are run to make sure that we don't deploy broken code. To run them at all, levels in the pipeline is an excellent idea that minimizes chances of error. Now, once the service meets SLAs, it's now time to deploy it on a real environment. A good practice that I usually follow is production servers should not have version controls. Depending on whatever tool we use (OpenShift, Kubernetes, Docker, and so on) we pass those tools to start the image. We then need to start integration testing, which will include things such as checking whether or not the container is healthy and checking with the service registry and API Gateway whether the service is registered or not. In order to make sure that nothing breaks, we need a rolling update where we deploy new instances and remove old instances one at a time. Our code base should be able to handle old/legacy code and it should be deprecated only after acceptance from every dependent. After completing integration testing, the next task involves running contract testing and acceptance testing. Once these tests have been successfully run, we can move from staging to production or going live. If the pipeline fails, the previous last successful source code is deployed back as part of a rollback strategy.

The entire process should be automated as we are more prone to error. We will look at CI/CD and how they make our life a lot easier. CI/CD promises that we could deploy a feature whenever it is complete and still be pretty confident that it won't break the product. The pipeline we looked at has loads of tasks and stages associated with it. Let's look at the following stages:

- **Dev stage/feature branch**: We start our development by creating feature branches. We keep the master as it is and only keep verified and tested code in the master branch. This way our production is a replica of the master branch and we can do any number of experiments in the development branch. If something fails, we can always revert back to the master branch and discard or delete a branch.

- **Testing stage/QA branch**: Once our development is done, we push the code to the QA branch. Once our development is done, we push the code to the QA branch so it can be tested. Modern development approaches go one step beyond and we go with TDD/BDD. Whenever we push the code to QA we run test cases to get exact code coverage. We run some lint tools, which give us an idea about code quality. After all that, if these tests are successful, then only, do we push the code to the QA branch.

- **Release stage/master branch**: Once our QA is done and our test cases coverage are passed, we push the code to the master in hopes of getting it pushed to production. We again run our test cases and code coverage tools and check whether something has been broken or not. Once successful, we push the code to the production server and run some smoke testing and contract testing.

- **Released/tag**: Once the code is pushed to production and it runs successfully, we create a branch/tag for the release. This helps us to make sure that we can return to this point in the near future.

Doing such processes at each and every stage manually is a cumbersome process. We need automation as humans are prone to error. We need a continuous delivery mechanism where a single commit in my code ensures me that the code deployed is safe for my ecosystem. In the next section, we are going to look at continuous integration and continuous delivery:

- **Continuous integration**: It is the practice of integrating or merging a new feature from other branches to the master and making sure that new changes don't break the existing features. A common CI workflow is that, along with the code, you also write test cases. Then you create a pull request representing the change. Build software that can run tests, check for code coverage, and decide whether the pull request is acceptable or not. Once the **Pull Request** (**PR**) is merged, it goes into the CD portion—that is continuous delivery.

- **Continuous delivery**: It is an approach wherein we aim to deliver a small, testable, and easily deployable piece of code seamlessly at any point in time. CD is highly automatable, and in some tools, it is highly configurable. Such automation helps in quickly distributing components, features, and fixes to customers and gives anyone an exact idea as to how much and what is present in a production environment.

With constant improvement in DevOps and the rise of containers, there is a rise in new automation tools to help with the CI/CD pipeline. These tools integrate with day to day tools, such as code repository management (GitHub can be used with Travis and CircleCI, and Bitbucket can be used with Bitbucket pipelines) to tracking systems such as slack and Jira. Also, a new trend is emerging, which is serverless deployment, where developers just have to worry about their code and deployments and other headaches would be sorted by the providers (for example, Amazon has AWS and Google has GCP functions). In the next section, we are going to look at various available deployment options.

Deployment options

In this section, we will look at some of the famous deployment options available and look at each of their strengths and weaknesses. We will start with the world of containers and look at why everything is dockerized these days. So, let's get started.

Before we get started, let's get acquainted with DevOps 101 so as to understand all terminologies that we will be using.

DevOps 101

In this section, we will look at some basic DevOps fundamentals. We will understand what is a container and what advantages it has. We will see the difference between containers and VM machines.

Containers

As cloud computing advances, the world is seeing the re-entry of containers systems. Containers have become widely adopted due to simplification in technology (Docker follows the same commands as GIT). Containers give private spaces on top of operating systems. This technique is also termed as virtualization in the system. Containers are easy mechanisms to build, package, and run compartmentalized (software residing and limiting to that container only). Containers handle their own filesystem, network information, inbuilt internal processes, OS utilities, and other application configuration. Containers ship multiple software inside it.

Containers have the following advantages:

- Independent
- Lightweight
- Easy to scale
- Easy to move
- Lower license and infrastructure cost
- Automated via DevOps
- Version controlled just like GIT
- Reusable
- Immutable

Containers versus Virtual Machine (VMs)

While a birds eye's view would seem both are stating the same thing, containers and VMs are hugely different. VM's provide hardware virtualization, too, such as number of CPUs, memory storage, and so on. VM is a separate unit along with OS. VMs replicate the full operating system, thus they are heavyweight. VM offers complete isolation to the processes running on it, but it limits the number of VMs that can be spun up as it is heavyweight and resource consuming and it will take effort to maintain it. Unlike VMs, containers share kernels and host systems and thus resource utilization of containers is very less. Containers are lightweight as they provide an isolation layer on top of a host operating system. A developer's life becomes much easier as container images can be made publicly available (there is a huge Docker repository). The lightweight nature of containers helps to automate builds, publish artifact anywhere, download and copy on a need basis, and so on.

Docker and the world of containers

Virtualization is one of the biggest trends right now in DevOps. Virtualization enables us to share hardware across various software instances. Just like microservices supports isolation, Docker provides resources isolation by creating containers. Using a Docker container for microservices makes it possible to package the entire service along with its dependencies within a container and run it on any server. Wow! Gone are the days of installing software in each environment. Docker is an open source project used to pack, ship, and run any application as a lightweight container without much hassle to install everything on a new environment again. Docker containers are both platform and hardware agnostic, making it easy to run a container anywhere, right from a laptop to any server without using any particular language framework or packaging software. Containerization is nowadays referred to as dockerization. We are already dockerized starting from `Chapter 2`, *Gearing up for the Journey*. So let's understand the overall process and concepts involved.

We already saw the installation of Docker in `Chapter 2`, *Gearing up for the Journey*. Now, let's dive deep into understanding Docker.

Docker components

Docker has the following three components:

- **Docker client**: Docker client is a command-line program that actually talks with the Docker daemon residing inside the Docker host through either socket based communication or communication over REST APIs. A Docker client with CLI options is used to build, package, ship, and run any Docker container.
- **Docker host**: Docker host is basically a server-side component that includes a docker daemon, containers, and images:
  - Docker daemon is a server-side component that runs on the host machine and contains the script for building, packaging, running, and distributing Docker containers. Docker daemon exposes RESTful APIs for the Docker client as one of the ways to interact with itself.
  - Along with the Docker daemon, Docker host also includes containers and images running in that particular container. Whatever containers are up and running, Docker host contains a list of those along with options such as starting, stopping, restarting, log files, and so on. Docker images are those that are either built or pulled from public repositories.

- **Docker registry**: The registry is a publicly available repository, just like GitHub. Developers can push their container image there, make it some common library, or use it as version control among a team.

In the following diagram, we can see the overall flow among all three Docker components:

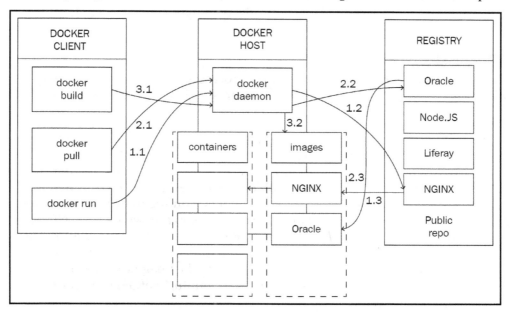

Docker components and flow

The following is a typical Docker flow:

1. Whenever we run any command such as `sudo docker run ubuntu /bin/echo 'hello carbon five!'`, the command goes to a daemon. It tries to search whether there is any existing image with the name Ubuntu. If not it goes to the registry and finds the image there. From there it will download that container image inside the host, create a container, and run the `echo` command. It adds the Ubuntu image in the list of images available inside the docker host.

2. Most of our images would be on top of available images in the Docker Hub repository (`https://hub.docker.com/`). We don't reinvent the wheel until and unless it is very much required. Docker pull issues a command to Docker host to pull out a particular image from the repository and make it available in the list of images in Docker host.

3. The `docker build` command builds Docker images from a Dockerfile and an available context. A build's context is the set of files that are located in the specified PATH or URL mentioned in Dockerfile. The build process can refer to any of the files in the context. For example in our case, we downloaded Node.js and then did `npm install` based on `package.json`. Docker build creates an image and makes it available in the list of images inside Docker host.

Docker concepts

Now that we have understood the core Docker processes, let's move on to understanding various concepts involved in Docker. These concepts will make our lives easy to write Docker files and create our own microservice container image:

- **Docker image**: A Docker image is just a snapshot of the components that make up Docker's business capability. It is a read-only copy of OS libraries, applications, and its dependencies. Once an image is created it will run on any Docker platform without any problems. For example, a Docker image for our microservice would contain all components required to fulfill the business capability achieved by that microservice. In our case, web server (NGINX), Node.js, PM2, and database (NoSQL or SQL) are all configured for runtime. So, when someone who wants to use that microservice or deploy it somewhere, they just need to download the image and run it. The image would contain all layers right from Linux kernel (`bootfs`) to OS (Ubuntu/CentOS) to application environment needs.
- **Docker containers**: A Docker container is just a running instance of a Docker image. You download (or build) or pull a Docker image. It runs in a Docker container. Containers use the kernel of the host operating system on which the image has been run. So they essentially share the host kernel with other containers running on the same host (as seen in the preceding diagram). Docker runtime ensures that containers have their own isolated process environment as well as filesystem and network configurations.
- **Docker Registry**: Docker Registry is just like GitHub, a central place where Docker images are published and downloaded `https://hub.docker.com` is the centrally available public registry provided by Docker. Just like GitHub (a repository providing version control), Docker also provides a public and private images repository that is specific to a needs basis (we can make our repository private). We can create an image and register it to Docker Hub. So, next time when we want the same image on any other machine, we just refer to the repository to pull the image.

- **Dockerfile**: A Dockerfile is a build or a scripting file that contains written instructions on how to build a Docker image. There can be multiple steps documented, starting right from obtaining some public image to building our application on top of it. We already have written Docker files (recall `.Dockerfile` in `Chapter 2`, *Gearing up for the Journey*).

- **Docker Compose**: Compose is a tool provided by Docker to run multi-container Docker applications inside one container. Taking the same example of our product-catalog microservice, we need a MongoDB container as well as a Node.js container. Docker compose is just the tool for that. Docker compose is a three-step process wherein we define the application's environment in Docker file, we make other services run together in the isolated environment through `docker-compose.yml`, and we run the app using `docker-compose up`.

Docker command reference

Now that we have had a look at Docker concepts, let's go through Docker commands so we can add them in our playground:

Command	What does it do
`docker images`	See all Docker images available on my machine.
`docker run <options>` `<docker_image_name>:<version> <operation>`	Launch a Docker image into a container.
`docker ps`	Check whether the Docker container is running or not.
`docker exec -ti <container-id> bash`	See what's inside the Docker image by actually running on bash prompt. Able to use commands such as `ls` and `ps`.
`docker exec <container_id> ifconfig`	Find out the IP address of a Docker container.
`docker build`	Build an image based on instructions in `.DockerFile`.
`docker kill <containername> && docker rm <containername>`	Kill a running Docker container.
`docker rmi <imagename>`	Delete a Docker image from local repository.
`docker ps -q | x args docker kill | xargs docker rm`	Kill all running Docker containers.

Setting up Docker with NGINX, Node.js, and MongoDB

Now that we know fundamental commands, let's write Dockerfile and Docker compose file for a product-catalog service with NGINX in front to handle load balancing, in the same way we wrote `docker compose up` for MongoDB and Node.js in Chapter 4, *Beginning Your Microservice Journey*. You can follow along with the example in `chapter 9/Nginx-node-mongo`, which is just a copy of a product-catalog microservice with NGINX added on top, so that services are only accessed through NGINX. Create a structure like the following:

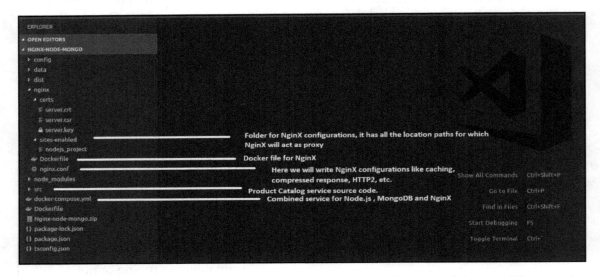

NGINX-mongodb-node.js file structure

Now let's write some rules:

1. We will create Dockerfile for Node.js. It will be the same as what we previously used.

2. We will write Dockerfile for NGINX. We basically tell NGINX to enable rules for applications defined in the `sites-enabled` folder:

```
FROM tutum/nginx
RUN rm /etc/nginx/sites-enabled/default
COPY nginx.conf /etc/nginx.conf
RUN mkdir /etc/nginx/ssl
COPY certs/server.key /etc/nginx/ssl/server.key
COPY certs/server.crt /etc/nginx/ssl/server.crt
ADD sites-enabled/ /etc/nginx/sites-enabled
```

3. Next, we define some hardening rules inside NGINX, so as to take care of our load balancing as well as caching and other needs. We will write our rules in two places—`nodejs_project` and `nginx.conf`. In `nodejs_project` we define all the proxy level settings and the NIGINX server settings. Write the following code inside `nodejs_project`:

```
server {
listen 80;
server_name product-catalog.org;
access_log /var/log/nginx/nodejs_project.log;
charset utf-8;
location / {
proxy_pass http://chapter9-app:8081;
proxy_set_header Host $host;
proxy_set_header X-Real-IP $remote_addr;
proxy_set_header X-Forwarded-For $proxy_add_x_forwarded_for;
}}
```

4. Let's see some of the example rules for configuring NGINX for production grade (hardening our web server). We will write these rules inside `nginx.conf`. For compressing all input and output requests coming to our NGINX server, we use the following code:

```
http {...
gzip on;
gzip_comp_level 6;
gzip_vary on;
gzip_min_length 1000;
gzip_proxied any;
gzip_types text/plain text/html text/css application/json
application/x-javascript text/xml application/xml
application/xml+rss text/javascript;
gzip_buffers 16 8k;
...
}
```

The preceding parameters simply configure any inbound or outbound HTTP requests with those attributes. Say, for instance, that it will gzip the response, gzip all sorts of files, and so on.

5. Whatever resources are exchanged between servers, we have the option to cache those, so each time we don't need to query again. This is caching at the web server layer:

```
http {
proxy_cache_path /var/cache/nginx levels=1:2 keys_zone=one:8m
max_size=3000m inactive=600m;
proxy_temp_path /var/tmp;
}
```

6. Lastly, we create our `docker compose` file to start MongoDB, Node.js, and NGINX to define. Copy the `docker-compose.yml` file from source to execute the build.

7. Open up the Terminal to hit `docker-compose up --build` to see our deployment live in action.

All internal ports will be blocked now. The only accessible port is the default port, which is `80`. Hit the `localhost/products/products/products-listing` URL to see our deployment live in action. Hit the URL again, which will load the response from the cache. See the following screenshot:

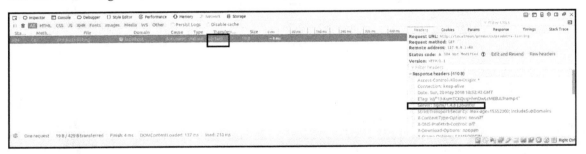

Cache response

Now that we are up and running with a container image that includes the web layer, in the next section we will look at our build pipeline and how WebHooks plays an important role in it.

WebHooks in our build pipeline

WebHooks are something that can be used for binding events in the project whenever something is happening. Say a pull request is merged and we want to immediately trigger a build—WebHooks does our job for that. A WebHook is essentially an HTTP callback. You can configure WebHook in your repository by going to settings and adding WebHook. A typical WebHook screen looks as follows:

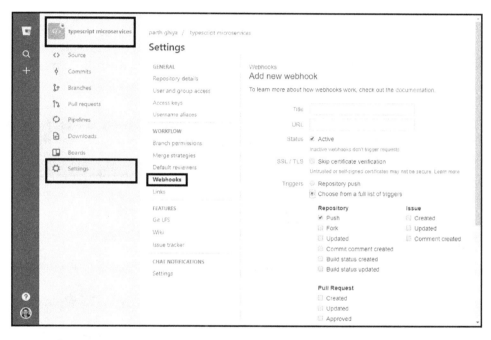

WebHook

As seen in the preceding screenshot, it has various triggers for things such as **Push**, **Fork**, **Updated**, **Pull requests**, **Issues**, and so on. We can set alerts and trigger various actions on the basis of this WebHook.

In the next section, we will see a new trend emerging in microservices development, which is serverless deployment.

 Please check extraced source/pipeline to see end to end pipeline in action.

Serverless architecture

The new trend emerging these days is serverless topology. It does not actually mean serverless or no server. Servers are abstracted from the users and users only focus on development aspects and leave everything else to the vendors. AWS Lambda is an example of a serverless architecture where you just package the microservice as a ZIP and upload it to AWS Lambda. Amazon takes care of other things, including spawning up enough instances to handle bulk service requests.

A Lambda function is a stateless function. It handles the request by invoking AWS services. We are simply billed on a number of hit requests and time taken to serve those requests. Similarly, Google has cloud functions. However, this pattern has the following pros and cons:

- Pros:
  - We just focus on the code and we don't need to worry about low-level infrastructure details. AWS has a built-in gateway to be used with Lambda functions.
  - Extremely elastic architecture. It automatically handles load requests.
  - You pay for each request rather than renting out the entire VM and paying monthly.

- Cons:
  - Few supported languages only. No freedom of polyglot environment.
  - These are always stateless applications. AWS Lambda cannot be used for queue processing like RabbitMQ.
  - If the application doesn't start quickly, serverless architecture is not the fit for us.

That's pretty much about deployment. In the next section, we will look at logging and how to create customized centralized logging solutions.

Logging

Microservices being totally distributed as a single request can trigger multiple requests to other microservices, and it becomes problematic to track what was the root cause of a failure or a breakdown or the overall flow of request across all services.

In this section, we will learn about how to track different Node.js microservices by doing logging the right way. Recall the concepts of logging and types of log, which we saw in `Chapter 4`, *Beginning Your Microservice Journey*. We are going to move ahead in that direction and create a centralized log store. Let's start by understanding our logging requirements in a distributed environment and some of the best practices that we are going to follow to handle distributed logging.

Logging best practices

Once in post development, let's say any issue comes up. We would be completely lost as we are not dealing with a single server. We are dealing with multiple servers and the entire system is constantly moving. Whoa! We need a full proof strategy as we can't just wander here and there, checking each and every service's logs. We are completely clueless as to which microservice runs on which host and which microservice served the request. To open up log files across all containers, grepping the logs and then relating them to all requests is indeed a cumbersome process. If our environment has auto scalability enabled, then debugging an issue becomes exponentially complex as we actually have to find the instance of microservice that served the request.

Here are some of the golden rules for logging in microservices that will make life easier.

Centralizing and externalizing log storage

Microservices are distributed across the ecosystem to ease up development and enable faster development. As microservices run on multiple hosts, it is unwise to have logs at each container or server level. Rather we should send all the generated logs to an external and centralized place from where we can easily get the log information from a single place. This might be any another physical system or any highly available storage option. Some of the famous options are the following:

- **ELK or Elastic stack**: The ELK stack (`https://www.elastic.co/elk-stack`) consists of Elasticsearch (a distributed, full-text scalable search database that allows storing large volumes of datasets), Logstash (it collects log events from multiple types of sources, and transforms it as per need), and Kibana (visualizes log events or anything that is stored in Elasticsearch). Using the ELK stack, we can have centralized logs in Elasticsearch powered by utilities from **Kibana** and **Logstash**.

- **CloudWatch (only if your environment is in AWS)**: Amazon CloudWatch (`https://aws.amazon.com/cloudwatch/`) is a monitoring service for resources and applications that are running on your AWS environment. We can utilize Amazon CloudWatch to collect and track metrics, monitor log files, set some critical alarms, and automatically react to changes in deployments in AWS resources. CloudWatch has the ability to monitor AWS resources, which includes Amazon EC2 instances, DynamoDB tables, RDS DB instances, or any custom metrics that your application generates. It monitors log files of all the applications. It provides system wise visibility into utilizing resources and monitors performance and health.

Structured data in logs

Log messages go beyond just raw messages and should include several things, such as the timestamp; the log level type; the time taken for requests; metadata, such as device type, microservice name, service request name, instance name, filename, line number; and so on, from which we get the right data available in the logs to debug any issues.

Identifiers via correlational IDs

We generate a unique identifier or a correlation ID when we are making the very first service request. The generated unique ID is passed downstream to other calling microservices. That way, we can use the uniquely generated ID coming from the response to get logs specified to any service request. For that, we have a so-called correlation identifier or uniquely generated UUID to pass it to all services that the transaction goes through. To generate a unique ID, NPM has module UUID (`https://www.npmjs.com/package/uuid`).

Log levels and logging mechanisms

Based on different aspects of an application, we need different log levels in our code, along with enough logging statements in code. We will use `winston` (`https://www.npmjs.com/package/winston`), which will have the ability to change log level dynamically. Furthermore, we will use async log appenders so that our thread won't be blocked by log requests. We will leverage **Async Hooks** (`https://nodejs.org/api/async_hooks.html`), which will help us track the life cycle of resources during our process. An Async Hook enables us to tap any life cycle events by registering callbacks to any life cycle events. At resource initialization, we get a unique identifier ID (`asyncId`) and parent identifier ID (`triggerAsyncId`) that created the resource.

Searchable logs

The logs files collected at a single place should be searchable. For example, if we get any UUID, our logging solution should be able to search based on that to find out the request flow. Now, let's look at a custom logging solution that we are going to implement and understand how it will take care of our logging problem:

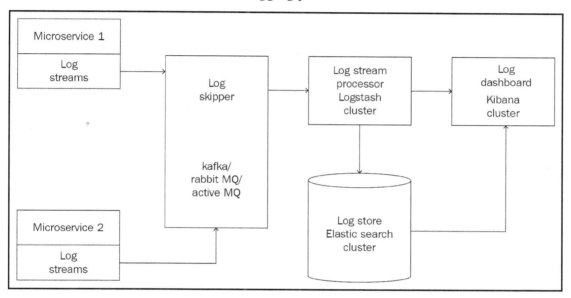

Log custom flow

The diagram explains the core components along with their defined purpose. Let's look at all the components along with their purposes before moving on to the implementation part:

- **Log Dashboard**: It is the UI front piece of our customized central logging solution. We will be using Kibana (`https://www.elastic.co/products/kibana`) on top of Elasticsearch datastore as it provides many out-of-the-box features. We will be able to search indexed logs with whatever parameters we have logged.

- **Log Store**: To facilitate real-time logging and storing huge amount of logs we will use Elasticsearch as the datastore for our customized logging solution. Elasticsearch allows any client to query on any parameters based on text-based indexes. One of the other famous options is using Hadoop's `MapReduce` program for processing logs offline.

- **Log stream processor**: Log stream processors analyze real-time log events for processing quick decision making. For example, if any service is throwing a 404 error continuously, stream processors come in handy in such cases where they are capable of reacting to a specific stream of events. In our case, a stream processor gets data from our queue and processes it on the fly before sending it to Elasticsearch.

- **Log shipper**: Log shippers usually collect log messages, which come from different endpoints and sources. Log shippers send these messages to another set of endpoints or write them to datastores or push them to stream processing endpoints for further real-time processing. We would be using tools such as RabbitMQ and ActiveMQ for processing streams of logs. Now that we have seen the architecture of our custom implementation, in the next section we will see how to implement that in our current application. So, let's get started.

Centralized custom logging solution implementation

In this section, we are going to look at the practical implementation of customized log architecture, which we have seen in the previous section. So, let's commence our journey. As a set of pre-requisites, we will need the following software installed:

- Elasticsearch 6.2.4
- Logstash 6.2.4
- Kibana 6.2.4
- Java 8
- RabbitMQ 3.7.3

Setting up our environment

We talked about quite a number of software in the previous section. We need to make sure that each software is installed properly and up and running on their respective ports. Also, we need to make sure that Kibana knows about our Elasticsearch host and Logstash knows about our Kibana and Elasticsearch host. Let's get started:

1. Download Elasticsearch from: `https://www.elastic.co/downloads/elasticsearch` and extract it in the location of your choice. Once extracted, start your server by `eitherelasticsearch.bat` or `./bin/elasticsearch`. Hit `http://localhost:9200/` and you should be able to see the JSON tagline: **You Know, for Search** along with the Elasticsearch version.

2. Next up is Kibana. Download Kibana from: `https://www.elastic.co/downloads/kibana` and extract it to the location of choice. Then open `<kibana_home>/config/kibana.yml` and add the line `elasticsearch.url: "http://localhost:9200"`. This tells Kibana about Elasticsearch. Then start Kibana from the `bin` folder and navigate to `http://localhost:5601`. You should see the Kibana dashboard.

3. Download Logstash from `https://www.elastic.co/downloads/logstash`. Extract it to the location of your choice. We will check Logstash installation by writing a simple script. Create one file, `logstash-simple.conf`, and write the following code. You can find this snippet in `Chapter 9/logstash-simple.conf`:

   ```
   input { stdin { } }
   output { elasticsearch { hosts => ["localhost:9200"] }
   stdout { codec => rubydebug }}
   ```

   Now hit `logstash -f logstash-simple.conf`.

   You should be able to see Elasticsearch information printed out. This ensures us that our Logstash installation is running perfectly.

4. Next, we need to install RabbitMQ. RabbitMQ is written in Erlang and it requires Erlang installation. Install Erlang and make sure that environment variable `ERLANG_HOME` is set. Then install RabbitMQ. Once installed, start the `rabbitmq` service as follows:

```
rabbitmq-service.bat stop
rabbitmq-service.bat install
rabbitmq-service.bat start
```

5. Now hit the URL `http://localhost:15672`. You should be able to log in using guest/guest credentials, which are by default, and be able to see the RabbitMQ dashboard.

If you are not able to see the server, you probably need to enable the plugin, as follows:

```
rabbitmq-plugins.bat enable rabbitmq_management
rabbitmq_web_mqtt rabbitmq_amqp1_0
```

We have successfully installed RabbitMQ, Logstash, Elasticsearch, and Kibana. Now we can move onto our implementation.

Please check extracted source `/customlogging` to see our solution in action. The solution makes use or previous architecture as explained.

Distributed tracing in Node.js

Distributed tracing is like tracing a particular service request that spans across all of the services that are involved in serving that request. These services construct a graph like they form a tree rooted at the client that starts the initial request. Zipkin provides an instrumentation layer to generate IDs for a service request, based on which we can trace data from all applications by using that ID. In this section, we will look at how to use Zipkin. You can find the complete source at `Chapter 9/Zipkin`:

1. Spin up our first microservice or any single microservice project from `Chapter 4`, *Beginning Your Microservices Journey*. We will add the `zipkin` dependencies to it:

```
npm install zipkin zipkin-context-cls zipkin-instrumentation-
express zipkin-instrumentation-fetch zipkin-transport-http
node-fetch --save
npm install @types/zipkin-context-cls --save-dev
```

2. We now need a Zipkin server. We will configure it to use a Zipkin server along with its defaults and just install its jar. Download the `jar` from `https://search.maven.org/remote_content?g=io.zipkin.java&a=zipkin-server&v=LATEST&c=exec` or you can find it in the extracted source in the `server` folder under `chapter 9/zipkin`. Once downloaded, open the Zipkin server as follows:

```
java -jar zipkin-server-2.7.1-exec.jar
```

The following screenshot shows a Zipkin server:

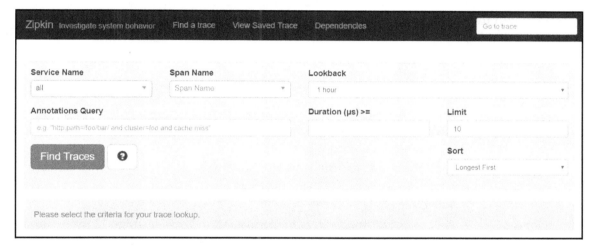

log Zipkin

As seen in the screenshot, the Zipkin server has lots of options, including providing a collector for receiving trace information, storage, and UI options to examine it.

3. Now, we will configure multiple Express servers so as to observe how Zipkin instruments the whole thing. We will first set up Zipkin on a single microservice followed by multiple microservices later on. Our code from the previous chapter adds any product information in our MongoDB database. We will be configuring Zipkin here. We need to tell Zipkin where to send tracing data (that's pretty obvious! This will be our Zipkin server running on 9411) and how to send tracing data (that's the question—Zipkin has three support options HTTP, Kafka, and Fluentd. We will be using HTTP). So basically we send a POST request to the Zipkin server.

4. We need some imports to configure our Zipkin server. Open Express.ts and add the following lines of code:

```
import {Tracer} from 'zipkin';
import {BatchRecorder} from 'zipkin';
import {HttpLogger} from 'zipkin-transport-http';
const CLSContext = require('zipkin-context-cls');
```

- Tracer is used to give information such as where and how to send tracing data. It handles generating traceIds and tells the transport layer when to record what.
- BatchRecorder formats tracing data to be sent to the Zipkin collector.
- HTTPLogger is our HTTP Transport layer. It knows how to post Zipkin data over HTTP.
- CLSContext object refers to Continuation Local Storage. Continuation passing is the pattern where the function calls the next function in a chain of functions with the data it needs. An example of this is Node.js custom middleware layer.

5. We're now putting all the pieces together. Add the following lines of code:

```
const ctxImpl=new CLSContext();
const logRecorder=new BatchRecorder({
logger:new HttpLogger({
endpoint:`http://loclhost:9411/api/v1/spans` }) })
const tracer=new Tracer({ctxImpl:ctxImpl,recorder:logRecorder})
```

This will set up Zipkin essentials along with a tracer that will generate a 64-bit trace ID. Now we need to instrument our Express server.

6. Now, we will tell our `express` application to use `ZipkinMiddleware` in its middleware layer:

```
import {expressMiddleware as zipkinMiddleware} from 'zipkin-
instrumentation-express';
...
this.app.use(zipkinMiddleware({tracer,serviceName:'products-
service'}))
```

The name of service in our case `'products-service'` will actually come in tracing data.

7. Let's hit our service to see what is the actual result. Run the program, make a POST request to `products/add-update-product`, and open up Zipkin. You will be able to see `products-service` (the name of the service under which we registered to Zipkin server) in the **Service Name** dropdown. And when you do a search query you will be able to see something like the following:

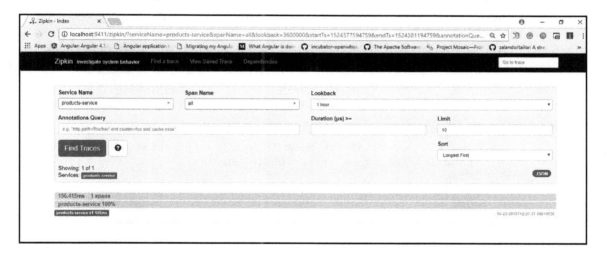

Zipkin service log

This is how it looks when we are dealing with one microservice. You get traces about successful as well as failed service calls here too, as seen in the figure. We want to wrap our head around services that have more than one microservices involved.

For those, who are directly running the code; please ensure that the following lines are commented out in the `ProductsController.ts` let file—`userRes= await this.zipkinFetch('http://localhost:3000/users/user-by-id/ parthghiya');` and `console.log("user-res",userRes.text());`.

8. Let's assume in our case that we have one more microservice involved based on our business capability that plays with owners authenticity. So, whenever a product is added, we want to check whether the owner is an actual user or not.

 We will just create two projects with dummy logic.

9. Create another microservice project with a user and create a GET request with `@Get('/user-by-id/:userId')`, which basically returns whether a user exists or not. We will be calling that microservice from our existing project. You can follow along from `chapter-9/user`.

10. In the existing project, we moved out the configurations of Zipkin to the external file so it can be reused throughout the project. Check out the source code of `ZipkinConfig.ts`

11. In `ProductController.ts`, instantiate a new object of Zipkin instrumentation fetch, as follows:

```
import * as wrapFetch from 'zipkin-instrumentation-fetch';
this.zipkinFetch = wrapFetch(fetch, {
tracer,
serviceName: 'products-service'
});
```

12. Make a fetch request, as follows:

```
let userRes= await
this.zipkinFetch('http://localhost:3000/users/user-by-id/parthg
hiya');
```

13. Open up the Zipkin dashboard and you will be able to see the following:

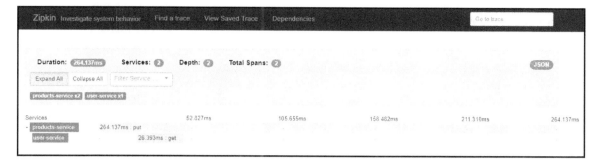

Zipkin combined

The overall report can be viewed by clicking on the request:

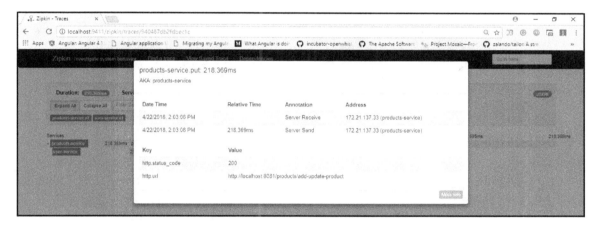

Tracing report

Tracing is an invaluable tool that helps to diagnose problems when they occur by tracing out any request across the entire microservices ecosystem. In the next section, we will look at monitoring microservices.

Monitoring

Microservices are truly distributed systems with a vast technological and deployment topology. Without proper monitoring in place, the operational team may soon run into trouble managing large-scale microservice systems. To add complications to our problem, microservices dynamically change their topologies based on load. This demands a proper monitoring service. In this section, we will learn about the need of monitoring and look at some monitoring tools.

Monitoring 101

Let's start by discussing Monitoring 101. Monitoring, in general, can be defined as a collection of some metrics, predefined **service level agreements (SLAs)**, aggregation, and their validations and adherence to prefixed baseline values. Whenever there is a service level breach, a monitoring tool has to generate an alert and send it across to administrators. In this section, we will look at monitoring to understand the behavior of a system from a user experience point of view, and the challenges of monitoring, and to understand all aspects involved in Node.js monitoring.

Monitoring challenges

Similar to logging issues, the key challenge in monitoring microservices ecosystems is that there are too many dynamic parts. Being totally dynamic, the key challenges in monitoring microservices are as follows:

- Statistics and metrics are distributed across many services, multiple instances, and multiple machines or containers.
- Polyglot environment adds more difficulties. A single monitoring tool does not suffice all the required monitoring options.
- Microservices deployment topologies differ in huge variations. Several parameters such as scalability, auto configuration, circuit breaker, and so on, change the architecture on-demand basis. This makes it impossible to monitor preconfigure servers, instances, or any other monitoring parameters.

In the next section, we are going to look at the next part of monitoring, which is alerting. We cannot alert every time due to errors. We need some definitive rules.

When to alert and when not to alert?

No one is excited to wake up at 3.00 AM in the morning on Sunday. The general rule for alerting can be if something is not stopping customers from using your system and increasing your funds, then the situation is not worth waking up at 3.00 AM. In this section, we will look at some instances and decide when to alert and when not to:

- **Service goes down**: Had it been monolithic, this would surely be a huge blow but, being a good microservice coder, you already have set up multiple instances and clustering. This would impact just a single user who would get functionality back on again service request and would prevent the failure to cascade up. However, if many services go down then this is definitely something worth alerting.

- **Memory leak**: Memory leaks are another painful thing, as only after careful monitoring can we actually find the leak. A good microservice practice suggests setting up the environment so that it should be able to decommission an instance once it surpasses a certain memory threshold. The problem will fix itself on system restart. But if processes are running out of memory quickly then it is something worth alerting.

- **Slow services**: A slow usable service is not worth alerting until or unless it occupies a huge resource pool. A good microservice practice suggests using an async architecture with event-based and queue-based implementations.

- **Increasing 400s and 500s**: If there is an exponential increase in the number of 400s and 500s then there is something fishy worth alerting. 4xx codes usually indicate erroneous services or misconfigured core tools. This is definitely worth alerting.

In the next section, we will get the actual implementation of monitoring tools available in the Node.js community. We will see hands-on examples with those in sections of Keymetrics and Prometheus with Grafana.

Monitoring tools

In this section, we will look at some of the available tools for monitoring and how those tools help us to solve different monitoring challenges. When monitoring a microservice, we are mostly interested in hardware resources and application metrics:

Hardware resources	
Memory utilization metrics	The amount of memory that is consumed by the application, such as RAM utilization, hard disk occupied, and so on.
CPU utilization metrics	How much percentage of total available CPU memory is it using at a given time.

Disk Utilization metrics	The I/O memory in a hard drive, such as swap space, available space, used space, and so on.
Application metrics	
Errors thrown per unit of time	The number of critical errors that are thrown from the application.
Calls made/service occupancy per unit of time	This metric basically tells us about the traffic on a service.
Response time	How much time is being utilized to respond to a service request.
The number of restarts of service	Node.JS being single threaded, this thing should be monitored.

The power of LINUX makes it easy to query hardware metrics. The `/proc` folder in Linux has all the necessary information. Basically, it has a directory for each of the running processes in the system, including kernel processes. Each directory there contains other useful metadata.

When it comes to application metrics it becomes hard to go with some inbuilt tools. Some of the widely used monitoring tools are as follows:

- AppDynamics, Dynatrace, and New Relic are leaders in application performance monitoring. But these are in the commercial segment.
- Cloud vendors come with their own monitoring tools, like AWS uses Amazon Cloudwatch and Google Cloud platform uses Cloud monitoring.
- Loggly, ELK, Splunk, and Trace are top candidates in open source segments.

We will now look at some of the available tools in the Node.js community.

PM2 and keymetrics

We already looked at the power of PM2 and how it helps us solve various issues, such as clustering, keeping Node.js processes running forever, zero downtimes, and so on. PM2 has a monitoring tool, too, that maintains several application metrics. PM2 introduced keymetrics as a complete tool with in-built features, such as the dashboard, optimization process, code manipulation from keymetrics, exception reporting, load balancer, transaction tracing, CPU and memory monitoring, and so on. It is an SAAS-based product with an option of free tier. In this section, we will use the free tier. So, let's get started:

1. The first thing we need to do is to sign up for the free tier. Create an account and once you log in, you will be able to see the main screen. Once registered we will come to a screen where we configure our bucket.

A bucket is a container on which multiple servers and multiple apps are attached. A bucket is something through which keymetrics define the context. For example, our shopping cart microservice has different services (payments, product catalog, inventory, and so on) hosted somewhere, and we could monitor all the servers in one bucket so that everything is easy to access.

2. Once we create our bucket we will get a screen like the following. This screen has all the information and necessary documentation required for getting started with keymetrics:

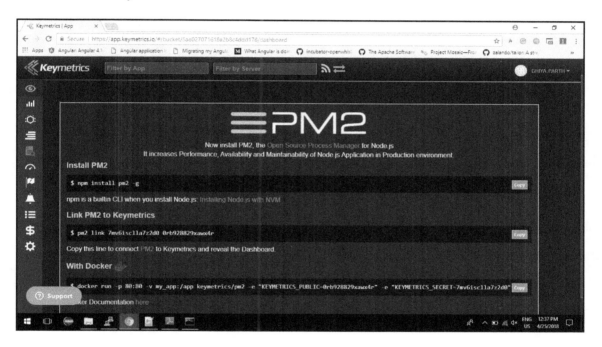

Keymetrics after bucket created

We can see commands for connecting PM2 to keymetrics and Docker with keymetrics, which we will be using further on:

```
pm2 link <your_private_key> <your_public_key>
docker run -p 80:80 -v my_app:/app keymetrics/pm2 -e
"KEYMETRICS_PUBLIC=<your_public_key>" -e
"KEYMETRICS_SECRET=<your_secret_key>"
```

Also as part of the installation, you will need the PM2 monitor. Once PM2 is installed, run the following command:

```
pm2 install pm2-server-monit
```

3. The next step is to configure PM2 to push data in keymetrics. Now, to enable communication between server and keymetrics, the following ports need to be opened: **Ports 80 (TCP out) and 43554 (TCP in/out) must be opened**. PM2 pushes data to port 80 on keymetrics, whereas keymetrics pushes data back on port 43554. Now, we will configure keymetrics in our product-catalog microservice.

4. Make sure that PM2 is installed in your system. If not, just install it as a global module by executing the following command:

```
npm install pm2 -g
```

5. Then link your PM2 with keymetrics by executing the following command:

```
pm2 link 7mv6isclla7z2d0 0rb928829xawx4r
```

6. Once open, just change your `package.json` script to start with PM2 instead of a simple node process. Just add the following script in `package.json`:

```
"start": "npm run clean && npm run build && pm2 start
./dist/index.js",
```

Once started as a PM2 process you should be able to see the process started and the dashboard URL:

PM2 start with keymetrics

7. Head over to keymetrics and you will be able to see the live dashboard:

Keymetrics dashboard

8. It gives us interesting metrics, such as CPU usage, available memory, HTTP average response, available disk memory, errors, processes, and so on. In the next section, we will look at utilizing keymetrics to solve our monitoring challenges.

Keymetrics to monitor application exceptions and runtime problems

Although PM2 does a pretty good job of keeping the server up and running, we need to monitor all unknown exceptions that occur or potential sources of memory leaks. PMX provides just the module for that. You can follow the example in `chapter 9/pmx-utilities`. Initialize `pmx` as usual. Just whenever there is an error, notify `pmx` with the `notify` method:

```
pmx.notify(new Error("Unexpected Exception"));
```

This is enough to send out an error to keymetrics to give it information about application exceptions. You will receive email notifications, too.

PMX monitors constant usage of the service, too, in order to detect memory leaks, if any. Check the route `/memory-leak`, for example.

The following shows several important keymetrics highlighted:

Pmx utilities

Adding custom metrics

Lastly, we will see how to add our own custom metrics based on our business capabilities and on a need basis. Most of the time, we often need some customization or we are not able to use out of the box functionalities as such. Keymetrics provides us with probes for this. A probe in keymetrics is a custom metric that is sent to keymetrics programmatically. There are four kinds of probes that we will see, with examples:

- **Simple metrics**: Values that can be read instantly, that is, used to monitor any variable value. It is a very basic metric where the developer can set a value to the data that is pushed to keymetrics.
- **Counter**: Things that increment or decrement, that is, downloads being processed, a user connected, number of times a service request is hit, the database goes down, and so on.

- **Meter**: Things that are measured as events/intervals, that is, requests per minute for an HTTP server, and so on.
- **Histogram**: It keeps a reservoir of statistically relevant values especially biased towards the last five minutes to explore their distribution, such as monitoring the mean of execution of a query into a database for the last five minutes, and so on.

We will be using pmx (https://www.npmjs.com/package/pmx) to see examples of custom metrics. PMX is one of the leading modules for PM2 runner that allows exposure of metrics that are associated with the application. It can reveal useful patterns that can help scale the service as per demand or to efficiently utilize resources.

Simple metrics

Setting a PM2 metric value is just a matter of initializing a probe and setting a value in it. We can create a simple metric with the following steps. You can follow the source in chapter 9/simple_metric:

1. Copy our first microservice skeleton from Chapter 2, *Gearing up for the Journey*. We will add our changes here. Install pm2 and pmx modules as a dependency:

   npm install pm2 pmx —save

2. In HelloWorld.ts, initialize pmx with the following code. We will add a simple metric name 'Simple Custom metric' along with variable initializations:

```
constructor(){
this.pmxVar=pmx.init({http:true,errors:true,
custom_probes:true,network:true,ports:true});
this.probe=this.pmxVar.probe();
this.metric=this.probe.metric({ name:'Simple custom metric'
});}
```

We initialized pmx with a few options, such as the following:

- http: HTTP routes should be logged and PM2 will be enabled to perform HTTP watching for HTTP related metrics
- errors: Exceptions logging
- custom_probes: JS Loop latency and HTTP requests should be automatically exposed as custom metrics
- ports: It should show which ports our app is listening to

3. Now you can initialize this value anywhere using the following:

```
this.metric.set(new Date().toISOString());
```

You can now see it in the keymetrics dashboard, as follows:

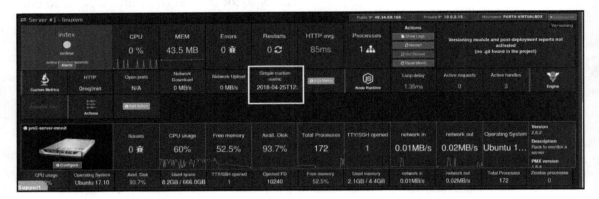

Simple metric

Counter metric

This metric is very useful in order to see things such as how many times an event has occurred. In this exercise, we will see the number of times that our `/hello-world` is invoked. You can follow along with the example in `Chapter 9/counter-metric`:

1. Initialize the project as before. Add the `pmx` dependency. Create one `CustomMiddleware` with the option of routing controller:

```
import { ExpressMiddlewareInterface } from "routing-
controllers";
 const
 pmx=require('pmx').init({http:true,errors:true,
custom_probes:true,network:true,ports:true});

const pmxProbe=pmx.probe();
 const pmxCounter=pmxProbe.counter({
    name:'request counter for Hello World Controller',
    agg_type:'sum'})

export class CounterMiddleWare implements
ExpressMiddlewareInterface {
    use(request: any, response: any, next: (err?: any) => any
):any {
```

```
        console.log("custom middle ware");
        pmxCounter.inc();
    next();     }}
```

2. Add that annotation before `HelloWorld.ts` and run the application:

```
@UseBefore(CounterMiddleWare)
@Controller('/hello-world')
export class HelloWorld { ... }
```

You should be able to see something like the following:

Counter metric

Meter

This metric allows us to record when an event actually occurs and the number of occurrences of events per time unit. Calculating average is quite useful as it essentially gives us an idea about the load in the system. In this exercise, we will look at how to utilize meter metrics:

1. Initialize project as usual. Install the `pmx` and `pm2` dependency. It consists of the following keywords:

   - **samples:** This parameter corresponds to interval based on which we want to measure the metric. In our case, it is the number of calls per minute, hence `60`.

   - **timeframe:** This is how long we want to hold the keymetrics data, the overall time frame over which it will be analyzed.
     Add the following code in the constructor to initialize meter metric dependency:

     ```
     this.pmxVar=pmx.init({http:true,errors:true,custom_probes:true,
     network:true,ports:true});
       this.probe=this.pmxVar.probe();
       this.metric=this.probe.meter({
     ```

```
name: 'averge per minute',
samples:60,
timeframe:3600 })
```

2. In route, `@Get('/')` will initialize this mark. This will give us an average number of calls per minute for the route `<server_url>/hello-world: this.metric.mark();`.

3. Now, run this metric. You will be able to see the value in the keymetrics dashboard. Similarly, you can use histogram metric.

In the next section, we will look at the more advanced tools available.

Prometheus and Grafana

Prometheus is a famous open-source tool, which provides powerful data compression options along with fast data querying for time series data analysis for Node.js monitoring. Prometheus has built-in visualization methods, but it's not configurable enough to leverage in dashboards. That's where Grafana steps in. In this section, we will look at how to monitor a Node.js microservice using Prometheus and Grafana. So let's get our hands dirty with coding. You can follow along with the example in `Chapter 9/prometheus-grafana` in the source:

1. As always, initialize a new project from `chapter-2/first microservice`. Add the following dependencies:

   npm install prom-client response-time --save

   These dependencies will make sure that we will be able to monitor the Node.js engine as well as be able to collect response time from the service.

2. Next, we will write some middlewares to be used across the microservice stages, such as injecting in Express, and using after middleware. Create a `MetricModule.ts` file and add the following code:

```
import * as promClient from 'prom-client';
import * as responseTime from 'response-time';
import { logger } from '../../common/logging';

export const Register=promClient.register;
const Counter=promClient.Counter;
const Histogram=promClient.Histogram;
const summary=promClient.Summary;
```

3. Next we will create some custom functions to be used as middlewares. Here, we will create one function; you can check out other functions in `Chapter 9/prometheus-grafana/config/metrics-module/MetricModule.ts`:

```
//Function 1
 export var numOfRequests=new Counter({
    name:'numOfRequests',
    help:'Number of requests which are made through out the
service',
    labelNames:['method']
 })
/*Function 2  to start metric collection */
 export var startCollection=function(){
    logger.info(" Metrics can be checked out at /metrics");
    this.promInterval=promClient.collectDefaultMetrics(); }

/*THis function 3 increments the counters executed */
 export var requestCounters=function(req:any,res:any,next:any){
    if(req.path!='metrics'){
       numOfRequests.inc({method:req.method});
       totalPathsTakesn.inc({path:req.path});
    }    next();}
//Function 4: start collecting metrics
export var startCollection=function(){
   logger.info(" Metrics can be checked out at /metrics");
    this.promInterval=promClient.collectDefaultMetrics();}
```

Take a look at the following functions mentioned in the preceding code:

- The first function starts a new counter with variable
- The second function starts Prometheus metrics
- The third function is a middleware that increments the number of requests
- The function counter except for metrics route

4. Next, we add the metrics route:

```
@Controller('/metrics')
 export class MetricsRoute{
    @Get('/')
    async getMetrics(@Req() req:any,@Res()
res:any):Promise<any> {
        res.set('Content-Type', Register.contentType);
        res.end(Register.metrics());    };}
```

5. Next, we inject middleware in our `express` application. In `express.ts`, simply add the following LOC:

```
..
this.app.use(requestCounters);
this.app.use(responseCounters)
..
startCollection()
```

6. Node.js setup is done. Now it's time to start Prometheus. Create one folder called `prometheus-data` and inside it create one `yml config` file:

```
Scrape_configs:
 - job_name: 'prometheus-demo'
   scrape_interval: 5s
   Static_configs:
     - targets: ['10.0.2.15:4200']
       Labels:
         service: 'demo-microservice'
         group: 'production'
```

7. Spawn up the Docker process by running the following:

```
sudo docker run -p 9090:9090 -v /home/parth/Desktop/prometheus-
grafana/prometheus-data/prometheus.yml prom/prometheus
```

8. Your **Prometheus** should be up and running and you should see a screen like the following:

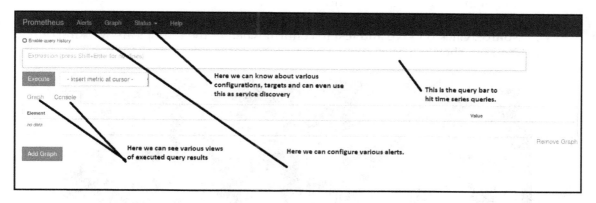

Prom dashboard

9. Perform something on your application or use some stress testing tools, such as JMeter or `https://www.npmjs.com/package/loadtest`. Then open up Prometheus and, in the query shell, write `sum(numOfRequests)`. You will be able to see live graph and results. These are the same results that can be seen when we hit `<server_url>/metrics`. Hit the following query to try to see Node.js memory usage the `avg(nodejs_external_memory_bytes / 1024 / 1024) by (service)`.

10. Prometheus is great, but it cannot be used as a dashboard. Hence, we utilize Grafana, which has excellent and pluggable visualization platform features. It has built-in Prometheus data source support. Hit the following command to open up Docker images of Grafana:

```
docker run -i -p 3000:3000 grafana/grafana
```

Once up, go to `localhost:3000` and add `admin/admin` in username/password to log in.

11. Once logged in, add a data source with Prometheus as type (open up the **Add Data** source screen) and enter your IP address: `9090` in the HTTP URL (your Prometheus running URL) and `Server (Default)` (the way you are accessing Prometheus) in the **Access** text box, so as to configure Prometheus as a data source. Click on **save and test** to confirm whether the settings are working or not. You can checkout the following screenshot for better understanding:

Grafana

12. Once the data source is configured, you can have custom graphs or anything, and design your own custom dashboard through GUI tools. It will look as follows:

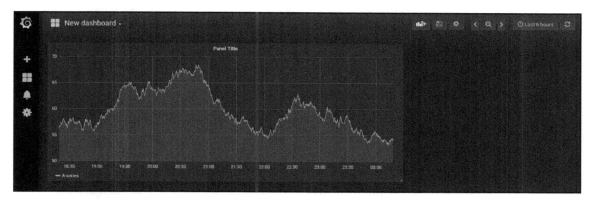

Grafana

Prometheus is a powerful tool for not only monitoring single Node.js applications, but it can be used in a polyglot environment too. With Grafana, you can create the dashboard that fits your needs best.

These are prominent tools used in deployment in Node.js Monitoring. There are other tools, too, but integrating them involves need of Polyglot environment. For instance, `Simian Army`. It is widely used and promoted by Netflix to handle various cloud computing challenges. It is built with a variety of simian army monkey tools to maintain network health, handle traffic, and locate security problems.

Production-ready microservice criteria

We are quickly going to summarize a production-ready microservice and its criteria:

- A production-ready to go microservice is reliable and stable for service requests:
    - It follows a standard development cycle adhering to 12-factor app standards (recall `Chapter 1`, *Debunking Microservices*)
    - Its code is thoroughly tested through linters, unit test cases, integration, contract, and E2E test cases
    - It uses CI/CD pipelines and incremental build strategy
    - There are either backups, alternatives, fallbacks, and cache in place in case of service failures
    - It has stable service registration and discovery process as per standards

- A production-ready to go microservice is scalable and highly available:
  - It has auto scalability based on load coming at any time
  - It utilizes hardware resources efficiently and does not block resource pool
  - Its dependencies scale with the application
  - Its traffic can be rerouted on a need basis
  - It handles tasks and processes in a performant nonblocking and preferably asynchronous reactive manner
- A production-ready to go microservice is ready for any unprepared catastrophe:
  - It does not have any single point of failure
  - It is tested for resiliency through enough code testing and load testing
  - Failure detection, stopping the failure from cascading, and remediation towards failure have been automated along with auto scalability
- A production-ready to go microservice is properly monitored:
  - It has its identified keymetrics (custom metrics, errors, the memory occupied, and so on) monitored constantly not only pertaining to microservice level, but also expanding to host and infrastructure level
  - It has a dashboard that is easy to interpret and has all important keymetrics (you bet, PM2 is our only choice)
  - Actionable alerts defined by signal providing thresholds (Prometheus and time series query)
- A production-ready to go microservice is documented:
  - Comprehensive document generated through tools such as Swagger
  - Architecture is audited frequently and well reviewed to support polyglot environment

Summary

In this chapter, we learned about the deployment process. We saw some go live criteria, a deployment pipeline, and finally got acquainted with Docker. We saw some Docker commands and got acquainted with the world of dockerization. Then we saw some of the challenges involved with logging and monitoring when dealing with huge distributed microservices. We explored various solutions for logging and implemented a custom centralized logging solution using the famous ELK stack. In the latter half of the chapter, we saw monitoring tools, such as keymetrics and Prometheus.

The next chapter will explore the final part of our product: security and scalability. We will see how to protect our Node.js applications against brute force attacks and what exactly our security plan should be. Then, we will look at scalability and scale our microservice through AWS—auto scalability.

Hardening Your Application **10**

It is very difficult to get security right. There always seems to be some open door for intruders to sneak in. Security mistakes are made all the time, such as the famous **WannaCry ransomware attack** (causing $5 billion of damage), **Ethereum theft** ($32 million heist), and so on. Such attacks always make us take extra steps toward security to avoid such disasters. As microservices are dynamic, any of the instances can go down leading to business loss.

With a focus on handling security and autoscaling, this chapter explores some security fundamentals and microservice best practices to make the system more secure and robust, and make it easy to handle any amount of traffic. With the advent of containers, we will be looking at security at the container level too, as well as the application level. This chapter also focuses on autoscaling with the aim of making the application available at any time to handle any load, with zero downtime during new deployments. This chapter covers the following:

- Questions you should be asking while applying a security mechanism
- Security best practices for individual services/applications
- Security best practices for containers
- Scaling your application

Questions you should be asking while applying security

In a constantly evolving world, we can't have a predefined set of rules to apply in microservice design. Rather, we can have some predefined questions that we can ask ourselves to evaluate the overall system and processes. The following sections list of all the standard questions at various levels, which we can use as an evaluation checklist. Later, we will be upgrading our security as a solution to these questions.

Core application/core microservice

We will begin at the very core—our microservice. Whenever we write any microservice to satisfy any business capability, once it is designed, we need to take care of whether the service is exposed to any vulnerabilities or not. The following questions can be asked to get a general idea about security at the application level:

- Is the system properly secured at all places or just at the boundaries?
- If an intruder sneaks in, is the system powerful enough to detect that intruder and throw him out?
- How easy is it for an intruder to get inside the network by mimicking the usual behavior, get access to traffic, or overload traffic?
- Does each microservice trust other microservices even if they call them too much?
- Does your service contract have authentication or does the network handle authentication?
- Is the identity of the caller passed along to each of the microservices or is it just lost at the gateway?
- What are the measures to ensure that SQL injection doesn't occur?
- Is the system updated enough to store passwords in encrypted form?
- If we need to upgrade any password storage algorithm, can it be done without mass disruption to users?
- How is private and sensitive data handled in the system?
- Can your logging solution detect and analyze security breaches?

Middleware

The next level is our **middleware**. It's the central place or starting point, where all services will pass through. We need to make sure that middleware is secured and cannot be exposed to any risk, as it has various parameters such as messaging middleware, database access configured, and so on:

- Do we have the least privilege principle (that is, single database login across all services)?
- Does each service have access to only the data that it needs?
- If an intruder gets access to service database credentials, how much data access will they get?

- Do we have a single messaging middleware across all services?
- Does the messaging middleware or service bus have login credentials?
- Does the legacy system put the microservice system at risk?

API Gateway

The next level is our API Gateway. A gateway plays an important part in microservices as it is the starting point of any request and is used by all microservices as a means of communication between them. Hence, it should not be exposed to any other security vulnerabilities:

- Is there a TLS implementation?
- Does the TLS implementation remove downgrade attacks or weak cipher attacks?
- How do you make sure that internal websites and admin URLs are abstracted to the internet?
- What information is circulated through the authentication APIs of your gateway service?
- Do the rest of the services trust the gateway too much or can they find out when the gateway is breached?

Team and operational activities

The final phase is team and operational activities. Being distributed in nature, every team works independently. In this case, it becomes an essential prerequisite that each team has enough security training. The following questions help us to evaluate security at the operational level:

- How are security activities baked in to every development team?
- How do you ensure that everyone is aware of common security principles?
- What security training do you give to the team and do you update them regarding any vulnerabilities?
- What automation level do you use to ensure security controls are always in place?

In the next section, we will look at how we can harden the application and container, and go through various security best practices.

Security best practices for individual services/applications

A microservice architecture shifts around complexity. Instead of having a single very complicated system, there are a bunch of simple services with complicated interactions. Our goal is to make sure that complexity stays in check and within boundaries. Security is really hard to get right. There are countless ways to break into an application. Node.js is no different. In this section, we are going to look at the techniques to prevent security vulnerabilities. This section is meant to act as a basic checklist to ensure that our microservice addresses some of the biggest security threats. So, let's get started.

Checking for known security vulnerabilities

Due to a wealth of modules available in npm, we can directly work on the application and rely on the ecosystem for ready-made solutions. However, due to the huge modules, larger security vulnerabilities can occur at any time even for mature popular frameworks. In this section, we will look at some valuable tools that ensure no vulnerabilities are present in the packages that the application relies on, or even while updating:

Auditjs

A simple utility that audits an npm project using the OSS index v2 REST API to identify known vulnerabilities and outdated package versions.

Using this is very simple:

1. Install it as a dev dependency npm install auditjs --save-dev.
2. Add audit scripts in the npm scripts:

   ```
   scripts:{ ... "audit":"auditjs" ...}
   ```

3. Run the npm run audit command. The full example can be seen in the extracted folder under the chapter 10/auditjs folder.

 For more information you can visit the link https://www.npmjs.com/package/auditjs .

Snyk.io

This is another module that we can use to vet any modules against the vulnerability database maintained by `synk.io`. The major advantage of this module is that we do not need to install this for auditing. This module can be used as a pre-check before using any third-party module:

1. Install it globally—`npm install snyk -g`
2. Once installed, you will need to authenticate it by hitting `snyk auth`
3. Once `snyk` is set up, you can now vet any module using `synk test <module_name>`

 For more information you can visit the link `https://www.npmjs.com/package/snyk`.

The following are some useful commands:

`snyk wizard`	Finds and fixes known vulnerabilities in a project
`snyk protect`	Applies patches and suppresses vulnerabilities
`snyk monitor`	Records the state of dependencies, so that whenever new vulnerabilities or patches are launched, we can be alerted

Here is some further reading:

- There are lots of other modules available (we saw Node security earlier)
- `retire.js` (`https://retirejs.github.io/retire.js/`) is yet another module that does similar vulnerabilities checking, and it can even be used as a command-line scanner, `grunt`/`gulp` plugin, Chrome or Firefox extension, and so on

Preventing brute force attacks or flooding by adding rate limiters

Brute force attacks are common and often serve as a last resort for the hacker. They systematically enumerate all possible candidates for a solution and check whether each candidate satisfies the problems statement or not. To protect against this kind of attack, we have to implement some kind of rate limiting algorithm, which will effectively block an IP address from making an outrageous amount of requests, thus blocking the possibility of accidentally crashing the application.

You can find the rate-limiting implementation under the `Chapter 10/rate-limiter` folder, where we used the rate limiting algorithm with the Redis database.

Now, let's follow these steps:

1. Install `express-limiter` and `redis`:

   ```
   npm install express-limiter redis --save
   ```

2. Create the redis client and set express-limiter:

   ```
   let client = require('redis').createClient()
   ..
   let limiter = require('express-limiter')(this.app, client)
   ..
   //limits requests to 100 per hour ip ip address
       limiter({
           lookup:['connection.remoteAddress'],
           total:100,
           expire:1000*60*60
       });
   ```

3. Now, run the program. It will limit requests to 100 requests per hour, after which it will start to throw `429: Too Many Requests`.

Protecting against evil regular expressions

One of the most commonly occurring vulnerabilities is a poorly formed regular expression. A regex, if it takes exponential time when applied to non-matching inputs, is termed an evil regex and should be prevented. An evil regex contains groupings with repetitions, alterations with overlappings, and words inside the repeated group. Let's look at an example, `Regex : (b+)+, ([a-zA-Z]+)*, (a|aa)+`, and so on.

All these regexes are exposed to input `bbbbbbbbbbbbbbbbbbbbbbbbbbbbbbbbbbbbbbbb!`. These repetitions can be a hindrance as it may take seconds or even minutes to complete. Due to the event loop of Node.js, the execution won't go ahead, which will effectively result in the server freezing as the application is completely stopped from running. To prevent such disasters, we should use the safe-regex tool (`https://www.npmjs.com/package/safe-regex`). It detects potentially catastrophic exponential time regular expressions.

You can check the source code in the `safe-regex` folder. You can check the regex by just typing `node safe.js '<whatever-my-regex>'`.

Blocking cross-site request forgeries

A common way to intrude in an application is by putting data into the application via unsafe sites through a common phishing technique known as cross-site request forgery. An intruder making a phishing attempt can initiate a request via a form or other input that creates a request for an application through inputs exposed by the application.

To harden the application against this kind of attack, we can use CSRF token implementation. Every time a user makes a request, a new CSRF token is generated and added to the user's cookie. This token should be added as a value to the inputs in an applications template and this will be validated against the token the CSRF library generates when the user sends information. NPM provides the `csurf` module (`https://www.npmjs.com/package/csurf`), which can be used in express middleware directly and we can play accordingly with the `csurf` token.

Tightening session cookies and effective session management

The focus of the secure use of cookies cannot be understated in an application. This especially applies to stateful services that need to maintain a state across a stateless protocol such as HTTP. Express has a default cookie setting that can be configured or manually tightened to enhance security. There are various options:

- `secret`: A secret string with which the cookie has to be salted.
- `name`: Name of the cookie.
- `httpOnly`: This basically flags cookies, so that they can be accessible by issuing a web server in order to prevent session hijacking.
- `secure`: This requires TLS/SSL to allow a cookie to be used only in HTTPS requests.
- `domain`: This indicates specific domains only, from which the cookie can be accessed.
- `path`: The path cookie is accepted from an application's domain.
- `expires`: The expiration date of the cookie that is being set. If a timely expiration is not available, the resource consumption will be very high and resources will never be freed.

In the following example, we will securely set cookies using express-session and thus have effective session management. You can follow along with the example under `typescript-express-session`:

1. Clone `first-microservice` from Chapter 2, *Gearing up for the Journey*, and install `express-session` and `@types/express-session`.

2. In `express.ts`, add the following code, which will make our application use cookies with the following secured parameters:

```
this.app.use(
  session({
    secret: 'mySecretCookieSalt',
    name: 'mycookieSessionid',
    saveUninitialized: true,
    resave: false,
    cookie: {
      httpOnly: true,
      secure: true,
      domain: 'typescript-microservices.com',
      path: '/hello-world',
```

```
        expires: new Date(Date.now() + 60 * 60 * 1000)
    }
})))
```

This module effectively helps us to handle stateful sessions by providing various options, such as cookie flags, cookie scopes, and so on.

Adding helmet to configure security headers

The `helmet` module (`https://www.npmjs.com/package/helmet`) is a collection of 11 security modules that prevents a varying number of attacks against an express microservice. It's easy to use, as we just have to add two lines of code. Adding some basic configurations can help to protect the application against possible security mishaps. You can use helmet by simply adding:

```
this.app.use(helmet())
```

 The source code for this can be found in `chapter-10/typescript-express-session`.

The `helmet` module has a whopping 12 packages that act as some middleware to block malicious parties from breaking or using an application. These headers include headers for `helmet-csp` (headers for content security policy HTTP header), `dns-prefetch` protocols, `frameguards`, `hide-powered-by`, `hpkp`, `hsts`, `ienoopen`, `nocache`, `dont-sniff-mimetype`, `referrer-policy`, `x-xss protections`, `frameguard` to prevent `clickjackings`, and so on.

Another option for securing headers is `lusca` (`https://www.npmjs.com/package/lusca`), which can be used in combination with express-session. An example can be found in the `chapter-10 /express-lusca` directory.

Avoiding parameter pollution

In Node.js, if there are no defined standards for handling multiple parameters of the same name, the de facto standard is to treat those values as an array. This is extremely useful because for a single name when the expected outcome is a string, it types changes to an array if multiple parameters with the same name are passed. If this isn't accounted for in query handling, the application will crash and bring the whole thing down, making this a possible DoS vector. For example, check this link: `http://whatever-url:8080/my-end-point?name=parth&name=ghiya`.

Here, when we try to read `req.query.name`, we expect it to be a string, but instead we get an array, `['parth', 'ghiya']`, which will bring down the application if not handled with care. To ensure that the application won't fail you, we can do the following things:

- Various policies implement polluting mechanisms differently; for example, some may take the first occurrence, some may take the last occurrence
- Use TypeScript types to validate the request. If the types fail, stop the request by giving parameters errors
- Ensure that parameters in HTTP GET, PUT, or POST are encoded.
- Strict Regexp must be followed in URL rewriting.

You can check the complete list and how it is handled at `https://www.owasp.org/index.php/Testing_for_HTTP_Parameter_pollution_(OTG-INPVAL-004)`.

Securing transmission

If an application has any moving parts (HTTP methods such as POST, PUT, and DELETE) that include anything right from logging or sending a tweet which mutates the information from the client, using HTTPs is a vital implementation to make sure that the information isn't modified in mid-transit. Cost can be an easy excuse for not investing in an SSL certificate. But now there are new, completely free, SSL certificate resources, such as **Let's Encrypt** (`https://letsencrypt.org/`). Also, a Node.js application should not be directly exposed to the internet and SSL termination should be handled prior to the request coming to Node.js. Using NGINX to do this is a highly recommended option, as it is specially designed to terminate SSL more efficiently than Node.js. To effectively set an express application behind a proxy, refer to this: `http://expressjs.com/en/4x/api.html#trust.proxy.options.table`. Once the HTTP is set up, we can use `nmap`, `sslyze`, or `OpenSSL` to test HTTP certificate transmission.

Preventing command injection/SQL injection

An injection attack can occur when an intruder sends text-based attacks that exploit the syntax of an interpreter. SQL injection consists of the injection of a partial or complete SQL query through user input, which can expose sensitive information and can be destructive as well. Similarly, command injection is a technique that can be used by an attacker to run OS commands on a remote web server. Through this approach, even passwords can be exposed. To filter against these kinds of attack, we should always filter and sanitize user inputs. Using JavaScript statements such as eval is also another way to opens up a door to injection attacks. To prevent these attacks, we can use `node-postgres` if you are using `postgres` (https://www.npmjs.com/package/pg), which provides positional query parameters. Common techniques to defend against injection include the following:

- To escape SQL injection, one of the techniques that can be used is escaping user input. Many libraries provide this out of the box.
- Parameterizing SQL queries is another way to avoid SQL injection, where you create a using positional query parameters and fill in the positional query parameters with values.
- `eval()` with user input is one of the ways to inject commands and should not be used at all (in the next section, we will write a `linter`, which will avoid this).
- Similarly, the express application is vulnerable to MongoDB attacks. Not explicitly setting the query selector will result in our data being vulnerable to a simple query.

We have `db.users.find({user: user, pass: pass})`, where `user` and `pass` are coming from a POST request body. Now being type-less, we can simply pass query parameters inside this query, such as `{"user": {"$gt": ""}, "pass": {"$gt": ""}}`, which will return all users along with their passwords. To resolve this, we need to explicitly pass the query selector, which will make our query `db.users.find({user: { $in: [user] }, pass: { $in: [pass] }})`.

TSLint/static code analyzers

In this section, we will look at one of the ways to analyze all the written code and check it against a list of security vulnerabilities. We will include this as one of the stages of our deployment plan. We will write a `linter`, have a `.tslint` file where all the rules to be checked against are mentioned, and then we will run the lint. So, let's get started. **TsLint** is one way to check and validate the source code. It is a static analysis code tool that runs on Node.js in order to keep your source code clean, find possible bugs, uncover security issues, and enforce a consistent style across all your teams:

1. Clone our `first-typescript-microservices` from `Chapter 2`, *Gearing up for the Journey* and inside it, add the following commands:

   ```
   npm install tslint --save
   npm install tslint-microsoft-contrib --save
   ```

2. Next, we will write `tslint.json` with the basic rules that we want to evaluate it against. Copy the rules from `https://github.com/Microsoft/tslint-microsoft-contrib/blob/master/recommended_ruleset.js`.

3. Next, we will write an initialization script:

   ```
   "analyze":"node ./node_modules/tslint/bin/tslint
       -r node_modules/tslint-microsoft-contrib/
       -c tslint.json
       -s src/**/*.ts"
   ```

4. We can now leverage this script anywhere because when we run this, it will throw an output of all the errors found while evaluating against that rule set.

5. We can add a `--fix` flag in the preceding script, which will automatically take the necessary measures in most cases.

You can find the source code under the `chapter 10/tslinter` folder. In this section, we looked at some of the things that need to be done when hardening our application against all sorts of possible attacks. In the next section, we will have a look at some of the container-level securities that can be applied.

Security best practices for containers

With the advent of containers, cloud-native applications and infrastructure need quite a different approach to security. Let's have a look at the best practices. This is the age of the **cloud-native** approach. The cloud-native approach refers to a process that packages software in standard units called containers and arranges these units in microservices that communicate with each other to form applications. It ensures that running applications are fully automated for the greater good—standard speed, agility, and scalability. Let's look at the security considerations that need to be addressed to have a comprehensive security program.

Securing container builds and standardizing deployments

This phase focuses on applying control to developer workflows and continuous integration and deployment pipelines to mitigate the security issues that may occur after containers have been launched. Here is the standard set of practices:

- Apply a single responsibility rule even at the container level. A container image should only have the essential software and application code needed to minimize the attack surface of every container launched from the image.
- Images should be scanned for known vulnerabilities and exposures. There is a common vulnerabilities and exposure database (just like the application level) on which we can validate the image (https://github.com/arminc/clair-scanner).
- Once images are built, they should be digitally signed. **Signing images** (https://docs.docker.com/datacenter/dtr/2.4/guides/user/manage-images/sign-images/#initialize-the-trust-metadata) with private keys provides assurances that each image used to launch a container was created by a trusted party.
- As containers running on a host share the same OS, it is of utmost importance that they start with a restricted set of capabilities. Use modules such as SELinux.
- Use secret management techniques (a technique through which secrets such as sensitive data are only distributed to the containers that use them when they need them).

Securing containers at runtime

For runtime phase security, we need to check the following things—visibility, detection, response, prevention, stopping containers that violate policies, and so on. Here are some of the important factors that need to be taken care of:

- Analyze microservice and containers behavior
- Relate distributed threat indicators, and ascertain whether a single container is contaminated or it is spread across many containers
- Intercept to block unauthorized container engine commands
- Automate actions for responses

These are some of the essentials we need to do to ensure that our containers are safe against any vulnerabilities. In the next section, we will see a general checklist that can be used during our overall microservice development phase.

Security checklist

Microservices development is a platform of standard tools combined with lots of supporting tools and everything is on the move. In this section, we will look at an overall checklist, which we can use to validate our development, or which can give us a general idea of our microservice development.

Service necessities

The first and primary level of development is individual microservice development, satisfying some business capability. The following a checklist can be used while developing microservices:

- Services should be developed and deployed independently
- Services should not have shared data; they should have their own private data
- Services should be small enough that they are focused and can add big value
- Data should be stored in databases and service instances should not be stored
- Work should be offloaded to asynchronous workers whenever possible
- Load balancers should be introduced to distribute work
- Security should be layered and we don't need to reinvent the wheel; for example, OAuth can be used to maintain user identity and access control
- Security updates should be automated

- A distributed firewall with centralized control should be used (such as Project Calico)
- Monitoring tools, such as Prometheus, should be used
- Security scanners should be used for containers

Service interactions

The next level is communication among microservices. When microservices communicate among themselves, a checklist should be followed. This checklist helps to ensure that if any service fails, then the failure is contained and it doesn't spread through the entire system:

- Data should be transported in a serialized format, such as JSON or protobuf
- Error codes should be used carefully and actions should be taken accordingly on them.
- APIs should be simple, effective, and the contract should be clear
- A service discovery mechanism should be implemented to find other services easily
- Decentralized interactions over centralized orchestrators should be preferred
- APIs should be versioned
- Circuit breakers help to stop the error propagating throughout the entire system
- Service interactions should only be through exposed endpoints
- Authenticating all APIs and passing them through middleware gives a clearer picture of usage patterns
- Connection pools can reduce downstream impacts instead of sudden request spikes

Development phase

The next phase to take care of is during development. This checklist adheres to the 12 factor standards. The following checklist is of development standards, which help in a smoother development process:

- A common source code control platform should be used
- There should be separate prod environment
- A release less, release it faster principle should be followed
- Shared libraries are painful to maintain
- Simple services are easy to replace

Deployment

The deployment checklist focuses on the deployment era. It indicates how containers and images help in quicker deployments. It advises on key values and property configurations to manage deployments in different environments:

- Images and containers should be used
- Configure a mechanism to deploy any version of any service on any environment (CI/CD plus proper Git branches and tags)
- Configuration should be managed outside the deployment package, such as environment variables, key-value stores, external URL links, and so on

Operations

The operational checklist contains a list of best practices to be done at an operational level to make the after-release life of a system easy. It advises using centralized logs, monitoring software, and more. It shows how automation can make life easier:

- All logs should be in one place (ELK stack)
- A common monitoring platform for all services
- Stateless services can easily be autoscaled, as we don't have to replicate the session everywhere
- Automation is the key to quick development

That's pretty much it! In the next section, we will cover scalability and look at some of the scalability tools available before concluding the book.

Scalability

Today, in the world of competitive marketing, an organization's key point is to have their system up and running. Any failure or downtime directly impacts business and revenue; hence, high availability is a factor that cannot be overlooked. Day by day, the mountain of information is growing thanks to the in-depth use of technology and the numerous ways we use it. Because of this, load average goes beyond the roof. Day by day, data is growing exponentially.

In some cases, it is unpredictable that data cannot exceed up to some limit or a variety of users won't depart out of bounds. Scalability is a preferable solution to handle and meet unexpected demands at any point in time. Scalability can scale horizontally (we scale by adding more machines to a pool of resources) and vertically (we scale by adding more CPU/RAM to an existing machine). In terms of data, spanning database and loads of application queries over multiple servers. We can add instances in order to handle load, descale after period of time, and so on. It is easy to add horsepower to the cluster to handle the load. Cluster servers instantly handle failures and manage the failover part to keep your system available almost all the time. If one server goes down, it will redirect the user's request to another node and perform the requested operation. In this section, we will look at two of the most famous tools—Kubernetes and the AWS Load Balancer.

AWS Load Balancer

For load balancing, we should understand **Amazon Web Services Elastic Load Balancer** (**ELB**), which can help us to leverage load balancing. We should understand AWS ELB specifically; however, most of the concepts remain the same for the rest of the load balancing alternatives available. There are various alternatives available to achieve load balancing. A few of them are HAProxy, Apache Web Server, NGINX Http server, Pound, Google Cloud Load balancing, F5 Load Balancer, Barracuda Load Balancer, and many more. In general, the following is the architecture that depicts the flow of load balancing:

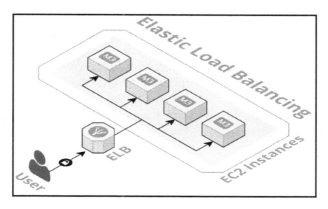

Load balancer

An ELB is one of the many available AWS services, which works to distribute incoming network traffic or application traffic to EC2 instances available in the network automatically. ELB also keeps an eye on the health of EC2 instances to provide high availability for the application by automatically adding or removing EC2 instances. It sends traffic only to instances that are available and in a healthy state. You can also configure ELB for internal load balancing or public-facing load balancing. ELB it becomes the face of the EC2 instances running behind wherever your application resides. Depending on the status or availability of the instances, a health check would mark it as either `InService`—if it's in a healthy state, or `OutOfService`—if it's in an unhealthy state. The load balancer would route traffic only to instances that are healthy. With the help of this health check, a load balancer provides us with a fault tolerant proof application and ensures the application's high availability 24/7, based on our configured parameters (high traffic, high resource utilization, and so on).

Benefits of using a load balancer

A load balancer helps us to provide a fault tolerant application, much better high availability, flexibility to the application, and security too, as we wouldn't be exposing backend systems directly to the user. Let's have a quick glance at some of the benefits of having a load balancer.

Fault tolerance

A load balancer helps to monitor the health of the backend instances. If one of the instances is unavailable, it would be marked as unavailable. Similarly, if the instances are healthy, it would be available to serve the requests. Traffic would be routed only to available healthy instances. This provides a fault tolerant application so the traffic reaching the application is not affected when we have unavailable instances in the backend. However, if none of your systems are unavailable in the backend to serve requests, the load balancer marks all the instances as unhealthy and users will be affected by an unavailable application.

High availability

What if we have an application running without a load balancer? If the number of requests to the application increases, our instances might not be able to handle the load of the requests and the performance of the application would deteriorate. Not only this, it might also affect the availability of the application. If we have a load balancer, it can route the traffic based on a round-robin method to all the instances and can easily distribute the load across the instances. This helps to overcome a situation of high availability and not restricting limited instances to be flooded with unexpected spikes, which might impact the business.

Flexibility

Although we discussed fault tolerance and high availability with presumed instances, our requests might go beyond the expected limit of the application. In fact, they can be below the limit as well. Either of these may lead to a business loss in terms of the additional cost of running instances or degraded application performance. To manage either of these scenarios, many load balancers, especially in public clouds such as AWS ELB, Google Cloud Load Balancing, and a few more, provide the flexibility to have the auto-scaling of instances based on certain criteria, such as memory or CPU utilization, which can, add or remove a number of instances in the load balancer when it scales up or down. Load balancing with such features helps to ensure that we manage unexpected spikes of either high or low efficiency.

Security

Load balancers can also be configured to be not only public-facing instances; they can be configured to be private-facing instances as well. This can help in cases when there is a secured network or site-to-site VPN tunnel. This helps to guard our instances against public interfaces and limit them only to a private network. With the help of a private-facing load balancer, we can also configure for internal routing of backend systems without exposing them to the internet.

A load balancer has various features, such as configuring protocols, sticky sessions, connection draining, idle connection timeout, metrics, access logs, host-based routing, path-based routing, load balancing to multiple ports on the same instance, and HTTP/2 support.

We looked at many features of load balancers, but we have one more important feature to look at. Yes, you are right; it's the health check. Health checks work as heartbeats for the load balancer and our application. Let's have look at health checks in a bit more detail to understand why they are heartbeats for the load balancer.

Health check parameters

To discover and maintain the availability of EC2 instances, a load balancer periodically sends pings (attempted connections) or sends test requests to test EC2 instances. These checks are called health check parameters. The following is a list of all health check parameters. Health checks help us to determine if an instance is healthy or unhealthy. Let us look at a few of the common configuration options available in health checks for most load balancers. The configuration options naming convention will vary from one load balancer to another; however, conceptually the following configuration parameters are available.

Unhealthy threshold

In unhealthy attempts, it is expected to validate by the number of times the load balancer doesn't get a positive response from the backend. For instance, if we have configured a value of five unhealthy attempts, the load balancer would mark the instance unhealthy only if it doesn't get five healthy responses from the instance.

Healthy threshold

This is exactly opposite to unhealthy attempts; it is expected to validate by the number of times the load balancer gets a positive response from the backend. For instance, if we have configured a value of two healthy attempts, the load balancer would mark the instance available only if it gets two healthy responses from the instance.

Timeout

A health check may be configured to check a URI. Let's say `/login.html` is supposed to be checked by a load balancer for a healthy response but doesn't respond within the time specified in the timeout. It would be considered an unhealthy response. This configuration would help us if there is an instance that may be affected due to limited system resource availability and not responding as per the expected time which we would have expected. Ideally, it is suggested to configure the timeout near to the actual response time from the instance for effective use.

Health check protocol

We can configure the health protocol type in diverse ways. We can have a health check based on a HTTP response, HTTPS response, TCP response, or HTTP/HTTPS body response. These are the most commonly available health check types, available in most load balancers.

Health check port

We can also configure health check ports. We can configure health checks based on various protocols, as we have just discussed, but if we have custom ports for the application, the load balancer can be configured accordingly. For instance, if we have an HTTP server in our backend instance running on port 81 instead of the default port 80, we can configure HTTP as the health check protocol with the custom port 81 defined in the health check port.

Interval

This configuration parameter determines after how much time a health check should count heart beats for our backend instances. In general, it is configured in seconds, so if we configure an interval of 10 seconds, the load balancer will keep on repeating its check every 10 seconds.

Configuring a load balancer

Now that we know about our health check parameters, let's configure a load balancer. You will need to create an account on AWS and launch one instance:

1. Open up your instance and then go to the **Load Balancing | Load balancers** tab.
2. Create a load balancer. You will be able to choose from an application load balancer, network load balancer, or classic load balancer. The uses of these are shown in the following screenshot:

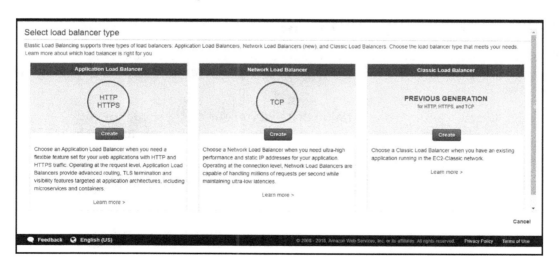

Types of load balancer

3. The next step is to configure the load balancer and add health checks as per your requirements. All the steps can be seen in the following screenshot:

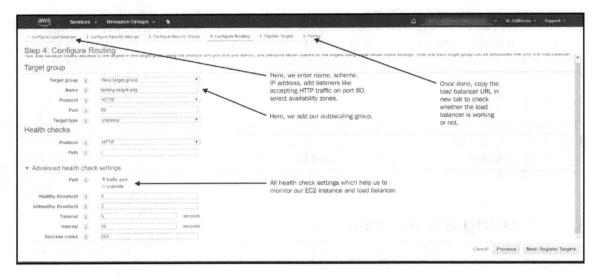

Configuring the ELB Load Balancer

5. You can specify the health parameters as per the theory discussed. Health checks ensure that request traffic is shifted away from failed instances.

Autoscaling – practical hands on with AWS

Now, we will do **autoscaling** using *AWS autoscaling groups*, a load balancer, and configuration properties. So, let's get started. Here is the overall process that we are going to follow:

1. Create a launch configuration that will run our `first-typescript microservice` from `Chapter 2`, *Gearing up for the Journey*, to start the HTTP server

2. Create an autoscaling group

3. Create an autoscaling policy to increase instances by two when the CPU load is greater than 20% for a minute
4. Add the criteria for removing the autoscaling group.
5. Auto-terminate the instances

So, let's get our hands dirty.

Creating the launch configuration

Log in to the AWS console and navigate to the EC2 dashboard. Select the launch configuration to start the wizard. Create the launch configuration accordingly to the wizard:

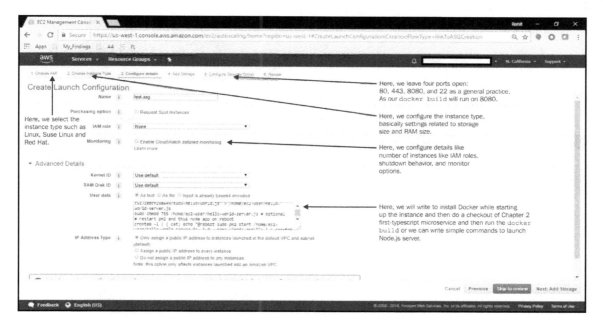

Launch configuration

We should have EC2 instances ready to host our `first-typescript-microservices` application.

Creating an autoscaling group and configuring it with autoscaling policies

Now we have a blueprint ready, we need the building base that is our autoscaling group. Create an autoscaling group and the following instance will appear. Enter appropriate values:

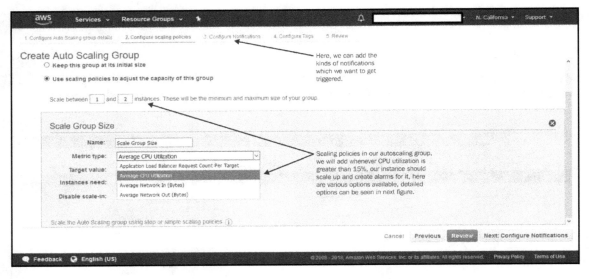

Creating an autoscaling group

This is how the wizard will look for configuring scale-up and scale-down strategies:

Increase Group Size

Name:	Increase Group Size
Execute policy when:	awsec2-test-asg-group-CPU-Utilization Edit Remove
	breaches the alarm threshold: CPUUtilization >= 15 for 60 seconds
	for the metric dimensions AutoScalingGroupName = test-asg-group
Take the action:	Add ▼ 1 instances ▼ when 15 <= CPUUtilization < +infinity
	Add step (i)
Instances need:	1 seconds to warm up after each step

Create a simple scaling policy (i)

Decrease Group Size

Name:	Decrease Group Size
Execute policy when:	awsec2-test-asg-group-High-CPU-Utilization Edit Remove
	breaches the alarm threshold: CPUUtilization <= 15 for 60 seconds
	for the metric dimensions AutoScalingGroupName = test-asg-group
Take the action:	Remove ▼ 1 instances ▼ when 15 >= CPUUtilization > -infinity
	Add step (i)

Autoscaling and auto terminating policies

After reviewing, click **OK** and your AWS scaling group is now ready.

Creating an application load balancer and adding a target group

The next step is to create an application load balancer and attach a target group to it. So, create a new ELB (we can use the one we created earlier for health check configurations). Add a name for the target group and in **Step 5** of the figure (Configuring ELB Load Balancer), register the instances that were launched by the autoscaling group:

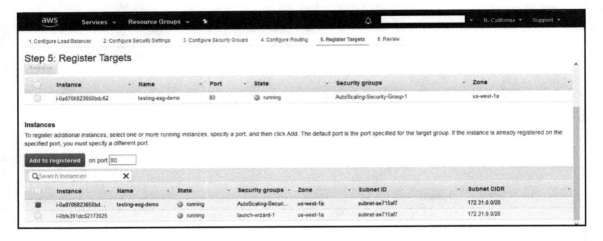

Attaching instances to load balancers

The next step is to associate this target group with our autoscaling group. To do this, edit your autoscaling group and add the target group by name (there should be an autocomplete dropdown). We are all done with configuring AWS.

Time to test

To do load testing, I would prefer a simple load test module (`https://www.npmjs.com/package/loadtest`) rather than setting up the entirety of Jmeter. Install the module by simply installing `npm install loadtest -g`.

Next, just to run the stress test, we can hit the following command:

```
loadtest -c 100 --rps 250 <my-aws-load-balancer-url>
```

Here, -c means concurrent requests and --rps means requests per second for each client. This will trigger an alarm to increase the CPU count by 2. Go to the AWS console after the alert time/wait period has elapsed to check your newly created instances. You will be able to see instances when the load has increased and after the load has decreased, it will automatically start to drain and terminate.

We successfully autoscaled our instances up and down based on policies.

 AWS has an interesting terminology—spot instances. These enables us to reuse unused EC2 instances, which can lower our EC2 instances significantly. Since the span of autoscaled instance is not that large, using a spot instance while scaling up is highly advantageous, and beneficial from a monetary perspective too.

Scaling with Kubernetes

Kubernetes is an open source system for automating deployments, scaling, and managing containerized applications. At the time of writing this book, the Kubernetes Version was **1.9.2**. In this section, we will look at some of the basic features provided by Kubernetes and the terms used in it. So, let's get started.

What problem does Kubernetes solve?

With Docker, we have commands such as docker run, docker build, or docker stop. Unlike these commands, which perform operations on a single container, there is no command like docker deploy to push new images to a group of hosts. To solve this problem, Kubernetes is one of the most promising tools. Kubernetes provides powerful abstractions that completely decouple application-wise operations, such as deployment and scaling. Kubernetes sees the underlying infrastructure as a sea of computers in which we can put containers.

Kubernetes concepts

Kubernetes has a client-server architecture, where the Kubernetes server runs on the cluster on which we deploy our application. We interact with the Kubernetes server using the *kubectl CLI*:

- **Pods:** Our running containerized application with environment variables such as disks. Pods are born and die quickly, such as at deployment times.
- **Node:** A node is a physical or virtual machine running Kubernetes, on which pods can be scheduled.
- **Secret:** We separate out our credentials from environment variables.
- **Service:** This exposes our running pods by labeling them to other applications or to the outside world on the desired IP and port.
- Kubernetes process

 For development purposes, we can use *minikube* and *kubectl*. At the production level, the ideal way is to use **GCP's** (**Google Cloud Platform's**) inbuilt Kubernetes. Trying to run `minikube` and `kubectl` inside VMBox wont be possible as it would become nested virtualization. You can download Kubernetes on NativeOS as per instructions found here `https://kubernetes.io/docs/setup/`.

In this section, we will get our application running with Kubernetes before winding up. You will need a Google Cloud Platform account for this exercise. Google provides a $300 credit free tier. So, let's get started:

1. Kubectl is a CLI tool for running commands against Kubernetes and we need the Google Cloud SDK. Install the Google Cloud SDK and Kubectl, and initialize your SDK with the `gcloud init` command.

2. The next step is to set up a project, so create one project in the web UI and set the default project ID while working with the CLI by running:

   ```
   gcloud config set project <project_id>
   ```

3. Revisit `Chapter 2`, *Gearing up for the Journey*, to gather the `docker build` and `docker run` commands locally:

   ```
   sudo docker build -t firstypescriptms
   sudo docker run -p 8080:3000 -d firsttypescriptms:latest
   ```

4. Next, we will create a cluster with three instances where we will deploy our application:

```
gcloud container clusters create <name> --zone <zone>
```

For example, the `gcloud container clusters create hello-world-cluster --zone us-east1-b --machine-type f1-micro`. F1-mico is the smallest available unit. We can connect the `kubectl` client Kubernetes server with:

```
gcloud container clusters get-credentials hello-world-cluster --zone us-east1-b
```

5. We now have a Docker image and server cluster, in which we want to to deploy the image and start the containers. So, build and then upload the image using the following code:

```
docker build -t gcr.io/<PROJECT_ID>/hello-world-image:v1 .
gcloud docker -- push gcr.io/<PROJECT_ID>/hello-world-image:v1
```

6. To deploy, create the following `deployment.yml` file from following `gist` (https://gist.github.com/insanityrules/ ef1d556721173b7815e09c24bd9355b1), which will create two pods. To apply this, run the following command:

```
kubectl create -f deployment.yml --save-config
```

Now, when you do `kubectl get pods`, you will get three pods. To check the logs of the system, we can hit `kubectl logs {pod-name}`.

To expose it to the internet and to add scalability to the load balancer, hit the following command:

```
kubectl expose deployment hello-world-deployment --type="LoadBalancer"
```

In this section, we deployed our application on Kubernetes with three replicas on which we can autoscale or close down unwanted instances, just like AWS.

Summary

In this chapter, we went through our hardening layer. We looked at all the vulnerabilities our service is exposed to, and we learned about how to address them. We looked at some fundamentals, such as rate limiting, session handling, how to prevent parameter pollution, and more. We got acquainted with security at the container level and went through all the best practices for handling microservice security before moving on to scalability. We looked at Kubernetes and the Amazon load balancer, and got hands-on with both.

So far, you have learned how to build microservices using TpeScript on the Node.js platform and learned about all the aspects of microservice development, right from developing, the API Gateway, service registry, discovery, inter-service communication, Swagger, deployment, and testing. The objective of the book was to give you a practical hands-on guide to the microservice development and an understanding of the basic aspects to get you up and running. I really hope this book covers the empty space that is missing in the Node.js community, when compared to the Spring Cloud and Java community.

Other Books You May Enjoy

If you enjoyed this book, you may be interested in these other books by Packt:

TypeScript High Performance
Ajinkya Kher

ISBN: 978-1-78528-864-7

- Learn about the critical rendering path, and the performance metrics involved along the same
- Explore the detailed inner intricacies of a web browser
- Build a large scale front end applications and learn the thought process behind architecting such an effort
- Understand the challenges of scalability and how TypeScript renders itself to the cause
- Learn efficient usage of TypeScript constructs to deliver high performance and avoid common mistakes and pitfalls that can hamper performance
- Monitor performance, resolve and detect performance bottlenecks in production, and learn the tools involved

Mastering TypeScript - Second Edition
Nathan Rozentals

ISBN: 978-1-78646-871-0

- Gain an insight into core and advanced TypeScript language features including inheritance, generics, asynchronous programming techniques, promises, decorators and more
- Integrate your existing JavaScript libraries and third-party frameworks by writing and using declaration files
- Target popular JavaScript frameworks such as jQuery, Backbone, Angular, Aurelia, React, Node, and Express
- Create extensive test suites for your application with Jasmine, Protactor, and Selenium
- Organize your application code using modules, AMD loaders, Require and SystemJs
- Explore advanced object-oriented design principles, including Dependency Injection
- Understand and compare the various MVC implementations in Aurelia, Angular, React and Backbone
- Build a complete single-page web application that incorporates CSS animations to enhance your customers' browsing experience

Leave a review - let other readers know what you think

Please share your thoughts on this book with others by leaving a review on the site that you bought it from. If you purchased the book from Amazon, please leave us an honest review on this book's Amazon page. This is vital so that other potential readers can see and use your unbiased opinion to make purchasing decisions, we can understand what our customers think about our products, and our authors can see your feedback on the title that they have worked with Packt to create. It will only take a few minutes of your time, but is valuable to other potential customers, our authors, and Packt. Thank you!

Index

www.ingramcontent.com/pod-product-compliance
Lightning Source LLC
Chambersburg PA
CBHW080607060326
40690CB00021B/4612